Spinning into Control

Studies in Communication and Society

Series editors: Ralph Negrine and Anders Hansen
University of Leicester

Also published in this series:

TV News, Urban Conflict and the Inner City
Simon Cottle

The Economy, Media and Public Knowledge
Edited by Neil T. Gavin

Forthcoming:

Small Screens: Television for Children
Edited by David Buckingham

Spinning into Control

News Values and Source Strategies

Jerry Palmer

Leicester University Press
London and New York

Leicester University Press
A Continuum imprint
The Tower Building, 11 York Road, London SE1 7NX
370 Lexington Avenue, New York, NY 10017-6503

First published 2000

British Library Cataloguing-in-Publication Data
A catalogue record for this book is available from the British Library.

ISBN 0-7185-0251-5 (hardback)
    0-7185-0252-3 (paperback)

Library of Congress Cataloging-in-Publication Data
Palmer, Jerry.
    Spinning into control: news values and source strategies/Jerry Palmer.
        p. cm. — (Studies in communication and society)
    Includes bibliographical references and index.
    ISBN 0-7185-0251-5 — ISBN 0-7185-0252-3 (pbk.)
    1. Government and the press—United States. 2. Spin doctors—United States.
I. Title. II. Series.

PN4745.P35 2000
071'.3—dc21   00-038439

Typeset by BookEns Ltd, Royston, Herts
Printed and bound in Great Britain by Biddles Ltd, Guildford & Kings Lynn

Contents

Introduction

This book has its genesis in some chance reading more than twenty years ago. In 1979 the *Sunday Times* serialized sections of Henry Kissinger's memoirs, including one in which he described the tactics used by Nixon's 'advance men' (aides) to ensure prominent US television coverage of one of Nixon's European tours:

> Unfortunately, at the precise moment set for leaving, the advance men were struck with the realisation that there had been no crowd scenes of Nixon in Rome. This was not unusual. Foreign dignitaries have been visiting Rome since records were kept. But [Nixon's aide] Haldeman was not interested in historical comparisons. He applied the wisdom acquired in many years of barnstorming in America: nothing produces an emotional crowd like a traffic jam. It was decided on the spot that the President would take [Mrs Nixon] to her hotel by limousine. A motorcade was improvised and set off for the centre of Rome at the height of the rush hour while the rest of us waited … The operation could not have been more successful. Those of us not part of the motorcade did not see our leader again for two hours. A beaming Haldeman told us that the traffic jam had been monumental; the crowds enormous; their passions nearly uncontainable. All of this made great television film. (*Sunday Times*, 18.11.79: 35)

Kissinger himself was obviously amused by the antics – at least as he saw them retrospectively – of Nixon's aides, and my reaction was similar. But I was also puzzled: first, (a question whose *naïveté* now shocks me). Why would anyone bother to go to such lengths just to get a few seconds of TV time showing Nixon apparently being welcomed by some crowds in a foreign country? Second, if the 'barnstorming' element of the occasion was so obvious to Kissinger, why wasn't it equally obvious to the TV journalists covering the event? And if it was equally obvious to them, why were they going along with it – broadcasting this farce, this 'pseudo-event' as Daniel Boorstin (1961) had already christened this category of happening?

I record my naive curiosity for two reasons: because it at least represents a break with the common-sense attitude towards news, according to which news is 'what happens'; and second, because it introduces the subject matter of this book: the relationship between news journalism and the sources that journalists use in assembling the information that subsequently constitutes news. This relationship has two essential components: the reasons that journalists have for approaching sources, or more exactly, the reasons they have for choosing between sources, including all the potential sources not actually used; and the reasons that sources have for approaching journalists, or allowing journalists to approach them, or trying to avoid this contact. Both are complex entities.

Using the word 'reasons' here might be taken to imply a psychological approach to the subject, but we shall see that – in both cases – reasons are in fact part of the structured situations the participants occupy. I readily admit that there is an obvious psychological dimension to these matters too: some journalists are more diligent than others, some sources are more close-mouthed than others. Certainly these factors play a part in the interactions between sources and journalists, but I shall focus on the elements of such situations which are common features of source–journalist relationships in general.

In the years since my curiosity was aroused, much has been written on the subject, and it has become a subject of journalistic interest in its own right, as the role of 'spin doctors' has become a matter of political concern. Also, the news media themselves have changed in significant respects: increasing competition between press titles and broadcast news channels; new technology which has made broadcast news cheaper and faster; and – in the UK at least – massive changes in the organization of print journalism following the introduction of the new technology. It has been well argued that news photography has a fundamental impact on the criteria of newsworthiness (Goldberg, 1991). In addition, most national and many regional newspapers and broadcast news (e.g. BBC, CNN) maintain websites. Already one change is visible: on several occasions recently, newspapers have been able to beat broadcast news media to the first announcement of news, as incoming information has been posted directly onto a website. This process is not without risk. In early 1998 the *Dallas Morning News* found an ex-White House employee who was apparently prepared to testify to having seen President Clinton and Monica Lewinsky, in a 'compromising situation'; this information went straight onto the website. Unfortunately, the 'unimpeachable source' who had provided this information then retracted, saying only that he had seen them together (*Observer*, 15.2.98, Review: 'Scoop du Jour'). By then the

Dallas Morning News version was already in the public domain; taking the time to do the traditional editorial checking would – or might – have avoided journalistic embarrassment. News values, source strategies and editorial judgement are bound together in a dramatic way in this incident, driven by media competition and the edge given by a new technology.

Arguably, however, 'news' as a category of activity has changed less: the values which dictate which events are selected as 'newsworthy' and which are neglected contain substantial elements of constancy. What has changed is the processes by which the news reaches the public domain. However, we must immediately add the caveat that these values may not mean very little when divorced from the ongoing historical contexts within which they are applied, and perhaps especially inter-title or inter-channel competition.

This book is based primarily on case studies of information flows. Although some of the reasons for choosing this approach will only become clear as the examples are analysed, it can be said at the outset that the main reason is the hypothesis that news is best understood as a sequence of events unfolding through time. That is to say, it is only analyses that are themselves based on following sequences of events – rather than on either single events or on processes whose analysis is not sensitive to the passage of time – which are capable of revealing certain central features of news.

The processes discussed here have been discussed many times. In particular, questions of source motives and source strategies have been a central concern of recent analyses of the mass media, for reasons central to social scientific accounts of the world. News values have been less central to recent debates, but there is a relatively well-established – if dated – literature on the subject. There are relatively few systematic analyses of the relationship between these two themes, the terrain chosen for this book. Although it does not aim to present a systematic survey of the literature, it frequently references it. The central focus – at least for social scientists – is the role that information made public in the mass media plays in our society at large. My focus is more modest. It is concerned primarily with the structure of the processes by which information becomes news, although the results are addressed in Chapters 7 and 8.

The book is divided into three parts which correspond to the ways of approaching the central question. In the first, a series of examples and small-scale case studies are used to present an outline of the book's central concerns and a set of generalizations about them. Part II consists of two extended case studies and follows the protracted series of events of their 'media careers'. This protraction is a significant element. In Part III, I explore a major theoretical question: the relationship between information flows through the mass media and fundamental features of our society. What has been analysed as a process in the first two parts will here be analysed as a function, and in particular (following the logic of certain arguments derived from Habermas) I shall examine the extent to which the process is responsible for the function.

The analyses in this book are grounded in two methods of data collection: content analysis and interviewing. Content analysis is a tried-and-tested method for assembling data about the cumulative meanings in mass media output. It is my preferred method for analysing the news values associated with particular events, precisely because it reveals cumulative meaning, which I interpret (with some reservations, discussed in the conclusion to Part II) to be the best indicator of news values. My use of it is only original, if at all, in the use to which it is put. I use content analysis to show the results of the combined operations of news values and the behaviour of news sources which have tried (by appealing to news values) to gain publicity for their activities. The content surveys have been carried out in the traditional way.

My second method is interviewing, my preferred method for gaining access to information about the behaviour of news sources. In general, I have tried to check this information by comparing it either with the public record or with other interviews. However, as will be clear, in many instances interviewees had unique access to relevant information. As far as the selection of interviewees is concerned, the people I asked for interviews were the journalists involved, those either who were quoted as sources in the reports in question, or whose role as sources was inferable from what was reported. Once relevance was established, my prime concern was to persuade people to agree to be interviewed. I am very grateful to those who did, and I well understand the concerns of those who refused. Readers will easily recognize the points at which I have no quotes from sources whose accounts of events cry out for inclusion. On some occasions sources refused to be interviewed. On others, I did not want to intrude on individuals still grieving or embarrassed. I was certain that no one would be willing to add anything to what was already on the public record, since doing so would expose them to even more difficult situations.

Of course, there are also many occasions when either a source's identity is a well-kept secret, or a source's activity is hidden by silence. When it is a secret, academic diligence is of little use; in the second case, although in theory diligence is indeed useful, in the absence of some indication of the invisible activity, one is unlikely to get anywhere. In the case of events which are covered by published memoirs and similar records, it is sometimes possible to find these traces, but, on the whole, the case studies that I have chosen have not benefited from this; where such material does exist, I have referred to it.

A brief annotated list of the main newspapers and broadcast outlets referred to in this book appears as an Appendix (pp. 165-6). I have not included a list of those I interviewed, as many interviews were off the record. The content analyses on which some of the material in this book is based can be found on the website of London Guildhall University (`www.lgu.ac.uk`) by following the links 'Departments', 'Teaching Departments', 'Communications'.

All translations from foreign languages which are not attributed in the bibliography are by myself.

'... go to work, to do spin ... '

Primary Colors, Anonymous (Joe Klein)

But now I often saw the [Duchess of Guermantes] at her window, or in the courtyard or in the street; if I could not manage to fit the name 'Guermantes' onto her, to think that she was Madame de Guermantes, I blamed the inability of my mind to carry out the act I asked of it; but she, our neighbour, seemed to be guilty of the same mistake, without worrying about it, without even suspecting it might be a mistake. Thus Madame de Guermantes' dresses showed the same care over fashion as if – believing herself to be woman like any other – she aspired to the sort of elegance of self-presentation in which other women, of any sort, could be her equal, or even outstrip her; in the street I noticed her admiring glance at a well-dressed actress; and in the morning, just as she was about to walk out of the house ... I could see her looking in the mirror, playing the inferior role of the elegant woman, playing it with a conviction entirely lacking in dissociation or irony, with passion, with poor grace, with pride, just like a queen who has agreed to play a serving-girl in a court comedy; forgetting her natural grandeur, she checked that her veil was just right, straightened her sleeves, made sure her coat sat right ...

Marcel Proust, *Le Côté de Guermantes*

To the memory of my family, who were journalists

James Palmer († 1961) *The Western Morning News, The Cornishman*
Cyril Palmer († 1963) *The Daily Mail*
Norman Palmer († 1972) *The Daily Mail, News of the World, The Daily Telegraph, The Observer*
Vera Palmer († 2000) *The Western Morning News*

PART I

News Values and Source Strategies: An Overview

———

CHAPTER 1

The News Encounter

―――――

On 28 January 1986 the space shuttle *Challenger* exploded a few minutes after take-off, killing all the astronauts on board. The nature of the event meant that it was televised and the moment of the explosion was caught on film; it was broadcast live in the US, and was featured on the front pages of newspapers and in TV news bulletins. One of the reasons why the photographs were so prominently used was because photographs of the actual moment of a disaster are extremely rare: a camera must be present and pointed in the right direction at the right moment. If the filming of an event has not been pre-scheduled the photographic record is made by sheer chance, as in a case discussed by Harold Evans (1978): a stowaway fell out of an aeroplane soon after take-off just as the owner of a new camera was trying it out in the vicinity of the airport and happened to film the body falling through the sky. So coincidental was this that the photographer did not even realize what was on the film until it was developed. The *Challenger* disaster obviously fits the first eventuality. Such photographs are a rarity: if a disaster could be predicted it could be avoided, or its results minimized. When the Soufrière volcano on the Caribbean island of Guadeloupe was about to erupt in 1976, the authorities evacuated the island and the German film-maker Werner Herzog moved in to film the event. The result is an eerie documentary of a deserted town, a solitary journey up to the rim of a volcano about to explode, and a bizarrely inconsequential conversation with the only inhabitant who was not evacuated because nobody had found him and he did not know what was about to happen. The eruption eventually occurred, no one was injured, and news coverage was minimal: an accurately predicted disaster can be avoided.[1]

As a result of their unpredictability, most photographs of disasters are photographs of the aftermath. The photographer's job is to select the subject matter, angle, framing and other elements of composition to best convey an impression of 'disastrous-ness'. Photographs of the aftermath of train and road crashes are a commonplace example, as are the many photographs of the aftermath of murders published by US tabloids during the inter-war years. As a result of these various factors, photographs such as those of the *Challenger* explosion have a considerable rarity value as photographs, as well as the value given by the importance of the event.

The significance of these details for my purposes is twofold. In the first place, the events in question are usually considered 'newsworthy' – they are in conformity with news values. This is in part because of the importance of the event (disasters involve destruction and suffering) and in part because of the dramatic nature (and sometimes rarity) of the photographic record. Photographs of any significant 'first time' obviously fit the same principle – the first man on the moon, the Earth rising over the moon's horizon. However, the mere existence of the photograph itself may have news value, as in the instance of the publication of the first underwater photographs of the wreck of the *Titanic* (whose presence on the seabed was scarcely news) under the headline '*Titanic:* the first seabed picture' (*Evening Standard,* 5.9.85). In part, such values derive from the nature of photography, since it directly implies the act of witness, and is regularly taken to constitute an important element of proof, despite well-known instances of photographic 'doctoring'.[2]

In the second place, the rarity of journalists themselves actually witnessing such an event indicates the way in which they are dependent upon sources. In the case of the *Challenger* explosion, journalists were filming the event because they were given access to it by the authorities – indeed, were encouraged to film it for publicity purposes. In the case of the photograph of the man falling out of an aeroplane, journalists were dependent upon the photographer offering the photograph to the news media. In the case of 'routine' disasters ('routine' in the statistical sense) such as road crashes, news organizations depend upon notification by chance observers or by the police or emergency services. Similarly, news of the explosion of Pan Am flight 103 (blown up by a terrorist bomb over Lockerbie, Scotland in December 1988) reached the BBC Scottish television newsroom within three minutes, phoned in by an AA patrolman who witnessed it; an anonymous informant phoned the BBC television newsroom in London shortly afterwards (Deppa, 1993: 69–70).

Without news sources there is no news. While this principle may be obvious, it is worth stressing because the dependence of journalists upon sources does not only explain the fact that a story is covered at all: it may well explain *how* the story is covered, or at least some elements of the way in which coverage occurs. The space shuttle disaster provides an obvious example: the photographs of the *Challenger* explosion were of very high quality since the cameras were favourably placed and photographers had plenty of time to organize the technical details of coverage. Other relevant elements were made available in advance through the source which had allowed access in the first place: background information concerning the crew, their photographs, technical information about the flight, etc.; this availability allowed extended coverage of the incident. The shot of the stowaway falling out of a plane, on the other hand, is extremely grainy and out of focus and little is known about the circumstances surrounding the death.

In a well-known analysis of source–journalist interactions, Sigal (1973: 120-9) demonstrated that most of the coverage analysed was dominated by journalists' routine dependence upon official sources; his analysis is worth considering in detail. Sigal distinguishes three types of source–journalist relationships: routine, informal and enterprise. 'Routine' means events such as on-the-record interviews and press conferences organized in order to present information to the media. 'Informal' means background briefings to groups of journalists, non-government proceedings, leaks and other news reports (for example, agency reports). 'Enterprise' means personal interviews, eyewitness accounts, and individual research and analysis. On this basis, Sigal finds that front-page stories were mainly sourced by routine access (58 per cent). In a second stage, he distinguished primary and secondary channels of sourcing: primary channels are the person quoted in the lead paragraph and/or the person responsible for the timing of the information release; secondary are all the others. Table 1 shows the results of this two-stage analysis.

Since 70 per cent of primary sources are routine, Sigal argues that news organizations rely overwhelmingly on official sources for their primary material, but use enterprise methods to check their primary

Table 1 Source–journalist interactions (percentages)

		Channels	
Sources	*All*	*Primary*	*Secondary*
Routine	58.2	70.7	49.7
Informal	15.7	19.3	13.3
Enterprise	25.8	9.9	36.6
Totals	99.7	99.9	99.6

Source: adapted from Sigal, 1973: 121-3; missing items unidentifiable.

sources for accuracy. This interpretation is plausible given the relative constancy of the role of informal sources, the reduction in the reliance on routine sources in secondary channels and the concomitant increase in the use of enterprise channels at the same point.

However, Sigal's analysis is subject to caution. Whether his results would be replicated in news channels other than the ones he uses (front-page stories in the *New York Times* and the *Washington Post*) is open to question. Gans' source analysis – which includes one network television newsroom – points in the same direction (1980: 128–34), as do Gieber and Johnson's (1961), but no analysis based on tabloid news pages is available for comparison. Schlesinger and Tumber (1994: 168, 173–5) report from a survey of national UK daily crime reporters that news people regard the official contact points between news media and the Metropolitan Police in London as a hindrance to getting reliable and up-to-date information about police operations. They prefer to pursue unofficial contacts with police officers. Sigal would presumably count such contacts as enterprise, but it is unclear from Schlesinger and Tumber's comments whether they consider them to be primary or secondary sources; it is possible that such a sourcing pattern for a major category of news stories would affect Sigal's figures.

Similarly, Sigal's placing of other news reports in the informal category needs development. Certainly it is true – not to mention obvious – that journalists use other news reports as a major source of information (e.g. Schlesinger, 1987; Breed, 1955; Tuchman, 1978: 20–4); placing these in a separate category from news conferences, etc. is reasonable, as the events have already been subject to journalistic processing when they appear in, for example, a news agency report. However, at some point all such reports must be the result either of a journalistic eyewitness account, or of a source–journalist encounter. Since Sigal did not follow individual stories back along their sourcing chain to their starting point, his analysis ignores many sources which might be either routine or enterprise, or indeed another version of informal sourcing. This too might alter the results of his analysis.

Lastly, Sigal's analysis does not distinguish between the degrees of importance of different sources and indeed different stories. Some stories contribute to shifts in public opinion and others set the tone for large swathes of coverage of a given subject; in this process, journalists may seek different sources, or seek different types of information from established sources. Famously, Morley Safer's TV report of American soldiers setting fire to Vietnamese villagers' huts contributed to a modification of reporters' attitudes towards the Vietnam War, even though the bulk of TV reporting of the US war effort continued to be largely positive (Hallin, 1986: 132–3, 147–58). Chapter 5 shows how a single tabloid report of a sexual scandal in Britain set the tone for months of reporting. Similarly, where reporters use more than one source, the tone of the coverage may be dominated by an interpretation which derives more from one source than others, or even by sources not named or even indicated in the reported version of events (Cockerell *et al.*, 1984: 135; Miller and Williams, 1993: 126–7). For example, in the UK coverage of Northern Ireland, academic studies of elements of the situation are often based, at least in part, on Northern Ireland Office (i.e. UK Government) briefing papers; the academic studies are then quoted by the Northern Ireland Office as 'independent commentary' in press releases; the academics in question are then approached by journalists as independent experts (Miller, 1993: 86–7). The complexity of the sourcing chain and the provenance of particular elements of reporting defy the classifications used in an analysis such as Sigal's.

In this analysis we can see ambiguities that arise in the source-journalist relationship. However, no one doubts that sources make great efforts to ensure that coverage is indeed in line with the profile of events for which publicity is being sought. For example, the desirability of technically perfect photographic coverage and control over other elements of the media profile of events for publicity purposes, leads media relations personnel to maximize their chances by arranging 'facilitation'. Figure 1.1 shows the arrangements for journalists to observe President George Bush, visiting US troops in the Gulf in 1990, prior to the launch of the Desert Storm operation against Iraq.

The purpose of such arrangements is to ensure that photographs of the subject are suitable for publication (from the source's point of view), both in the sense of technical adequacy and by reducing the chances of an unflattering portrayal; such photo-opportunities are a normal part of national political life. The fate of US presidential candidate Bob Dole in 1996 is a reminder that handling is central to modern politics: his fate was sealed the moment he fell off a badly constructed podium in full view of the cameras. The image was widely carried in newscasts and newspapers and was understood to symbolize a badly thought-out campaign (see also Seymour-Ure, 1989). Detailed planning does not always prevent things spinning out of control.

Photography is a particularly clear instance of the dependence upon sources, since a photograph entails the presence of a photographer, whereas the written record may be retrospectively constructed through interviews. However, the nature of the dependence is not dissimilar, and the press conference (or confidential press briefing) is not in principle different from the photo-opportunity in this respect. It is well known that in British politics many press briefings do not

THANKSGIVING DINNER WITH THE FIRST MARINE DIVISION COMMAND POST
Dharan, Saudi Arabia
Thursday, November 22, 1990

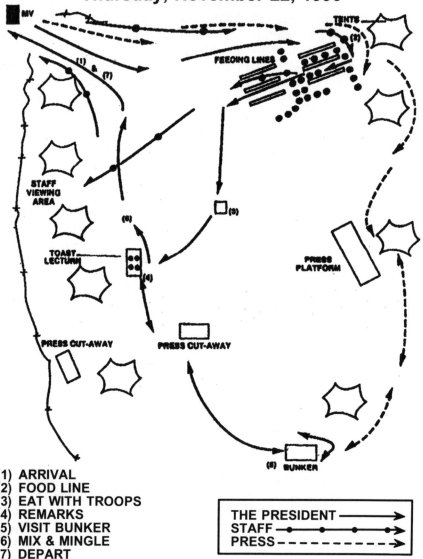

(1) ARRIVAL
(2) FOOD LINE
(3) EAT WITH TROOPS
(4) REMARKS
(5) VISIT BUNKER
(6) MIX & MINGLE
(7) DEPART

THE PRESIDENT ———→
STAFF •—•—•—•—→
PRESS – – – – – – →

Figure 1.1 Revealed: Bush's plan for attacking turkey. Photo-opportunity details for Bush's Thanksgiving dinner.
Reprinted with kind permission of the *Observer*.

officially exist, and journalists resort to coded circumlocutions to indicate their sources. The purpose of such arrangements is to permit deniability on the part of the source; this is said by proponents of the system to increase politicians' confidence in speaking to journalists.[3] Most news from official sources emerges from policy change or dispute. Interpreting it requires determining what the change or dispute is about. It requires making inferences about the source of the issue under consideration as she or he would see it, the target of the words, and his or her possible reasons for uttering them (Sigal 1973: 188).

It is relatively rare to see journalistic accounts of details of the briefing process. Jo Revill – health correspondent of the London *Evening Standard* – published a detailed account of the way in which the Labour Government spin doctor attached to the Department of Health and Social Security constantly intervened in a press conference to try to ensure that journalists' coverage of the event was 'on-message', in other words supportive of the interpretation favoured by the Government (3.11.97).[4] The way in which stories are sourced is becoming a legitimate topic for journalistic enquiry in its own right.[5]

A particularly tangled skein is to be found in two accounts of policy trailing in the last week of February 1998 in the UK. Following well-publicized disagreements within the Labour Government in previous months about welfare reform (which had centrally involved the role of Harriet Harman, the minister responsible), reports appeared in many newspapers discussing the possibility that the forthcoming Budget would effectively countermand some of the reforms which had attracted internal party opposition. In a review of these reports in the *Observer* (1.3.98) the political reporter Patrick Wintour suggested that these stories had been placed by Harman herself in an attempt to shore up her fraught position in the Cabinet, citing patterns of sourcing and contacts with well-placed journalists; on the following day, in the *Guardian*, Polly Toynbee, the journalist centrally refer-enced by Wintour, denied that the information had come from Harman.[6]

The 'leaked' story is a particularly clear example of journalists' dependence upon sources: the value of a leak is that it supposedly guarantees that the information is sufficiently significant that someone does not want it published, and that it cannot be made available through the usual routine channels. In fact, many leaks are phoney, in the sense that they are authorized by the very person who apparently does not want the information to be made public; commonly, this is done to test public reaction to a potential future decision, or to distract public attention from some feature of the event that might be more controversial; many examples of this process are to be found in academic commentaries on political communications.[7] Anatomies of leaks by participants are rather rare (since the hidden nature of the mechanism of information release is the most important component of the whole process), but the Labour Party politician Roy Hattersley gave a clear analysis of one in which he was a passive participant. Here the leak was apparently calculated to make a particular policy decision more difficult for its proponents, but in fact its 'premature' issue was intended to ensure that it could not be modified in the way that its opponents wanted: the subtlety of the event was that one group was apparently to blame for underhand tactics to spoil a policy, whereas in truth it was their opponents who were pre-empting the first group's tactics (*Guardian*, 22.12.97). An attempt at something similar in December 1997 misfired: someone, still unidentified in May 2000, leaked the details of the then forthcoming Freedom of Information Act. It was supposed that the leak came from someone in the Ministry responsible, since it was also leaked that the Minister's advisers had lunched with the journalist in question a few hours before the leak. The second leak was clearly intended to reinforce the attribution of the first. However, the leaked document was not in fact the final draft agreed by the Ministry; the leak had therefore not been by someone privy to the final version, which indicated that the leak was not a pre-emptive strike.[8]

These examples suggest that, in Sigal's phrase, 'Sources make the news' (1986). However, source behaviour is subject to the filtering norms of journalistic selection and interpretation. While we will see many instances of this in a variety of different circumstances, one clear example will suffice to show what is meant: the rules of decorum which restrict the use of excessively distressing images. It was often said after the Gulf War that the photographic coverage was 'sanitized' by the use of footage supplied by the military which showed 'smart' bombs hitting targets with pin-point precision and (at least implicitly) sparing unnecessary civilian casualties; against the background of this criticism the *Observer* printed a photograph of the charred head of an Iraqi soldier killed during the retreat from Kuwait, arguing that the revulsion it caused was part of the understanding of what this war was like.[9] Although decorum is not the most often stressed feature of news values, it is one of the clearest examples of the autonomy of editorial judgement: editors reject or accept material on the grounds that journalistic norms dictate what is or is not an acceptable representation of events in the outside world. Whether these rules of decorum increase or decrease source control over media agendas can only be established on the basis of individual instances; in the case of the Gulf War, sanitization was arguably in the interests of the Allied governments, and it also gave added force to the *Observer* image. An even stronger example of the way in which the contrast between sanitized images and those which are (arguably) more realistic serves political purposes, is the American TV news coverage of the American military intervention in Somalia. Carefully constructed photo-opportunities gave the illusion of effortless superiority. When things went wrong and a dead American soldier was dragged through the streets, the TV images were doubly shocking.[10]

The preplanned event shown in Figure 1.1 involved President Bush eating Thanksgiving dinner with US troops in the desert. Clearly an event like this is intended to indicate presidential concern with the morale of troops, both to those troops and especially to the wider public reached through the media. Such events, organized in order to be witnessed via the news media, were christened 'pseudo-events' by Daniel Boorstin (1961). His analysis – as his title suggests – condemns these events as phoney, in the sense that if it were not for the presence of the media, they would not occur at all. A similar analysis suggests that, but for the presence of the media, President Bush would not have eaten turkey with his troops. However, there is a particular and long-lived category of events which are not dependent upon the media for their existence – since they pre-date the existence of the media – and which are in some respects difficult to distinguish from these modern pseudo-events. Ceremonies of every kind – coronations, parades, weddings, processions – exist in order to be witnessed; without the act of witnessing, they would lose much of their meaning. Clearly the fact that a ceremony exists in order to be witnessed does not turn it into a pseudo-event, and Boorstin's category is in danger of developing into an unjustified denunciation of traditional ceremonial. Is it possible to draw a distinguishing line between traditional ceremony and the modern pseudo-event? On what grounds could they be distinguished?

Clearly, the degree of public importance of the (pseudo) event could be used to establish a distinction, but whose estimate of importance should we accept? Promoters of events are unlikely to concede their triviality. Central to the modern pseudo-event is the presence of the news media as intermediaries in the act of witnessing. The presence of the media implies not just that there is a ceremony which requires public witness, but that the ceremony in question is newsworthy as well, in other words that the 'public' witness is of a particularly privileged kind: members of the British royal family 'enjoy' the 'privilege' of broadcast cameras at their weddings and funerals; ordinary mortals usually do not. Therefore the organizers of any such event must conform to journalistic judgements of what constitutes a newsworthy event if they wish to benefit from the attentions of the media: what characterizes a pseudo-event, in other words, is its deliberate construction according to media norms rather than the norms of ceremony and public witness. On the other hand, it is difficult to argue that the construction of an event according to journalistic norms is in itself enough to make it a pseudo-event: the organization of the funeral of Diana, Princess of Wales, clearly included the facilitation of media coverage, but it cannot be argued that it only existed in order to be broadcast. It is difficult to arrive at entirely watertight definitions of such phenomena because much modern ceremonial is closely linked to its dissemination via the mass media; yet we cannot say that ceremonies that are not designed with such dissemination in mind are more genuine than those which are. A more legitimate conclusion is that in a world where much information transmission is via the mass media, it is inevitable that certain categories of events become 'mediatised' in a manner integral to their construction; this sociological observation arguably makes ethical arguments about (in)authenticity irrelevant.[11]

This category of event and its relationship to the modern news media show us that the preceding argument is somewhat one-sided. Although it is true that journalists are dependent upon sources, it is equally true that sources are dependent upon journalists, in that source desire to obtain publicity through news media can only be realized in so far as the event and/or the message disseminated by the source are in conformity with news values. During the first week of December 1997, the Labour Government tried very hard to launch a series of new political initiatives with maximum publicity – notably the creation of the Social Exclusion Unit and Education Action Zones. However, there was great competition for media space from an event that was totally incompatible with the Government's plans: allegations that the Paymaster-General, Geoffrey Robinson, had benefited from an offshore trust fund (a device for reducing tax liability) in a way that was arguably incompatible with the Government's own stated political priorities. Journalists' sense of news priorities was far from in accordance with Government priorities in this instance, although no doubt in accordance with the priorities of whoever it was who called their attention to Mr Robinson's affairs in the first place. The choice of the sources who were to enjoy access to news space was made in accordance with journalistic criteria, and not – or not primarily – to benefit the sources.

A substantial amount of recent academic writing about the mass media focuses on source behaviour and studies the relationship between sources and journalists as an empirical process. Here the main elements are the resources available to the two parties in question, the motives of the sources in terms of the role that publicity plays in particular contexts, and the balance between conflicting sources' access to the media. The conclusion usually reached is that 'sources make the news'. Such studies certainly illuminate the ways in which particular items reach the public domain via the news media, and others fail to do so, by showing how and why sources approach journalists, or allow themselves to be approached. However, journalists' motives must be understood in terms of news values and news values are not an empirical entity: it is news reports, and the behaviour of participants in the news-gathering process, which can be observed. The value system which regulates their behaviour is not in itself directly observable. Its nature must be inferred from what is observable, in much the same way that a language is not observable, and its structure must be deduced from the linguistic competence of its speakers. But this value system is none the less real for not being directly observable – just as a language is real despite the fact that it exists only as an ideal object.[12] Since this value system dictates journalists' judgements about what to include in (and exclude from) media accounts of events, it influences the success or failure of sources in their approach to journalists, and may be presumed to influence decisions about their communications strategies. In a brief case study (pp. 17–25) we shall see both how this 'ideal object' does influence participants' behaviour, and some of the problems involved in inferring what the role of news values is in particular contexts.

The analysis of news must be conducted not just in terms of encounters between sources and journalists, but also in terms of these encounters mediated by the system of news values. Metaphorically, we could say that negotiations between journalists and sources about what the media will include or exclude are conducted in the currency of news values.

From the source point of view, access to the media has many purposes. In general, it is a resource-efficient way of reaching a wide public. This is commonly an intermediate goal, The primary purpose is to place a message with a particular public, although it may also be the case that the message is not 'targeted', and the sender's purpose is only to ensure that the information in question is in the public domain.[13] As with any communication channel, the number of intermediate stages between the sender of a message and its intended receiver affects the chances of the message reaching its destination in its original form. News media reports of events are usually simplified, objective descriptions which may give little attention to the motives or purposes of participants. Those who use the news media as intermediaries are obliged to construct their original message – which may in fact be an event, not a representation of that event – in a way that minimizes the risk of distortion.

We may call the moment at which a source meets a journalist the 'news encounter'. It is central to the process by which events become news because the interdependence of sources and journalists is typical of news organizations. Indeed, in a sense the newspaper in the modern sense of the word was brought into existence by the regularization of the reporter–source relationship (Schudson, 1978: 18–25; Curran and Seaton, 1985: 11–45). The history of the news media as autonomous organizations is based in part in a particular relationship between journalists and news sources, which is in turn part of the 'objective method' of news reporting (see Chapter 2).

We should stress what is certainly obvious – that the news encounter necessarily consists of two participants: the source and the journalist. Of course, in practice, the two participants each frequently consists of more than one individual: a newsroom is a large number of individuals, and sources are frequently, if not usually, a collective entity, as when, for example, a government organization, a business corporation or a political party holds a press conference. Even if the number of speakers is reduced to one, that person is speaking on behalf of an organization, in a way authorized by that organization. The distinction between the roles of organizations and those of individuals cannot be ignored, of course, and we shall see many occasions and many ways in which it is significant for an understanding of the processes by which events become news. However, it is a convenient shorthand to speak of the news encounter as involving a single journalist and a single source, while recognizing that both may be the collective bearers of organizational imperatives rather than autonomous individuals. Moreover, regardless of these numerical and organizational issues it is clear, if only on *a priori* grounds, that both parties to the news encounter are there for their own reasons. We may assume that the journalist is there in order to collect information that may become news (although journalists may be present by coincidence, or as a result of some purely private arrangement). Sources have their own reasons for approaching journalists or allowing themselves to be approached (we should include in this category, contradictory though it will sound, the desire to avoid being a news source, i.e. the desire to avoid being approached by a journalist). Also, many potential news encounters never occur because neither journalists nor sources make any move to contact each other, either through indifference or ignorance or a mixture of both (Goldenberg, 1975: 125). In a case study of the Brent Spar affair (Chapter 6), we shall see that one of the protagonists missed opportunities for placing material favourable to their interpretation of events through simple lack of awareness of the significance of that material.

This fundamental principle is of course obvious, but it is heavy with implications that are less so, and which can be formulated thus, in an approximate and initial way: the situation of the source leads him or her to have a particular interpretation of the event in which she or he is involved; this interpretation may or may not coincide with a journalist's reasons for being interested in the event. For the journalist, the criterion of relevance of events is their potential newsworthiness, but this is not necessarily a valid criterion for anyone else. A source who is seeking publicity via the news media (for whatever reason) will be forced to accept the criteria of relevance that constitute newsworthiness in order to interest the journalist in the information. This may (or may not) involve placing an interpretation upon the event or information which is at odds with the interpretation which has led the (potential) news source to seek publicity in the first place.

By the same token, it may be a rival organization's interpretation of an event which is in accordance with news criteria, and therefore comes to dominate news media accounts. A well-known example is the protest movements in the 1960s. The participants organized street demonstrations in order to bring their ideas and their organizations to public attention. Frequently, such demonstrations led to clashes with the police, and the demonstrations became the focus of news media coverage of the events. From the point of view of the organizers, the violence may well have been incidental to the purpose of the event. But from the point of view of the police, and of newsworthiness, the violence was of more importance than the reasons that the organizers had for setting up the event. There was a fundamental discrepancy between the interpretative frameworks of the parties to the news encounter (Gitlin, 1980; Halloran, Elliott and Murdock, 1970). A more commonplace example occurs regularly in business-page journalism, where company results are interpreted in the process of deciding what makes them newsworthy, often to the discomfiture of the corporations in question. By the same token, a source who is trying to avoid publicity may well consider the event an unfortunate mishap which is best kept as quiet as possible, whereas news criteria dictate that it is very interesting and should receive maximum publicity. The English actress and soap star Gillian Taylforth was said by the *Sun* to have been questioned by the police about an incident in which they claimed she was having sex with her lover in a parked car; she sued the paper for libel and lost. It is clear that her interpretation of the event and the newspaper's were divergent, not only in the sense that she claimed that sex had not occurred, but also in the sense that she would no doubt have preferred silence to any public interpretation at all. This situation is typical of that staple of tabloid journalism, the 'scandal' (see Chapters 4 and 5).

This simple outline of a principle, and the anecdotal examples that illustrate it, are intended only to introduce the subject matter of this book: the relationship between journalists and sources, the criteria of newsworthiness that drive journalistic enterprise, and the strategies used by sources in their endeavours to control the flow of information into the public domain via the news media. For sources, the passage of information into the public domain via the news media (as opposed to other information channels) is one action among alternatives, the advantages and disadvantages of which are to be weighed according to criteria deriving from the situation of those who control access to the information in question. For example, it is a commonplace of PR and marketing that the balance of advantage between advertising and publicity achieved through the news media is to be assessed according to the following criteria: in advertising, the advertiser gains a high degree of control over the nature of the message placed in the public domain (by paying for the space it uses), but may well sacrifice readers, as well as credibility, because of the public certainty that advertising shades the truth; in news, the information gains a high degree of credibility because of the reputation of news as an accurate source of information (especially in the case of television news), but the information source has reduced control over the nature of the message as it passes into the public domain: 'the strength of editorial coverage is its credibility and independence. The weakness is that because you are not paying for the exposure you do not control it' (Stone, 1995: 162).

Clearly, the presence of vast quantities of advertising demonstrates that often the decision goes the other way, as the situation dictates, depending on the nature of the message, the situation of the communicator, and the intended audience. In the jargon of the communication industries, all strategists exercise control over the relationship between 'above the line' and 'below the line' budgeting. What is implicit in these criteria of evaluation of communications strategies is that an information source can exercise choice over the manner (or channel) in which information reaches the public domain, which of course includes the possibility of suppressing (or attempting to suppress) its passage entirely. In political histories, the passage of information into the public domain is similarly considered as part of a communications strategy pursued as part of some wider course of action. In histories of the Vietnam War, for example, information originating with the government is seen primarily in terms of the role that public communication played in the organization of the military and political pursuit of foreign policy objectives (e.g. Hallin, 1986: 15–19, 70–5). Miller gives an example from British government information policy on Northern Ireland. Stories interpreting IRA activity as linked to an international terrorist conspiracy (especially to Libya) derived from unattributable Northern Ireland Office and Foreign Office briefings, and were intended for foreign consumption, especially in the US (in order to strengthen the hands of those in the US who wanted to argue against settlement with the IRA). However, in order to achieve credibility abroad, it was important that they should be stressed in UK news media, even though such stories played no part in the development of internal policy (Miller, 1993b: 84–5).

From the point of view of professional journalists, what occurs in the news encounter is the search for news. Their part in the transaction is dictated primarily by the news organization's need for information compatible with its organizational imperatives, which may be summarized as 'newsworthiness' and the forms of action imposed by the methods of information-gathering and dissemination adopted. The source's motives are only relevant in so far as they influence the reliability of the information, although journalists may sometimes refuse to use information because they object to being used for source purposes. In March 1998 the previous Arts Editor of *The Times* stated that he had resigned because he objected to being made complicit in this process; in this instance the source was part of an organization, News International, owned by the same conglomerate as *The Times* (*Guardian* 'Media', 2.3.98; cf. Schlesinger, 1978: 72). From the point of view of the source, what occurs in the news encounter is part of a wider communications strategy, which is in turn part of some plan of action.[14]

In short, both journalists and sources have motives which lead them to interpret events in particular ways. Both also have at their disposal a variety of techniques for structuring the news encounter in ways calculated to maximize the chances of their interpretation being the one that obtains. Such techniques are composed fundamentally of each understanding the motives of the other: sources who seek publicity – or who seek to avoid it – must understand what drives the search for news, and what as a result constitutes news values, if they are to influence journalists and persuade them to interpret events in the way that is beneficial to their purposes. By the same token, journalists recognize that sources make themselves available to journalists – or seek to avoid availability – for reasons that influence the sources' conception of the meaning of events. This situation is represented diagrammatically in Figure 1.2.

In short, news must be understood in terms of the interactions between journalists and their sources – or sources and their journalists – mediated by news values. A brief case study will show how such interactions work in practice. In this instance, the story was exceptional, and the features which made it so foreground elements of the news encounter which are more difficult to observe.

On Saturday, 11 November 1995 Leah Betts collapsed and went into a coma during her eighteenth birthday party, at which her parents were present; before she lost consciousness she told them that she had taken an Ecstasy tablet. She was put on a life-support system but never

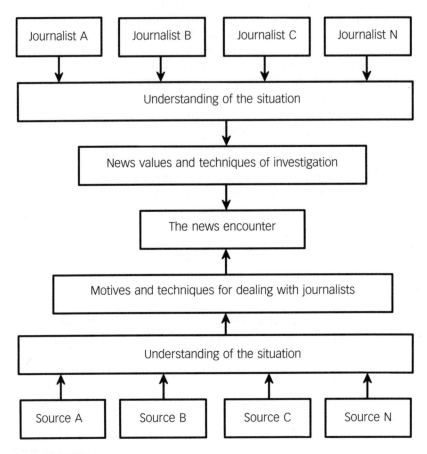

Figure 1.2 The news encounter

regained consciousness and was declared dead the following Thursday.

This was by no means the first occasion on which a young person had died after taking Ecstasy, and clearly the primary news value of the event was the fact of yet another death from this drug. However, the media interest in her case was more intense and protracted than in other instances: it occupied a prominent position in news coverage throughout her period of unconsciousness; her funeral was widely covered; and for many months her name was mentioned with reference to other drugs-related stories; indeed it still is. Her case was so highly profiled in news media that her photograph was used in an anti-drug campaign during the months following her death.

When she was taken to hospital – shortly after midnight on Sunday,

12 November – the local police press office was routinely alerted to the incident.[15] At midday the press officer handling the case consulted detectives dealing with drugs cases, because of fears that the tablet might have been contaminated (a common cause of death in drugs incidents) which would entail issuing a warning via the local media. By early afternoon the Essex police-recorded tape, which journalists use for an outline of current crime stories, carried the bare facts of Leah Betts' case, but without her name. The press officer also took the less usual step of contacting two news agencies – UK News and the Press Association – and calling their attention to the incident, because of fears that the tablet might be part of a contaminated batch.[16] At 4.00 p.m. he went to the hospital with the police family liaison officer to talk to the girl's parents. In discussion with them, he predicted that there would be considerable media interest, and asked how the parents wanted to handle the situation. They consented to appear at a press conference, and Leah's father offered to release a picture of his daughter on the life-support system. The police press office notified the media at around 5.00 p.m. that there would be a press conference at 7.00 p.m., which was attended by approximately fifteen journalists. A doctor, a hospital administrator and police representatives were in attendance. The initial batch of media reports immediately aroused intense further interest: according to the police press officer, the phone in his office did not stop ringing until 2.00 a.m. and his home phone started ringing again at 5.00 a.m. On Monday morning Leah's parents held another press conference at the hospital; until Leah Betts was officially declared dead the media were constantly present on the hospital grounds, in anticipation of updates on her condition. They were described by both the hospital and the police press officer as well-behaved and cooperative: there were no complaints of the kind of harassment that has been a feature of other incidents (e.g. Deppa *et al.*, 1993). The media turnout for her funeral was huge.

How can one explain the extent of the media interest in this incident? Clearly the nature of the arrangements to publicize it constitutes a partial explanation: the police press officer's prediction of media interest induced a pattern of behaviour on his part that would encourage such interest – to this extent, his prediction was self-fulfilling. Both the police press office and the hospital public information office made every effort to facilitate maximum coverage. Certainly (according to both the police and the hospital press officers) Mr and Mrs Betts' decision to cooperate fully with the media was crucial; their willingness to appear immediately at a press conference, to give continued access, and especially their offer of a photograph of their daughter provided the media with elements of coverage which to some extent distinguished this case from other similar ones. Her parents publicly stated on more than one occasion that their cooperation was motivated by a desire that something good should come of their daughter's death.

We can give a partial account of the scope of media interest in this event by referring to the institutional interaction between media personnel and the source organizations. However, this account still does not explain the intensity of the coverage, as it does not sufficiently distinguish this case from a number of others where facilitation did not produce massive media coverage; we need to refer to the news value of the story in order to go further. Approximately fifty young people had died from Ecstasy before Leah, and in none of those cases had there been such extensive reporting although in one earlier case the girl's mother made a photograph of her available, which was used as a poster in an anti-drugs campaign in the locality.[17] Evidence of the exceptional nature of the attention given to Leah Betts is to be found in the massive and sustained increase in the number of reports in which 'Ecstasy' and 'death' are both mentioned after her death (Figure 1.3). Another indicator is the number of reports, and the time-scale of their distribution, devoted to other Ecstasy victims. Twenty-one other fatalities were reported in the press during the twelve months in question; the number of reports devoted to each of them varied from three to fifty-six, whereas Leah Betts was mentioned in approximately 500 reports. The story of Leah Betts received far greater coverage than that accorded to any previous drug coma or fatality in the absence of any other element of newsworthiness such as celebrity.

Moreover, the behaviour of news sources is partly premised upon their own understanding of the news value of the story. The initiatives of the press officers were, by their own accounts, more or less routine, but had included the prediction of extensive media interest. Many grieving parents had made statements to the press, even if not as many as the Betts. But the Bettses' willingness was in part evoked by the predicted level of media interest, a prediction which turned out to be accurate. From an explanatory point of view, the significant feature of the story is the immediacy of media interest as shown by the extraordinary volume of phone calls received by the police press officer immediately after the initial press conference. It was this interest that gave the Bettses the opportunity to use the media exposure for their own purposes. Thus while the availability of sources is indeed central to the news process, this availability cannot by itself explain the news profile of events: a large part of the explanation must be reserved for news values, the features of the event that fitted with journalistic criteria.

In the case of the earlier examples cited – the *Challenger* explosion

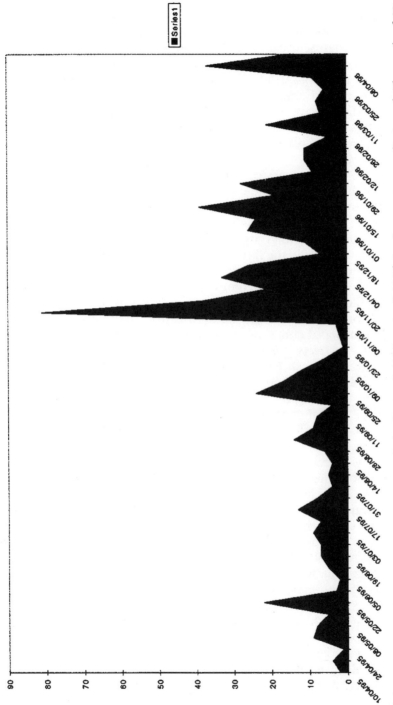

Figure 1.3 Reports mentioning 'Ecstasy' and 'death', April 1995 to April 1996. Irrelevant reports eliminated. The peak of 80 reports occurs in the week beginning Monday 13 November.

and the Lockerbie bombing – the news value of the events in question is sufficiently obvious that the principle involved can be readily overlooked. Their scope and public importance make the operation of this principle difficult to observe, because the 'fit' between event and news values is so complete. The case of Leah Betts does not have such an obvious news frame, because, rightly or wrongly, the death of a single non-famous person does not necessarily have a high news profile. Thus it is clearer in this instance that we need to enquire into its news value and the way in which that value created a particular 'event profile'.

Analysis of the internal structure of the coverage of Leah Betts' death shows that the intensity of news interest is to be explained by the long-term interest in the occurrence of death from Ecstasy ingestion in combination with a particular perception of Leah Betts herself. The dramatic frame provided by a family celebration under parental supervision, her youth, the fact that she was (in the words of the police press officer) 'the girl next door', as opposed to a stereotypical member of a drug-using subculture: all of these elements contributed to the profile of the story.[18] In this sense the story can be seen as a crystallization of parental fears about this feature of youth culture, or more general social concerns about the nature of this culture (see for example, *Daily Telegraph*, Leader, 12.3.96).

The content analysis shows that the material which contributed to her portrayal as 'the girl next door' was prominent during the opening days of the reporting of her case, but that these themes declined in prominence thereafter. (We shall return to this matter shortly.) It might appear to be natural to the point of inevitability that this should indeed be the focus of news interest in her story, but events usually present a range of possible foci – indeed, the deaths of other young drug victims were not given the degree of unequivocal sympathy so central in this instance. An alternative possible focus could have been other elements in Leah Betts' lifestyle; the event could also (in theory) have been interpreted from within a perspective which stressed the pleasures of drug-taking (although this is more or less unthinkable in mainstream media) or a policy-oriented perspective which stressed the option of decriminalization. In fact, the attention given to the story in combination with its unambiguous interpretation as a warning against drug use *per se* made any of these perspectives impossible for some time. We can see here that the combined role of news values and news sources not only explains the fact that a story is covered at all, but also explains how it is covered: in this instance the profile of the event as it appeared in the media was in accordance with the intentions of the news sources. Initial reporting was primarily focused around three elements: the personal tragedy for the family involved, the dangers of drug abuse, and attempts to apprehend the supplier. The first two are closely connected to the portrayal of her as the 'girl next door'.[19] It was this focus which led the police press officer who handled the case to stress that it was a good example of the 'constructive power of the media'. In other words, the coverage was unambiguously themed around the dangers of drug abuse and the accounts of both the victim and her family were entirely sympathetic.

We should of course add into the equation the much-reproduced photograph of Leah in intensive care. While the availability of the photograph was certainly central, its content was also crucial: it shows her on a life-support machine. Since photographers could not enter the intensive care unit, one of the medical staff took a single photograph which was pooled.[20] In fact, its news value resulted from a combination of availability and content. Its news value is implied by the recognizability it achieved. That it did indeed impact on public awareness is attested by the fact that it was used, without Leah's name, in an anti-drugs campaign some months later, accompanied only by the single word 'Sorted'. According to the ad agency responsible for the campaign, the intention was to use the picture's instant recognizability. All the feedback suggested that this supposition was justified.[21]

The intensity of media interest in Leah Betts is also to be seen in the form of its protraction.[22] All reports of her coma and death mention its cause, and her death became linked with the fates of other young people who suffered ill-effects from Ecstasy in the following months, giving a more than routine news profile to other similar events. Content analysis shows that mentions of Leah continued for a substantial period after her death (my analysis followed her story for six months), and that after the first few days, the percentage of each report devoted directly to her fell sharply and constantly.[23] As the story was defined in the first day's reporting, the themes which demonstrated Leah Betts' ordinariness were prominently featured, but as the days went by, these elements became less prominent. Reporting of her death increasingly took the form of mentions of it in the context of linked events, and focused more and more on story elements which were not directly related to her personal history. Nonetheless, the originally central element continued to be mentioned briefly, throughout the six months covered by the analysis, to remind readers of the overall significance of the story as a whole. This indicates both the extent of news relevance in her story and the way in which this relevance operates: it is the linkage between this case and other similar events which provides the impetus.

Subsequently, mentions of her became mixed with mentions of other related stories, especially the murder of three suspected drug dealers, the near-death of another young woman, the export of her liver to Spain, and a controversy provoked by a Glasgow social worker's statements about Ecstasy. On each occasion that her name becomes linked with a completely fresh event, the level of media coverage surges upwards again (see Figure 1.3). What appears to happen in this instance – and probably in other similar instances – is that the original event acquired such a clear and well-established profile that it came to be used as a way of giving a particular profile to other events which could be seen to have something in common with the earlier event. The three dead men had police records, but at the time of the discovery of their bodies there was little to link them directly to the drugs trade, and nothing to link them with Leah Betts, other than the common location of Essex; but the possibility of a link was widely used in reporting and gave the case the unequivocal profile of a drugs killing. The young woman who was taken to hospital unconscious after taking Ecstasy (among a number of other things) did not die, but the quantity of reporting of the case was due to the comparison with Leah Betts.

The protraction of interest in her case makes it relatively easy for analysis to follow the way in which news values led to a profile of the event, which was then reproduced in subsequent reporting. As a result of the way in which the media life of her story was protracted, the original news values involved – the theme of 'the girl next door' – became less and less visible in subsequent coverage. This is because the basic premise of news is that 'yesterday's news is not news' and therefore any continued attention to an event will consist of updated information, in other words fresh but linked information; what actually gives rise to the continuity – the news value of the initial event – rapidly becomes lost to view even though it is present by implication in the protraction of the event.[24]

The nature of the protraction of the interest has particular relevance for our understanding of news values. The fundamental axiom about yesterday's news may frequently result in a story dying completely, but it also commonly results in the prolongation of a story by the supply of new material which can be attached to the original core of news interest. In newsroom jargon this 'gives the story legs' and this is indeed what happened in the case of Leah Betts. A contrary example is to be seen in the case of the story of a 'flesh-eating killer bug' that dominated the front pages of tabloid newspapers for the best part of a week in May 1994, and was also prominent in broadcast and broadsheet news agendas. During that week (by coincidence) I found myself in the House of Commons Press Gallery lift with a group of Westminster journalists who agreed that the story would not last past the weekend, as it did not appear to them to have the capacity for self-renewal that would make it last longer. They were absolutely right – it had completely disappeared from news pages by the following Monday. Leah Betts' story, on the other hand, became linked to a series of other events, as we have seen, and acted as the crystallization point for a whole series of public concerns. This resulted in reports of her coma and death being linked to reports of things to which no other Ecstasy victim's death had been linked. For example, the *Daily Mirror* (16.1.96) reported that staff at Eton had received the video of her funeral which would therefore be seen by Prince William; this story is driven partly by the enduring interest in Leah Betts, but also by news focus on the royal family, and the paper's desire to promote its own anti-drugs campaign. To the extent that news sources and journalists have an interest in either prolonging or killing a story, the operation of this principle is a matter of intense practical interest. From a theoretical point of view, it is crucial because it leads journalists to look for news material and it leads sources to offer such material. That is to say: the behaviour of news sources and journalists must be explained in part by the nature of the value system by which journalists make judgements of relevance.

In brief, this chapter has shown that central to the process by which events become news is an encounter between media personnel and news sources. The negotiation between these people over what will appear in the form of news output is conducted (at least partly) in terms of the 'fit' between an event and news criteria, which dictates whether an event will become news at all and how much attention will be given to it. The way in which the event will be profiled is dictated by the degree of concordance between specified features of it and the news criteria in question. The case of the news coverage of Leah Betts shows how this principle operates in practice in one instance – the protraction of news interest enables a clear understanding of the principle.

Such negotiations and interactions are the subject of this book, which essentially follows the method used in this chapter: news values are inferred from the nature of coverage of particular events; interviews with relevant people establish how sources and journalists behaved in the news encounters in question. In the chapters that follow, news values, source motives, and strategies are analysed as topics in their own right. There follow two extended case studies, which are intended to exemplify how news encounters functioned in the instances in question. In each instance, the general shape of the case study is this: I examine how events acquired their news profile by looking at the interaction of journalists (driven by news values) and sources (driven by the desire to profile an event in a particular manner).

CHAPTER 2

News Values

'Dog bites man' is not news, 'man bites dog' is.
> (John Bogart, editor of the *New York Sun*)

News is what somebody wants to suppress; all the rest is advertising.
> (attributed to Lord Northcliffe in MacShane, 1979: 46)

These aphorisms focus on particular elements of news but do not constitute a systematic analysis. Journalism textbooks provide definitions of the newsworthy features of events; the most famous is Macdougall's 'timeliness, proximity, prominence, consequence and human interest' (quoted in Romano, 1986: 59). However, such general principles are so general that without detailed discussion of examples they tell us relatively little. The earliest attempt to provide a more systematic definition was made by Galtung and Ruge (1970). They distinguish eleven features, or dimensions, of events which make them likely to be reported in news media.

1. *Frequency*: The event must be complete within the publication cycle of the news organization reporting it.
2. *Threshold*: The event must pass a certain size threshold to qualify for sufficient importance to be newsworthy.
3. *Clarity*: What has actually happened must be relatively clear.
4. *Cultural proximity*: It must be meaningful to the audience of the news organization in question.
5. *Consonance*: The event must be in accordance with the framework of understanding which typifies the culture of the potential audience.
6. *Unexpectedness*: Within the framework of meaningfulness identified in features 4 and 5, the event must be unexpected or rare.

7. *Continuity*: If an event has already been in the news, there is a good chance it will stay there.
8. *Composition*: Coverage of events is partially dictated by the internal structure of newsgathering organizations.
9. *Actions of the elite*: Events involving elite people or organizations are more likely to be covered than those of people perceived as unimportant.
10. *Personification*: Events that can be seen in terms of individual people rather than abstractions.
11. *Negativity*: Bad events are more newsworthy than good ones.

These features of events, singly or in combination, increase the chance of an event being considered newsworthy. Inevitably most reported events are characterized by more than one of these features; particular combinations define the type of story, or the 'angle' of the event, that is responsible for its newsworthiness.

The usefulness of these analyses of news values can be shown by considering one story which was prominent in the UK media in the days following Tuesday, 27 June 1995. The English film actor Hugh Grant, who had just shot to fame after the release of *Four Weddings and a Funeral*, was accused of 'lewd conduct' with a prostitute by the Los Angeles police; charges were brought and the police identification photograph was made available to the news media. Grant did not deny the charge.

First, the event was reported immediately after it occurred. The report was 'timely' in that sense, although it probably would have been 'timely' even if the information had been made public some time after the event, since the public availability of the information would itself still have had news value. However, this does not exhaust the question of timeliness. As Galtung and Ruge (1970) argue, it is important that the event in question should be complete within the cycle of publication of the news channel. They use the example of the construction of a dam: what is reported is the beginning of the project (funding agreement) and its completion (the opening ceremony); its gradual construction on a day-by-day basis would not usually provide events that are significant. Thus 'construction' comes to mean – in news terms – inception and completion. Similarly, court cases are commonly only reported (in national media) on the first and last days, with the exception of very high-profile trials; indeed, national media crime correspondents do not regularly attend in court on the intervening days; editors rely on agency reports.[1] Another example is the reporting of a protracted event such as a war: what is reported on a day-to-day basis is what has happened during the last twenty-four hours, or what has happened since the last news report. If the latter is the case, some element of explanation of what has occurred in the time lapse is necessary and this raises the further question of the time frame that surrounds the news cycle and is implied in reports (Schudson, 1986: 84). Hugh Grant's arrest has an implied time frame deriving from the reasons for his celebrity, but beyond that it is given only by the nature of the event.

The next value to consider is 'prominence', which we can equate in this instance with Galtung and Ruge's categories of 'threshold' and 'elite': it is Grant's fame that is responsible for the newsworthiness of the event. More exactly, it is Grant's fame in the UK and the US that is responsible. Well-known in journalism is 'McLurg's law' which establishes a ratio between the size of an event and its distance from (or relevance to) the news audience (Schlesinger, 1987: 117). Gans' survey (1980: 4-6, 12) of those whose actions were reported in US news media shows that roughly 75 to 80 per cent were 'knowns', as he calls them; 20 to 25 per cent were 'unknowns'. The majority of the knowns were in fact a group of approximately fifty people, all 'high Federal officials'; the identity of these knowns is certainly affected by his sample of news media, all of which had national as opposed to regional circulations in the US, but the general principle is not in doubt. All the media in question were non-tabloid, which would also have had an effect.

In discussing 'prominence' we have already opened up the topic of 'proximity', which Galtung and Ruge call both 'proximity' and 'consonance'. In the case of Grant's arrest, prominence and proximity are effectively the same: it is his fame that is responsible for both. 'Consonance' in this instance is unproblematic since the event is perfectly comprehensible in terms of the cultural norms of our society: prostitution in relation to male sexuality, the bizarre lifestyles of the rich and famous. A category of event which poses greater problems for the cultural norms of our society, and which therefore makes the theme of 'consonance' more visible, is the religious miracle. In September 1995, all UK national newspapers reported a 'miracle' in which stone statues in Hindu temples appeared to drink milk. This constituted a problem for objective, factual news reporting since miraculous events are only partially consonant with the norms of modern Western culture. As a result UK newspapers were divided over whether to report this as a miracle or as a sham. On 27 September 1995 the London *Evening Standard* presented a summary of press reporting and commented that the nature of the event posed problems for normal news procedures. Other mysterious events such as UFO sightings may pose the same problem, depending on the credibility of the source.

In the case of Grant's arrest, we can also consider the questions of 'proximity' and 'consonance' in relationship to 'consequence' and Galtung and Ruge's category of 'continuity'. Grant's arrest had consequence in relationship to his future as a star and especially the launch of his latest film: it was debated whether the scandal might fit well or badly with the public persona involved in the launch (*Guardian* G2, 29.6.95: 2–3; *Evening Standard*, 29.6.95: 13). Even more attention was paid to the potential consequences for his much-publicized relationship with Elizabeth Hurley, who was just about to be launched as the new 'face' of Estee Lauder beauty products. As a result, follow-up stories in the UK media focused on her (since Grant managed to hide for some days) and her reaction to the news: for example, photographs of her were interpreted through captions drawing attention to the emotional significance of her expression. Here we can see a fundamental news value principle in operation: the notion of 'consequence' operates both in the sense that an event may be considered newsworthy because of its likely consequences, and may remain newsworthy over time because of the way in which news attention produces material which enables a focus upon the unravelling of these consequences – Galtung and Ruge's 'continuity'. In the case of Grant's arrest, even the prostitute's version of events was newsworthy: she was paid $100,000 for her story by the *News of the World* (*Guardian* G2, 3.7.95: 13).

The event was also unexpected. Inevitably the 'unexpectedness' of events conflicts with their 'consonance', in the sense that consonance indicates comprehensibility whereas unexpectedness points in the opposite direction. It is the balance between the two that is crucial, as was noted many years ago by an American commentator: '[the journalist's] commodity is not the normal; it is the standardised exceptional' (Bent, 1927, quoted in Sigal, 1973: 66). This event was unexpected, not of course in the sense that it is unlikely that men should consort with prostitutes, but in the sense that it is a breach of the normal moral framework of our society, and – perhaps – in a much more emotionally charged sense: Grant and Hurley had become prominent public symbols of glamour, and it seemed incomprehensible that someone with that status should be revealed so dramatically to be involved in something sordid. Here the factual reporting of an incident is linked to cultural themes that are more or less well articulated in public discussions and private conversations. The conventional distinction between factual news reporting and editorial comment or feature writing operates to maintain this distinction, although in some media – especially tabloid – the distinction between reporting and commenting is frequently blurred. As a result, the points about glamour and sordid behaviour are not found in the news reports, although they were made in commentaries at the time: this 'information' would be lacking in news reports even though – arguably – this was why so much attention was paid to the event.[2] Clearly the event was also negative, highly personalized and associated with elite people – here the importance of the event and the elite nature of Grant and Hurley's status are largely the same thing. Also, the 'personification' involved gave a personal identity to something that is otherwise publicly debated in the abstract.

By 'composition', Galtung and Ruge mean that news organizations balance coverage of different areas of activity in the world according to the subdivision of news organizations into sections. This claim is substantiated by Sigal's analysis of one year of the front pages of the *New York Times* and the *Washington Post*: he shows that 'whatever the variation in world events and news flow, … the front page [of these papers] had a tendency to contain an equal number of stories from the national, foreign and metropolitan desks' (1973: 30–1). This balance is not the result of an average over time (which would not be surprising) but is achieved on a daily basis. Tuchman observed the same process in a US regional daily (1978: 33). The explanation offered by all three studies is the bureaucratic nature of news organizations and the importance of giving different groups of journalists the amount of access to news space they expect. The Grant story happened to coincide with the election of a new leader of the Conservative Party caused by the Prime Minister's sudden and dramatic decision to resign his position as leader and seek re-election; while it is likely that the Grant story would have been newsworthy under any circumstances, its nature made it a welcome relief on the pages of newspapers and broadcast bulletins dominated by the minutiae of political debate and produced predominantly by specialist political staff.[3] Whether the balance found by Sigal would obtain in tabloid or broadcast news is unclear; certainly major news stories have the effect of 'unbalancing' the front pages.

There is a certain degree of inconsistency in these criteria which reduces their usefulness, despite the ease with which it has been possible to exemplify them. Some of the criteria are effectively elements of cognition, deriving from a social psychological approach to understanding data processing; they thus refer to subjective understanding of the world, whether on the part of the journalist or the reader – 'clarity' and 'proximity' are clear instances of such criteria.[4] Others are specific to media routines: 'page composition' and 'frequency' fall into this category; such criteria are not a part of the normal cognitive apparatus. As a result, there is a certain randomness in the way in which these criteria are able to account for news events, for there is no obvious reason why an element of universal cognitive processes, such as 'consonance', should be adopted as a criterion of news evaluation. If it is indeed clear that on occasions consonance is a relevant criterion – as in the instance of the milk miracle referred to above – it is obvious that the criterion of 'unexpectedness' is often close to incompatible with it: the tension between the two is clear.[5] Galtung and Ruge's criteria probably cannot constitute a systematic basis for the analysis of news, but are useful as an *ad hoc* set of elements with a partial explanatory value.

It is implied in the preceding analysis that the general principles which constitute 'newsworthiness' are only to be understood in relation to particular contexts. In each case, we have to ask what features of the event in question make it conform to the news criterion in question. As an example, we can take Galtung and Ruge's own instance of the construction of a dam, where what is reported is various stages in the construction which are complete within a single news cycle, such as the opening ceremony. Of course, it is true that the ceremony does indeed conform to this criterion in the way that they say. But that is not the only – or even the main – reason why the event is reported; it is also because the construction of the dam – 'summarised', as they put it, in the ceremony – passes a certain 'threshold' of importance or interest. The criterion of 'threshold' is rather obvious in the example of Hugh Grant, but in other instances such as the construction of a dam, what occurs is that the actual event chosen as the peg for the report only crosses the threshold because it is the event that fits within the news cycle while depending for its importance on its relationship to the longer-term process which it summarizes. In other words, in an instance such as the construction of a dam, the news judgement is that the overall event is important and/or interesting and that its overall significance justifies the attention given to the particular event reported (e.g. its inauguration).

But this analysis needs to be taken one stage further. By referring to the importance of the event, we are still essentially in the realm of the 'universal' news criteria listed above. But an event is only important in a particular context, or – if you prefer – it is important because of some dimension of the event. A dam may be important because it is large and expensive, or because it is a threat to wildlife or historic sites, or because it will transform people's lives for the better (or all of the above and many other reasons). Whatever is the case in a particular instance, it is that particular understanding of the significance of the event that will constitute its newsworthiness and that will provide the theme of the coverage. Thus the 'universal' criteria of newsworthiness are always to be understood in terms of their relevance to the structures of particular events.

For example, in the summer of 1995, a report of an abnormally high number of hospital admissions for asthma in south London was linked to the 'packaging' of some already published scientific studies of the effects of air quality on respiratory problems by a public relations company retained by various medical charities.[6] Here the timeliness is given by reported hospital admissions, which transforms the news value of the already published research; but by the same token, it is the wider frame of public concern about pollution and health which gives the fact about admissions its impact power: the news value of the events in question derives from the nature of their links to the context in which they occur. We have already seen the way in which the news coverage of Leah Betts' death could not be explained without reference to features of the social context in which the events occurred (the crystallization of parental fears about teenage drug use in 'ordinary' families, for example). This principle applies to all news stories in the sense that the general principles of newsworthiness discussed above can only operate within particular event-contexts. Thus Hugh Grant is famous, but being famous implies being famous for some particular kind of activity. In his case, it was his association with the world of glamour, produced through his personal relationships and his film persona. This fame – as opposed to any other fame – seemed incompatible with the sordidness of the event.[7] Increased hospital admissions for respiratory ailments passed the threshold test because of the context of well-developed public concerns about the impact of pollution.

Thus when we explore events in terms of their articulation of news values – in other words, when we analyse the information flows in which the public profile of events is constituted – we expect to do so in terms of the relationship between the events and the framework within which they occur. Such frameworks are interpreted according to the general news principles outlined above, but in order to explain the relationship between news values, source strategies and journalistic judgements, it is the features of particular contexts which need to be examined. In Chapter 1, I argued that news values were not an empirical entity, but an 'ideal object' akin to a language, in other words a semiotic system: they consist of a set of criteria which transcend individual judgements, but whose empirical existence is manifested in their application in particular contexts. Now we can see that news is doubly a semiotic system as well as an empirical one: it is cast in the terms of the 'universal' news values and also in the 'local' symbolic terms of understandings of the meanings of events or categories of events. As a result, the discussions of particular series of events in this book will concentrate primarily on the context-bound elements of news values rather than the 'universal' ones to be found in textbooks. But it is significant that news criteria always involve understanding events both in terms of their relationship to ongoing contexts and, simultaneously, in terms of their conformity to the 'universal' news values of timeliness, etc. In other words, news value consists of that aspect of an event which is in accordance with the timeliness, interest, importance, etc., of the event's relationship to its context. From the point of view of news sources, it is the capacity to define an event in terms where their own interpretation and news criteria converge which provides the motive for attempting to achieve a public definition of it via the news media.

Gans (1980: 145–80) defines newsworthiness in terms of the 'suitability' of events, of which there are three basic forms: 'substantive', 'product' and 'competition'. Substantive suitability consists of elements of story content, essentially its importance or interest; Gans' argument here is little different from Galtung and Ruge. 'Product' suitability is based in the relationship between the story and the format of the medium or channel reporting it. It may be, for example, the size of a story in relation to the audience's presumed interest in it; or it may be the availability of some particular element in the composition of the story. For example, in the case of Hugh Grant's arrest, his photograph was made available to the media close to the moment the story broke in a way which gave it a certain rarity value: the police identity photograph was made available to the media by the local police – a routine occurrence – and an enterprising agency photographer, realizing its potential, re-photographed it and promptly made it available on the Internet; the rapid availability of a photograph, which was the exact opposite of the usual film star 'glamour' pose, was clearly part of the profile of the story (*Decisive Moments*, BBC2, 28.12.95). In other words, the photograph was certainly 'timely', but it was also its pictorial impact which was significant, and this can only be understood in terms of the context – the contrast between a police identity photograph and a glamorous publicity photograph. In general, all other things being equal, television is more likely to give news attention to an event where film is available; this has led organizations that seek publicity via the news to ensure the availability of relevant, fresh video footage at times that fit with TV channels' output schedule (known as 'video news releases', their role in maximizing TV coverage of events fell somewhat into disrepute in the aftermath of the Brent Spar affair).[8] Competition suitability refers to the desire not to miss something that rival channels have got, and if possible to scoop them with an exclusive.

All of the above are features of events which make them potentially liable to attract editorial attention and to be selected for inclusion in news reports. However, journalists also distinguish between different categories of news: the most common are 'hard' news, 'soft' news, 'spot' news, 'diary' news, 'breaking' news and 'investigative' journalism.[9]

The reliability of information about events is another feature of decisions about their inclusion (or exclusion) in news reports, and thus part of news values. Reliability derives in part from the journalistic evaluation of the sources from which information is obtained, in part from corroboration. Information is considered to be reliable when it comes from a proven reliable source, or when it can be verified. Journalism textbooks often use 'triangulation' as a way of assessing the reliability of information, i.e. checking it with two independent sources. A reliable source may be one whom a reporter has come to trust through extended personal experience, or one whose institutional position makes him or her reliable because she or he is obliged to take public responsibility for any on-the-record statement. Thus any such statement, if made within the speaker's competence as the representative of an organization or a body of knowledge with a valid public profile, will be acceptable as 'true for all practical purposes' (Murphy, 1991: 12; cf. Gans, 1980: 128–31, 181–6; see also Chapter 7). In other instances, reliability may be more problematic: if information is given 'off the record', 'unattributably' or as 'background' only, the speaker is not obliged to take public responsibility for what is said; the role that such information flows play in political communications is well known, and the ethical implications have been widely debated in both the USA and the UK.[10]

Here we should distinguish carefully between two different news judgements: in one, the fact that 'X claimed such-and-such', where X is an important or interesting person, is a fact worthy of publication even if there is no reason to think that X is telling the truth, or no way of checking it; in another, journalists will only accept a piece of information as factually correct and worth printing if it can be shown that X was in fact telling the truth. The relationship between these two judgements is complicated and enormously varied according to circumstances. To take a simple fictitious example: if someone with large, well-defined public responsibilities (say, the prime minister) says that he thinks that X is the case, the fact that he has said so is in itself worthy of attention, even if he is mistaken or lying. But in other circumstances the process may be very different: during the events that subsequently came to public attention as the insider trading scandals on Wall Street in the late 1980s, two bankers tried to launch a price rise in some shares they had bought by publicizing the plan (which they knew to be true) that the company would shortly be the subject of a take-over bid; they did this by tipping off a Chicago business-page journalist. The journalist checked the story and decided it was not true, or at any rate unsubstantiable; it was not printed. It was printed only when the bankers substantiated it with details of private meetings which other sources corroborated (Stewart, 1991:

125). The journalist's care was no doubt due to the fact that attempts to launch rumours in order to move share prices ('ramping') is a well-known device (see Chapter 4). A more complicated example is the origin of the scandal concerning rigged quiz shows in the USA in the late 1950s (Stone and Yohn, 1992: 13–19). Here an actor who had been a contestant objected to what he saw and approached various people with a view to stopping it, including a newspaper reporter. The reporter persuaded him to write out an affidavit to give to the Federal Communications Commission and – without telling him – sent it to the FCC; sometimes together, sometimes separately, they approached various members of the quiz-show organization and their sponsors, and eventually the New York District Attorney's office. At the quiz-show offices the actor was eventually given a substantial amount of money in cash in return for signing documents, which he was not allowed to retain in copy form; the journalist's paper considered that without the documents the story was not printable. However, they subsequently ran the story on the basis that a complaint had been made to the FCC and the District Attorney. In this instance, the reporter clearly believed that the complaint was essentially true, but was having some difficulty in substantiating it because there was only one source and no documentation. By involving the two official bodies, even if only passively, there was the core of a story which had objective validity: a complaint had indeed been made, even if it had subsequently turned out to be unjustified. Clearly the hope was that publicity would unleash a further sequence of events which would bring the truth into the open and validate the complaint. In this instance, the 'objective method' of reporting only facts ('a complaint has been made') served the interests of truth rather well; but it is often said that this method makes journalists into accomplices of established public authorities because of the tendency to accept the fact that they say something as sufficient warrant for publishing it as if it was the truth (for example: Willis, 1991; Weaver, 1994; Hallin, 1986): in this account 'objectivity' and 'truth' are not at all the same thing (see Lichtenberg, 1991, for a cogent defence of the objective method against such criticisms).

So far this analysis has proceeded as if news values were uniformly distributed across media systems, but there is an important reservation to be made: the distinction between tabloid and broadsheet formats. These two formats have traditionally been associated with differences in news values: the type of event which might figure in tabloid formats might not pass the threshold criteria of broadsheet media, and vice versa.[11] Again the instance of Hugh Grant's arrest is a good example: this event in fact did figure in both types of media, because his arrest made it hard news, but had the event consisted of somebody less authoritative than the police asserting that Grant had been guilty of the behaviour he was in fact charged with, it is possible that the allegations might have been reported in the tabloids but not in the broadsheets. The actress Gillian Taylforth sued the *Sun* over a report in which the newspaper claimed that she had been questioned by the police over an incident of lewd conduct with her lover; the source of the allegation was certainly not official. The original report in the *Sun* appeared some time after the incident in question, and was little mentioned by broadsheet media until the court action.

The differences in news values are held to be considerable, as the tabloids are accused of sensationalization and triviality, implicitly suggesting that broadsheet journalism is characterized by the opposite of these attributes. For example, the commentator Roy Greenslade, writing in the *Observer* (14.7.96), made the accusation that the news values of UK national tabloids led to self-evidently inadequate coverage of the 'stand-off' between Ulster Loyalist marchers and the Royal Ulster Constabulary at Drumcree in the previous week: coverage was relegated to brief mentions on their inside pages. However, another recent journalistic commentary suggested that in the last ten years the differences between the tabloids and the broadsheets had been considerably eroded: both in layout design and choice of stories, the broadsheets had become more like the tabloids (Matthew Engel, *Guardian*, 3.10.96). For instance, the coverage of an event such as Hugh Grant's arrest would probably have received little coverage in the broadsheets before the 1990s.

There are no wide-ranging systematic studies of these differences but we can address the question by considering what the potential differences are. They fall into the two categories, which are effectively different dimensions of comparison:

1. the choice of stories covered, i.e. the decision whether or not to give any space at all to a particular event;
2. the treatment given to the story.

Both of these dimensions need further development.

Story choice can be seen primarily in terms of the importance, interest and meaning of the event in question relative to all the other events that are potential candidates for inclusion – this is the purpose of traditional studies of news values, summarized above. But it should also be seen in terms of the time in the life-cycle of the event at which editorial choice is to be made; this involves a calculation about whether treatment by other media makes coverage necessary, and – crucially – decisions about whether to continue coverage of the event after the first day in a potential news event life-cycle. Analysis of this variety can only be done on a longitudinal basis, following one or more stories through at least some part of their life-cycle. The Louise Woodward case study does this; the case studies in other chapters are all based on longitudinal analysis.

Treatment can be analysed in both quantitative and qualitative terms: the amount of coverage devoted to the event; its place in the paper (an indication of the importance attributed to the event); the choice of themes within the event which are deemed to constitute its meaning.

The quantitative comparisons, amount and position, need some refinement. The absolute amount of coverage devoted to a story in a newspaper is not a good indication of the importance attached to it since newspapers have very different amounts of space available for news reports (the 'newshole', to use US newsroom jargon), and therefore in my analyses the absolute size of reports is expressed in a device which makes allowance for this difference.[12] The qualitative comparison between themes can be quantified by measuring the amount of space devoted to each theme as a percentage of report space; some of the longitudinal studies in later chapters are based on this technique.

Analysis of a small and chronologically random sample reveals the following similarities and differences between the tabloid and the broadsheet press:

- There is substantial agreement between the two sectors about what constitutes the main story or stories on any given day. This does not imply that all papers always choose the same story as their lead story, but that more often than not there is majority agreement about the events to which substantial attention is to be given by the national press; exceptions are likely to come from scoops, from the fact of previous coverage producing a new agenda, and from the search for title identity. The latter probably derives mainly from commercial rivalry, where sector-specific rivalries dictate tactics rather than differentiation from other-format papers.

- Where stories are covered by a substantial proportion of the press – but neither universally nor with the degree of emphasis given to major events – story choice is not very likely to correlate with the tabloid/broadsheet distinction. Where this distinction is concerned, variations in story *choice* are less important than variations in story *treatment*; this is as likely to be a product of title identity or of idiosyncratic news judgement as it is of format.

- A large percentage of the stories to which not much attention is given are reported in only a small minority of the press, and it is difficult to discern any consistent pattern in their distribution.

- Where there are clear differences in story choice between the two press sectors they are predicated primarily on two features:

  The tabloid press carries substantially fewer foreign stories than the broadsheet. With the exception of major political stories, the criterion of choice for tabloid inclusion of such stories is either human interest (e.g. disasters) or UK involvement in some form; availability of photographs is also important here.

  The distinction between human interest stories and policy community stories; although both sectors carry both types of story, there is a clear difference of emphasis in this respect.

- Where the same stories are covered across both sectors, broadsheets extend coverage (beyond the tabloid limits) by including more material which refers to background information, policy context or a wider range of reactions to events.

This analysis probably over-emphasizes the similarities and underestimates the differences between the two sectors. First, in order to simplify the contours of the comparison, the mid-markets have been placed in the same category as the red-top tabloids; however, although the format of both is tabloid in the literal sense, this similarity hides a mass of differences; the mid-markets have a larger newshole. (In the case of the *Daily Mail* the difference is considerable – in our snapshots it covers more events than the *Independent*.)

Secondly, the analysis is based upon general news pages, and many of the most obvious differences between tabloids and broadsheets are to be found elsewhere – in sports coverage, in features, and in competitions and promotions; by the same token, this analysis omits pin-ups. In particular, the red-tops' constant attention to showbiz stories is omitted from the comparison because it is subsumed under variations in story choice. Also, the random sample which underpins this analysis does not include any days on which either of the red-top tabloids was campaigning on any issue. Overt campaigning is one of the striking differences between the two sectors. For example, the *Sun* ran a protracted campaign on behalf of the Dunblane parents' attempts to get a comprehensive ban on handguns following the massacre in the local primary school.

The content analysis in Curran and Seaton (1985: 114–5) which compares percentages of total space devoted to different types of content by title and across time can be reinterpreted to allow some comparisons which are relevant here (although the small number (two) of broadsheet titles in the sample must lead to caution). Most significant is the balance between human interest and public affairs reporting, where the figures are as follows: over all papers, average public affairs space is 18 per cent, average human interest space is 22 per cent; tabloids are consistently below the public affairs average, broadsheets are consistently above it, mid-markets are on or close to it. In human interest reporting, the mid-markets and the tabloids are consistently above average and the broadsheets well below it (figures for 1976). Tabloids consistently give roughly 8 to 10 per cent more space to photographs than broadsheets. This reveals a significantly different approach to news.

Thirdly, in an attempt to make valid comparisons about the treatment of topics, the analysis is disproportionately based on stories which were in fact shared across sectors. But equally interesting would be an analysis which looked at story choice based upon a selection of events which allowed the type of treatment which was typical of the paper's 'general approach' or identity, which is not separable from its sector position. For example, on 30.10.96 the entire national press with the exception of the *Sun* put on the front page the story of the disagreement between the then Education Secretary Gillian Shepherd and the Prime Minister about corporal punishment in schools. The *Sun* led on a story about a postman who had been sacked for looking through a woman's letter-box and seeing her in the nude, and relegated the 'caning' story to the inside pages. There were two possible reasons for this: the *Sun* had in fact broken the story about policy differences apropos corporal punishment in a brief exclusive report the previous day and perhaps felt it did not want to give it maximum prominence on the second day; but no doubt it is mainly a question of the type of treatment the two events lend themselves to.

Finally, very little attention has been paid to differences in news values deriving from political affiliation. This is largely an artefact of the actual days chosen for the snapshot analyses, where political differences were relatively low in salience; it is also possible that the nature of UK parliamentary politics in the final months of the Major government and the first few months of the Blair government blurred the traditional political allegiances of the press, albeit for different reasons. The relationship between news values and the political affiliations of newspapers is sufficiently complex to require separate analysis.

A balance between our two types of analysis suggests that in the case of major news stories there is a great deal of similarity between the two sectors where both story choice and the core of story treatment are concerned. However, as soon as we move away from this area of concern, the differences are marked. What is unclear – and needs a form of analysis that is more subtle than this one – is the extent to which differences in identity between titles and between sectors lead to both differences in the types of story chosen for coverage, and differences in emphasis within story treatment. The final section of this

Chronology of Louise Woodward's trial for murder

7–11.2.97	Baby Matthew Eappen goes into coma and subsequently dies; Woodward charged with murder
5–8.3.97	Initial court proceedings against Woodward
7.10.97	Full trial starts
30.10.97	Jury gives 'guilty' verdict
3.11.97	Judge announces review of verdict
11.11.97	Judge quashes verdict, substitutes 'manslaughter' charge. Woodward freed, pending appeal, but has to remain in Massachusetts

chapter follows a particular story that was universally and massively covered during one weekend in an attempt to see how such differences and similarities affect the coverage of one event: the trial verdict in the case of au pair Louise Woodward, charged in the USA with the murder of the baby she was caring for.[13] The October trial attracted attention in all UK national dailies and on television, following more sporadic coverage during the spring and summer.

The guilty verdict was delivered on Thursday evening, 30.10.97, at around 9.30 p.m. local time (2.30 a.m. Friday UK time); sentencing was the following morning. The already high volume of attention increased dramatically at the moment of the verdict. On Saturday and Sunday, all national newspapers carried coverage. No doubt the motive for the wide coverage was the extent of earlier coverage, and in particular extensive TV coverage of the trial while it was in progress, using live footage from the courtroom.[14] Thus the coverage at the weekend must be seen in the context of the continuation of interest from the earlier stages of the story, and in particular from the previous day's TV coverage. It is also – arguably – a tabloid story in the sense that coverage is dominated by or predicated on the sensational nature and human interest element of the events, as will be seen in the content analysis; yet analysis of the coverage of the whole case reveals that broadsheets paid as much and as regular attention to events as did the tabloids; indeed, in the period between the opening of court proceedings in the spring and the trial proper in the autumn, the *Daily Telegraph* provided the most regular coverage.

The thematic core of the story as it developed from the moment of the verdict can be seen by looking at the reporting in an evening mid-market paper which has a regional monopoly. The London *Evening Standard* covered the event extensively, devoting the entire first seven pages of editorial content to the story.[15] The front page had a banner headline and a photograph spanning the width of the entire page, the pooled courtroom photograph taken at the moment she reacted to the verdict by a photographer for the *Boston Globe* (*Decisive Moments*, BBC2, 31.12.97). They occupied more than 50 per cent of the page, the majority of its editorial content. The rest of the page reported the defendant's shock at the verdict, brief comments from both sets of lawyers, and a brief report of public reaction. Pages 2 to 7 contained the following material: details of the defendant's reactions and the length of the jury's deliberation, lawyers' comments, a portrait of her prison, UK attitudes to American trials, a report from the defendant's home village in England and columnists' comments.

In this coverage we can see clearly the core of the human interest elements of the story (shock caused by the verdict in both the defendant and others) and the way in which the extent of the interest leads to a search for extra details to flesh out the bare bones of the story as defined by the traditional hard news questions of 'Who? What? Where? When? How?' The core of the story is what drives it forward across time, but the drive results in the accumulation of ever-changing details. On Saturday, the national press added to the core as defined on Friday. The *Daily Mirror* overtly campaigned to define the verdict as unjust , and papers were able to add background material about the defendant's personal history and the reactions of those involved in the trial or observers of it. In addition, many papers carried analyses of the au pair system as it functions in the USA, including the information that the agency responsible for placing Louise Woodward was paying her defence costs (which had already been noted earlier in the year).

All newspapers took fundamentally the same line on the story: that the verdict was very surprising and (implicitly or explicitly) wrong. All tabloids explicitly reported the verdict as wrong, broadsheets and mid-markets followed the conventions of objective reporting by summarizing opinions and facts which pointed implicitly in the same direction. As well as the common core of reporting focused on the conduct and result of the trial, and the immediate reactions of those most directly concerned, the range of material covered was as follows: reactions of people less directly concerned (villagers in the defendant's home village, her ex-boyfriend, other friends, other au pairs); the range of protest against the verdict, and the organization of it; direct campaigning by the newspapers themselves; possible future tactics by the defence team; the opinions of the jurors and the judge; portraits of legal personnel and of the bereaved parents; legal and cultural differences between the USA and the UK; courtroom television; the regulation of the au pair system; and the difficulties of childrearing.

In this range of material we can see the same basic outline as was found in the *Evening Standard* coverage on the day the verdict was announced: a core of detail predicated on the human interest of the case, surrounded by a range of issues characterized by greater or lesser distance from the core. Thus the campaigning tactics adopted by some tabloids are very closely related to the human interest core because they presuppose that the human interest has sparked off great sympathy for the defendant (evidence of which was already available to the papers through details such as Sky viewing figures). The policy-oriented issues such as the regulation of the au pair system are clearly much further removed from the core of human interest. We could anticipate that tabloid coverage would be characterized by majority focus on the core of human interest material, whereas mid-market and broadsheet coverage would include a wider range of the potential issues. Analysis of individual titles' coverage broadly supports this contention.

The content analysis shows that on the day after the verdict the primary emphases of all titles' reporting are the trial, the verdict, predictions about the immediate future, and the reactions of those involved in some degree or other with the trial. The reactions of those directly involved received relatively little coverage on the day after the verdict, due to lack of access. All titles gave space to the subject of the defendant's future, but this elides significant differences, as it does not distinguish between human interest stories about what the defendant's life in prison would be like, and discussions of future defence tactics; the tabloid titles gave more attention to the former, less to the latter. Also, attention to reactions of those not directly connected with events – again a feature of all titles' reporting – fails to distinguish between lawyers' reactions to the verdict and that of other interested parties (e.g. friends and neighbours); again this balance roughly correlates with the tabloid/broadsheet distinction. The three themes which are most distant from the core of the story – differences in culture between the two nations, the US system of justice, and the international childcare system – are emphasized more in the broadsheets than the tabloids. The *Daily Mail* pays extensive attention to the childcare system, but its coverage is thematically distinctive in that its focus is the low value accorded to motherhood in the modern world rather than to the norms of paid childcare, a more dominant theme in the broadsheet titles.

On the Sunday – two days after the verdict – the primary focus did not shift. However, the story slipped down tabloid news agendas: fewer themes are mentioned, and the reduced amount of space given to the story as a whole, as well as its placing, indicates a changed priority. On the Sunday too the broadsheets consistently gave more space to those elements of the story that are furthest away from its core than did the tabloids; indeed, it is likely that the low availability of new material directly related to the core played a part in tabloid decisions to move it down their news agendas.

However, the relationship between tabloid and broadsheet coverage of these events cannot be resolved in these terms alone: other factors are equally important. In particular, they say nothing about the emotional tone of the treatment, and the extent to which this differed between tabloids and broadsheets. Several factors are relevant.

First, the question of language. It is often said that tabloid style is characterized by exuberant, dramatic use of language, and it is indeed easy to find examples: the two-column by half a column, white-on-black headline 'Your justice stinks' (*Sunday Sport*) contrasts easily with the three-line, three-column 'Jury believed nanny did not murder baby' (*Sunday Times*). However, informal analysis of the coverage of Louise Woodward's trial verdict shows that most of the tabloid reporting of the case is not sensationalist in its use of language. Yet 'most' may be misleading: it is true that words whose role is clearly to dramatize are relatively infrequent, but even one in a paragraph is capable of changing the overall impact of the writing. For example: 'In a stunning admission of the flimsiness of the case against Louise, juror Jodie Godber said they felt obliged to deliver a guilty verdict because of the judge's instructions to them' (*Mail on Sunday*, 2.11.97: 1).

Here the single word 'stunning' changes the impact of the whole paragraph. Indeed, what may be characteristic of tabloid style is not the constant use of such language, as is often alleged, but its relatively infrequent use, calculated to change the overall tone of reporting. Here the paragraph is close to the top of the story, which increases the impact.

Secondly, the role of pictures and other graphic devices. Large headlines and prominent photographs tend in general to increase the emotional impact of reporting. Traditionally, these have been associated with tabloid coverage rather than broadsheet; however, all the broadsheet Sundays used large headlines and photographs in their coverage. As we have seen, the photographs were largely TV-derived, and it seems likely – although unprovable – that the widespread circulation of courtroom TV coverage via UK broadcast news bulletins increased the relevance of photographs in newspaper coverage. It has been said that one of the ways in which the broadsheets have come increasingly to resemble the tabloids is in terms of layout and especially the use of large headlines and photographs.[16] The coverage of Louise Woodward's trial verdict by the Sundays supports this view. Whether this should be understood as a criticism is less clear. The advantage of contemporary layout norms, including photographs and headlines, is that items are very clearly signposted, enabling readers to follow patterns of interest in their reading of the paper's content; it is difficult to see how this could be viewed negatively.[17] However, the use of graphic devices may also inflect the interpretation of events offered by a report. The availability of a photograph may in itself lead to an expansion of news coverage, as we have already seen in the cases of the death of Leah Betts and Hugh Grant's arrest for 'lewd conduct'. The graphic devices may offer an interpretation of the event which is not in accordance with either the story as reported in the main body of the report, or with reality. For example, during the Korean war an American soldier was persuaded to pose for a photograph giving a dying Korean a drink of water; in fact, he was only willing to do so if it was done quickly and using the photographer's water ration (Evans, 1978: Introduction, n.p.). When a photograph is not misleading in this sense, and is entirely appropriate – as is clearly the case with the courtroom photographs of Louise Woodward – it may none the less be the case that the photograph acts as an incentive to the reader to interpret the event in terms predicated on, or dominated by, the evidence of personal emotions as revealed in the photography; the use of TV clips may have the same effect. In principle, the same is true of a headline: it inflects the interpretation of the report that follows. If a headline is not inaccurate in either of these two senses, its visual prominence is none the less an incentive to the reader to interpret the detail presented in the body of the report in the light of what it suggests. The headline is a significant relay in the construction of meaning, and the more one-dimensional and prominent it is, the more it is likely to have this effect. For example, a story in London *Evening Standard* (24.2.98) bore the headline 'Brother flies to join British nurse facing the electric chair', a story concerning a British resident of Florida who had shot her husband after discovering he was having an affair. While the headline is not misleading – since she was charged with murder which could if proved bring the death penalty in that state – it focuses attention on the question of penalty rather than guilt or innocence, which is (arguably) at least as important a question.

Thirdly, the role of broadcast media. As has been briefly suggested above, the Woodward trial was prominently featured in broadcast media, and the availability of live coverage from the courtroom (still forbidden in UK trials) certainly played a part. The availability of video footage is always a consideration in TV newsroom assessment of the value of particular stories (although by no means the only one). Here the focus on personal response as shown in facial expressions and body language, which is a necessary accompaniment of the norms of broadcast *mise-en-scène*, emphasizes elements of the events which are comprehensible in terms which derive from personal response, and may correspondingly marginalize elements of events which do not derive from it; of course, such other elements can always be re-emphasized through other journalistic devices, such as analytic commentary. In the case of the Woodward trial it is arguable that the widespread protests that followed the verdict (reported in most of the Sunday papers analysed here) derived from an empathy with the defendant which would have been far less likely were it not for the television coverage. To the extent that these factors are indeed operating, the norms of TV reporting are subtly altering the relationship between the different factors involved in public perceptions of the criminal justice system; the extent to which they impact upon the conduct of trials themselves is a more complex matter which must be debated elsewhere. The principle is the manner in which news agendas are driven by the circulation of information by different media appearing at different points in the daily news cycle, something which is only visible when individual stories are tracked across time.

This analysis suggests that the distinction between broadsheet and tabloid styles derives primarily from the selection of elements of a story in order to create a distinctive profile for events. Preference for the personal rather than the policy elements derives from event selection, but also from the use of pictures, which invite personalization, and from headlines which inflect the understanding of subsequent detail.

It is clear that this story was driven by the human interest elements: they form the common core that runs through all the coverage surveyed. To this extent we could say that the story was tabloid-driven, although we have already seen that in fact the broadsheets paid the same level of attention as the tabloids. However, it is also true that the level of public interest in the events was what allowed the broadsheets (and to a lesser extent the tabloids, see pp. 41-3) to expand the scope of their reporting beyond the narrative of the events and to bring to public attention matters that were peripherally relevant but also of wider public significance: for example, the regulation of au pair arrangements, or more generally the status of childcare arrangements in the USA and elsewhere. In the range of issue coverage the tabloids' focus was narrower than the mid-market and broadsheet media. However, in another respect, this distinction starts to break down, for the peripheral topics were indeed mentioned in all three.[18]

To summarize this chapter: news values transcend individual judgements, although of course they are to be found embodied in every news judgement made by particular journalists. These values are in effect a system of criteria which are used to make decisions about the inclusion and exclusion of material, and also – crucially and less obviously – about which aspects of stories to present in the form of news output. We have also seen that news values are far from a unified entity, since it is clear that they are divided by medium and by format, as well as by title identity. In particular, where the differences between broadsheet and tabloid formats in the UK national press are concerned, we can see that:

- there is a core of news values which are more or less shared across media and across sectors;
- this core is only operative in conjunction with an understanding of the significance of events in relationship to their contexts;
- this significance is subject to wide fluctuations of assessment between media sectors, but less so where major public events are concerned, to the extent that coverage of many such events is orchestrated around a consensual core;
- the history of stories – in other words, of the public profile of events in so far as it derives from the media – must also be seen in terms of the circulation of news between media and media sectors, and in particular across time.

Lastly, we should stress that this set of values constitutes a symbolic system which is the currency in which access to news space is negotiated, and therefore also in which access to below-the-line publicity is negotiated between journalists and sources. At this point we can turn to the subject of the motives and strategies of news sources.

CHAPTER 3

Source Strategies

In the preceding pages we have seen the extent to which and the ways in which journalists are dependent upon sources, as well as the ways in which the encounters between them are mediated by news values. We now view the situation from another angle: the reasons that sources have for entering into contact with journalists. We have already seen some examples of source motives, but we can go somewhat further than anecdotal examples in formulating the factors that structure the encounter from the source point of view.

The moment of the news encounter is commonly preceded by another where the decision is taken to enter it, and how to behave while there.[1] Analytically, we can distinguish two elements in source situations: the sources' purposes in entering the news encounter and the techniques used by sources for realizing their purposes.

Source purposes are not easily susceptible to generalization, since they derive from the detail of the situations, and in a sense can be summarized in the pithy words of a journalist: 'Detective chief inspectors tell journalists things in the same way City tipsters tell journalists things. For a reason.' (John Sweeney, *Observer* Supplement, 5.12.93). However, recent literature on source behaviour allows some measure of generalization from the case studies involved.[2]

The main themes which emerge from this literature are:

- the public right to know (which includes mandatory disclosure)
- the attempt to modify or improve the profile of an organization
- the desire to build credibility with the media
- policy development
- faction fighting
- damage limitation

Public right to know

Although constitutional guarantees of the public right to know are not homogeneous internationally, and are usually balanced by counter-vailing legislation protecting commercial and other professional confidentiality, state security, etc., there is a general presumption in democratic societies that some degree of practical recognition of the right to know is an integral part of the political order. Even in a state of war such considerations apply, albeit balanced by military considera-tions of secrecy and the desire to confuse the enemy through mis- or disinformation. At the beginning of the Falklands crisis, it appears that the Royal Navy Task Force which mounted the campaign to re-take the islands tried to exclude journalists entirely, and only agreed to do so at the insistence of the No. 10 Press Office. Its head, Bernard Ingham (1991: 286), argued that 'in the national and Government interest, the war should be reported from the front'. We should note that here the policy is not only dictated by the public right to know, but by desire to gain political credit; none the less the right to know was a potent argument against those who wanted to cut off information flows. The Gulf War also was reported from close to the front, albeit under conditions dictated primarily by US information strategy (Macarthur, 1992: 30–36).[3] The same argument applies to events such as disasters, where the public right to information is acknowledged. Since an information black-out is out of the question under such circumstances, the relevant organizations need a mode of operation which is capable of handling the potentially conflicting demands of news media, rescue organizations and those affected by the disaster. In other words, the public right to know has a profound impact upon the nature of such organizations (Deppa, 1993: 208). Schlesinger and Tumber report similar concerns on the part of senior police personnel who stress openness and accountability in police policy (1994: 112–13, 120–3). Mandatory revelation is clearly central to the public reporting of business activities: under UK legislation companies must publish their accounts at least once a year, and this obligation creates a framework in which decisions about what to reveal publicly are partly out of company control.

Although this principle may be clear, its applications are often the subject of uncertainty and controversy. For example, it was revealed on 9 July 1995 that the British Department of Health and the Department of Agriculture had been warned about the dangers of listeria infection in certain types of food two years before it had made these warnings public. Indeed, the Ministers had signed orders preventing disclosure of relevant documentation (Public Interest Immunity certificates) to people trying to establish Government negligence in court. The then Secretary of State for Health argued that Government had to balance the need to avoid unnecessary alarm among the public with the need for disclosure of relevant information (*Sunday Times*, 9.7.95; *Guardian*, 10.7.95). The regulations which control mandatory public disclosure of activities are far from homogeneous between countries, and, within countries, between different organizations and categories of activity.

Profile modification

For many organizations, news media publicity is a way of producing a particular profile. Under these circumstances 'information subsidy'[4] may well be a relatively cheap way of buying access to something that could not be acquired in any other resource-efficient way. Fishman (1980: 4–10) discusses the example of a reported 'crime wave' in New York in 1976, in which the focus was on black youths 'mugging' elderly white victims. The sequence of thematically linked reports began because a reporter had received a lot of help on a particular story from a particular police unit set up to deal with crimes with elderly victims, and which wanted more attention and resources. Despite reporters seeing police statistics indicating a reduction in such crimes, and despite many individual reporters having misgivings about the reality of the supposed 'crime wave', reports of individual incidents which fitted the common pattern continued because 'the crime wave was a force weighing heavily on [reporters'] judgments about what was news, and it simply could not be ignored' (1980: 5). The reporting pattern set up a symbiotic relationship, in which a report of one spectacular incident led to political attention to the event, which led to instructions for special monitoring of the actions of the specialist police unit and increased staffing, which led to an increased number of arrests for this category of offences, which produced more reporting and more political attention.[5]

A frequent tactic on the part of Government and voluntary organizations is 'flying a kite'. Here the news is leaked – or otherwise unofficially issued – that Government intends to introduce policy X, in such a way that the nature of the information flow makes it deniable. Frequently, policy X is in fact one from a range of options, and the purpose of the unofficial deniable announcement is to 'test the water', to see what public reaction will be. If it is excessively unfavourable, the option can be denied or quietly dropped; if favourable or only marginally unfavourable, other possibilities remain open. The purpose may even be to attract negative comment in advance so that the policy can be modified in a way that was already planned, and calculated to meet the criticisms that had been made public. Not uncommonly, governments ask voluntary-sector organizations to appear to make the policy proposal themselves, in order to create even further distance from the real policy-makers (Schlesinger and Tumber, 1994: 72–6).

Building credibility with the media

The release of information is often motivated by a desire to obtain or maintain credibility in the eyes of the media, or of particular news organizations. Credibility means conformity with media criteria of usefulness, which are essentially authority and productivity: the capacity to produce information that is reliable, interesting, timely and in a form that can be used. Organizations have an interest in ensuring the flow of information to news media which is analytically distinct from an interest in the actual information in question, because the reputation for reliability is useful in organizing their relationship with the media (or particular news organizations) in the long term; this reputation may be spectacularly useful at moments of crisis management.

In their analysis of relationships between news media and penal reform pressure groups, Schlesinger and Tumber found that building credibility with the media was a frequent focus of activity in pressure groups. Credibility derived from the accuracy and authority of the information they disseminated, the volume of information and the speed of their response to government initiatives (because journalists would approach them for comments on government proposals). Journalists often approach penal reform pressure groups to identify individuals involved in contentious legal proceedings (for example, deportation procedures for illegal immigrants) in order to personalize an abstract issue. In interviews with charities' press officers, I found the same process to be commonplace (Palmer, 1999). Willingness to cooperate helps to build the media credibility of the organization, but may be counter-productive for the individuals involved; therefore such decisions may involve complicated calculations, balancing different factors (Schlesinger and Tumber, 1994: 99–101).[6] By the same token, journalists may be willing to publicize something non-newsworthy that a fruitful source wants published in order to gain credit with the source, in the hope that this may produce even better information in the future (Sigal, 1973: 53–6).

Policy development and faction fighting

The previous literature abounds with examples of sources entering the news encounter in order to use publicity to pursue a particular line of policy or to gain advantage in a policy dispute. As Sigal says:

> most news from official sources emerges from policy change or dispute, and interpreting it requires
>
> - determining what the change or dispute is about;
> - making inferences about the source of the information and his position in public life;
> - making inferences about the face of the issue under consideration as he would see it;
> - identifying the target of his words;
> - identifying his possible reasons for uttering them. (1973: 188, 44-5)[7]

Princess Diana's famous interview with the BBC is subject to the same considerations: the key point is that her choice to confirm publicly what was already widely suspected, if not known, was clearly related to her intention to seek a legal separation. In this sense, we can say that the interview had two audiences – a mass audience and a fine-tuned target audience of one, her husband; her impact on the second depended upon her impact upon the first.

Damage limitation

All of these themes have a common element: the news encounter is the result of an initiative by the source, intended to open up communicative possibilities for the source's reasons. But another common reason for entering the news encounter is damage limitation, where the source's activities are already in the news, and in a way that is unfavourable to their purposes. This situation is fundamentally different from the preceding ones in that the initiative has been taken by someone else, and this has resulted in an initial definition of the situation which is not what was wanted.

Cockerell *et al.* (1984: 130–4) give an example of the first Thatcher government's reaction to an unplanned leak about a policy review document which discussed the possibility of wholesale commercialization and privatization of large segments of the welfare state. The policy review had been commissioned by the prime minister, and in her absence (on a state visit abroad) the then Chief Secretary to the Treasury Leon Brittan confirmed the accuracy of the leak. Subsequently other ministers confirmed its accuracy, and yet others denied a policy revision was under consideration. Some two weeks later, the Downing Street Press Office was denying that the policy review document had ever been discussed in Cabinet, and confirming that there was no intention of proceeding with any policy along the lines suggested. These denials found their way directly into headlines, and constituted an 'impressive damage-limitation exercise' (1984: 130-4).[8]

Source techniques

In this discussion we have seen some indications, from previous literature on news, of the range of motives which lead sources into the news encounter. We now turn to the techniques which are available to sources to maximize the chances of their intentions being realized.

Relevant personnel

In general, in the last fifty years, the growth of journalism as a profession has been matched by the growth in information officers and public relations personnel. But at least in the UK this hides significant differences. The recent growth in media has not been matched by an increase in government information officers, but the growth in private sector public relations personnel has been rapid.[9]

The parliamentary lobby system both brings journalists into contact with professional intermediaries between Government and the media, and places controls on what use journalists can make of the information they acquire (Negrine, 1989: 155-62; Cockerell *et al.*, 1984: 49-74).[10] Most public companies or corporations have departments responsible for external communication, and there has been a growing tendency for their importance within company structures to be upgraded over the last two decades, an upgrading marked by seats on the board of directors for the heads of such departments; since the late 1950s in the UK, an increasing number of companies have also used the services of specialist financial PR companies as intermediaries with the press and the public (Newman, 1984: 87-9, 211-14, 237-49).[11]

Public relations techniques

Apart from limiting physical access, the basis of source control over information flows through the news media is based in the standard techniques of public relations: drafting press releases and ensuring that they are written in a form that is relevant to the journalist; sending them out at a time appropriate for media deadlines; targeting news organizations, and individual journalists, who are likely to have an interest in the material and to deal with the topic in a way that is not incompatible with the purposes of the information release; organizing press conferences and receptions, and contacting journalists to encourage them to use particular material. Close knowledge of media routines, and especially deadlines, is a central professional skill (MacShane, 1979; Schudson, 1986: 81). More recently, video news releases (VNR) – in other words, publicity material prepared to be indistinguishable from television news footage – have been made widely available to television news.[12] In general, such 'information subsidies' place resource-rich groups in society at a competitive advantage in gaining access to media because they can afford to create the subsidies and distribute them to news media; 'resource-poor' groups regularly lack both the professional personnel and even the knowledge necessary to make advantageous contacts with news media (Gandy, 1982; Goldenberg, 1975). Such commonplace information flows are probably mostly used as starting points for reporting rather than the endpoint; writing in the early 1970s, Tunstall (1971: 179) asked specialist journalists how often they used PR material and the replies indicated a high take-up rate, but with the proviso that often it was only as the first stage of an investigation.

If the news encounter is to be more extended, a range of techniques is available. Press releases may have bullet-point summaries attached to catch attention and indicate a preferred interpretation; journalists whose initial attention is caught may be further briefed, attributably or otherwise depending on circumstances; in order to maximize the possibility of journalistic attention special events may be organized in such a way as to make them especially attractive in news terms – many years ago Daniel Boorstin (1961: 22–3) coined the term 'pseudo-events' to cover those events created especially to attract media attention (Negrine, 1989: 145). These standard techniques have more sophisticated counterparts: Sigal (1973: 110) gives the example of planting questions at a press conference by indicating to a journalist that a question on a particular topic will elicit newsworthy information.

More interesting, from our point of view, is the range of techniques available to sources to direct journalists' attention towards particular interpretations of stories that are likely to be considered newsworthy. The main techniques identified in the literature are:

- absorbing the journalist into the culture of the source organizations;
- appealing to journalists' conscience and asking for cooperation;
- timing and placing information release in such a way as to pre-empt coverage;

- tailoring information release to particular news values.

Absorption

Specialist reporters need to have an insider's understanding of the range of activities they are reporting on: a political reporter needs to understand the details of how a political system works and to have good contacts with relevant individuals; a science reporter needs some knowledge of scientific processes and a good knowledge of the scientific community. Insiders' knowledge is a two-edged sword, in the sense that it enables reporters to probe matters which might be impenetrable to someone without it, yet at the same time it may make them vulnerable to seeing the world through their sources' eyes.[13] For example, police sources in the UK and Canada want to be sure that sensitive information given to crime reporters will not be published in a form that may jeopardize the outcome of trials, since if it is prejudicial it may be alleged to prevent a fair trial (Ericson *et al.*, 1989: 126-36; Schlesinger and Tumber, 1994: 160-6); this leads them to choose journalists who share their understanding of the situation.[14] Clearly the 'reliability', from a source point of view, of particular journalists or indeed a whole news organization, is a measure of their absorption into the culture of the source organization and its usual environment. Indeed, sources may deny journalists' requests for information on the grounds that they do not trust them, or simply from distaste at their procedures: several people who faced journalists in the aftermath of the Lockerbie bombing refused to give information because they condemned their behaviour on ethical grounds (Deppa *et al.*, 21-2, 28, 54, 171-3).

Such absorption is almost inevitable to some extent because of the reporters' dependence upon sources, a dependence which is only mitigated by the fact that there are always other sources, and sources need journalists. In this equation, most studies have concluded that journalists' dependence on sources outweighs the reverse (Sigal, 1973: 55; Gans, 1980: 132-6; Negrine, 1993; Chibnall, 1977: 105; Golding and Middleton, 1982). Journalists may be unwilling to write stories likely to antagonize their regular sources and unwilling to refuse routine information from an official source because they may jeopardize their capacity for getting non-routine information at a later date (Gans, 1980: 132-6; Goldenberg, 1975: 96); even similar behaviour by another member of the same news organization may have this effect (Ericson *et al.*, 1989: 128). In the *Observer* (24.10.99) Andrew Rawnsley lamented the ease with which the Labour Government found 'friendly' journalists.

Appealing to journalists' conscience

Previous studies reveal three main grounds upon which successful appeals to journalists' conscience are made: national security, taste, and help in apprehending criminals to avoid danger to members of the public from criminal activity.

The British system of government control of public information flows is in part based upon appeals to journalistic conscience, in that the system of D-Notices (under which a government committee warns editors that publication of a particular item of information is (in its opinion) not in the public interest, and might breach the Official Secrets Act) is based upon negotiation with editors who compose part of the committee and therefore are privy to the items under discussion. When conflict over its interpretation arises, it is clear that voluntary cooperation is part of the system. The police ask for media cooperation over the reporting of sensitive operations, such as dealing with kidnappings, cooperation which often involves self-censorship by media organizations in the interests of police efficiency and usually in return for guarantees of extensive cooperation after the case is over (Chibnall, 1977: 186–8; Schlesinger and Tumber, 1994: 166; see also Leapman, 1992: 262).

Timing and placing of information release

The timing of information release to the news media is carefully calculated and frequently subject to a form of restriction usually called an 'embargo': the media are given information before it is made public in the wider sense, but are instructed not to make it publicly available until a specified time. The placing of information is also crucial. Media channels compete with each other for access to information, and releasing information to one channel (or even one individual) gives an advantage. Of course, journalists will be likely to publish that information as soon as possible unless they suspect that they are being unjustifiably used; of course, by the same token, giving a competitive advantage to one individual or channel places their competitors at a disadvantage, which may lead to a reduction in the esteem in which they hold the source in question if it happens too frequently (Goldenberg, 1975: 106; Jones, 1999: 84–6). Organizations with well-defined public responsibilities (such as Government departments) tend to treat media channels in an even-handed fashion, or at least go to some lengths to hide lack of even-handedness.[15] Earlier examples given in Chapter 1 suggest that this is often ignored for locally profitable reasons (cf. Jones, 1999: 11–12, 42, 84–6, 157–8).

In Britain, police operations are an example of an activity which is extremely sensitive to the timing and placing of information release, because of the risk that publicity may affect the outcome of a criminal prosecution.[16] As a result, police officers are extremely careful what they say to whom; however, restricting information to anodyne statements devoid of detail does not win the police any favours among journalists, and police information policy about operational matters must constantly negotiate the difficulties created by these opposing imperatives (Ericson, 1989: 126–8, 136; Schlesinger and Tumber, 1994: 160–6).

Timing may also produce other effects on news flows, for example using the dominance of news by a particular story to hide other stories by releasing relevant information at a time when they will attract little attention. On the day following the announcement of the trial verdict in the Louise Woodward case, which totally dominated news agendas, the government chose to release the information that it was not going to make extra cold weather payments to old age pensioners (*Guardian*, 1.11.97). The dramatic death of John Kennedy Jr. in the summer of 1999 served to disguise further welfare reforms.

Tailoring information release to particular news values

Channels and titles have different identities, and as a result potentially different news values. In the earlier discussion (see p. 35–46) of tabloid and broadsheet news values, we saw that the balance of emphasis between photographs and text is often very different in the two cases. It is well known that television news has a voracious appetite for video footage, in order to reduce the number of 'talking heads'.[17] 'Tailoring' information to the news values of particular news organizations – for example, by making visual materials available, or by including details likely to be useful for the construction of a story typical of the channel in question – is likely (all other things being equal) to increase the chances of the channel in question accepting the story. This technique may be very fine-tuned, for example to target individual titles or journalists by appealing to their known priorities (Palmer, 2000; cf. an example in Jones, 1999: 178–9).

Source strategies

We are now in a position to clarify what is meant by 'source strategies'. Sources act in the context of a particular situation, and use a particular technique to try to persuade journalists that their information is appropriate and useful for the journalist's purposes. The combination of motives and techniques is strategy. More exactly, a communication strategy is usually defined as the set of communication plans and the means for their implementation which enable an organization to proceed, through time, to realize a specified set of communicative goals. These are usually part of some wider strategy for the realization of a set of goals such as commercial purposes or policy implementation. Within 'strategy' defined in this wider manner the combination of motives and techniques outlined above is perhaps better categorized as 'tactics', since what occurs in any individual news encounter is likely to be aimed at the realization of only one among a number of small-scale goals. This is due to the nature of news agendas: since news is predominantly what has happened in the last twenty-four hours, it is inevitable that source behaviour in the news encounter will be subject to short-term considerations, and it is likely that on many occasions the longer-term strategic calculations within which these short-term objectives are framed will not be immediately visible. For example, charity press officers have said that they target individual journalists rather than entire news organizations in their ongoing attempts to build credibility with the media, offering, for instance, background briefings on relevant government and voluntary sector activities which may not in themselves realize any organizational goal, but which cumulatively may create trust and goodwill, a precious asset which can subsequently be used to realize particular organizational goals.[18] Charities rarely have large-scale advertising budgets and rarely have the means to exercise any influence over news organizations, except under exceptional circumstances such as disasters in remote areas, where they may control access. Building influence with the media must therefore largely take the form of building credibility, and given the scarcity of internal resources, choosing a limited number of relevant subject-specialist journalists is a plausible way of doing this. Whether individual journalists who are targeted in this manner are aware of source motives is a secondary matter.

Conclusion

The first three chapters have demonstrated the existence of a systematic process in which events acquire media profiles. In this process the news encounter is central. Here journalists meet sources and a negotiation is conducted, using the 'currency', metaphorically speaking, of news values. These values are not in themselves observable: what is observable are the results of their application to particular events; participants' understandings of their application may also be observable through interviews.

News values can be understood as a set of 'universal' criteria, of the variety often quoted in journalism textbooks and analysed in academic writing. However, these values are so general as to have a low information content about any given set of events, and we have seen that they always require the addition of an understanding of the event context, which gives rise to a set of 'local' news values, in other words the features of individual events or sequences of events which lead journalists to conclude that the events are newsworthy. New values are thus the combination of the 'universal' values which are the fundamental guiding principles of news judgement and the 'local' values constituted by the set of events in question.

Source motives derive from the position that they occupy in the world, and are amenable to some generalizations; however, these – like 'universal' news values – tell us little about the actual motives of actual sources in any given event. To understand the latter, we need to study particular events or event sequences and observe what sources actually do in these contexts. At the same time, there are a limited number of techniques available to sources to achieve their intentions, which are also amenable to generalization. The combination of motives and techniques constitutes a strategy (provided we include under the heading of 'motive' the overall situation of the source). In particular, sources attempt to use access to the news media in order to achieve event profiles that are in accordance with their purposes – and this may include, paradoxically, avoidance of contact with the media in order to achieve silence, or indeed any other technique which produces silence.

PART II

Case Studies

———

Introduction

In the first part of the book we saw thematic analysis illustrated by a series of small-scale examples. In the second part we move to a set of extended case studies. Their purpose is twofold:

- They give the opportunity to test various ideas about our central topic against sets of linked events, rather than seeking illustrations for analytic themes from the ebb and flow of events in general. The more systematic approach typical of the extended case study should strengthen the validity of the claims made in the central analytic points.
- They explore one of the central propositions in the overall analysis of the book: that news values are inseparable from the continuity or discontinuity of the flow of events through time. It follows that these elements of continuity and discontinuity enter into source strategy calculations. If this proposition is correct, then it is only through longitudinal studies, and perhaps especially case studies, that the function of news values can be clearly analysed.

It is these purposes that underlie the choice of case study material. Two problems are clear in any case study based analysis: their *suitability* to the purpose at hand and their *typicality* in relationship to the general field of analysis.

Where *suitability* is concerned, in each instance I have sought sequences of events in which the flow of information via the mass media was clearly central to the course of events (in one way or another). The role of mass-mediated information allows an assessment of the relationships between news values and source strategies. As a result of the central role of events with a common theme and some substantial duration, it is inevitable that the stories in question are all – by average journalistic standards – big stories.

Where typicality is concerned, it must be said that my choice of case studies is inevitably untypical of news output in general, precisely because the stories are ones with high news values and extended duration. However, since news is largely event-driven, no story will ever be typical of news output in general; what is typical is not the event or its coverage but the process which leads from the event to its coverage. Events in general do not have protracted media lives and short-lived events are potentially just as typical of the relationship between news values and source strategies as are the protracted media events I have chosen. However, there is no reason to suppose that where the basic news processes are concerned there is any fundamental difference between protracted media events and one-shot ones. This is so despite some obvious differences such as the extraordinary allocation of source and journalistic resources to protracted events. This type of difference is reflected in current newsroom terminology about such stories: references abound to 'feeding frenzy' or (in Continental newsrooms) the 'newswave'.

A related problem of typicality is to be seen at the lowest level of media attention to events: total omission of an event from media accounts. Where events are not covered, it is difficult in principle to know whether it is due to lack of media interest, or the capacity of potential news sources to hide what they are doing. Silence is as important a form of communication as its opposite; in the case of crisis public relations and damage limitation exercises it may well be the optimum result. Clearly events which do not have media lives, but which might have but for the efforts of news sources, are difficult to assess if one is not privy to the loop of information in which the possible results of different communications tactics are discussed. In particular, if silence or near-silence was sought and achieved, how could one know that an 'event' had taken place, or what its potential scope was? Assiduous reading of memoirs or similar documents may provide examples, some time after the event, but otherwise the analysis of news values and source strategies in such cases is difficult.[1]

The first case study is 'scandal'. This term can be applied to a wide range of human behaviour, and stories falling into this category have been common in the last ten years. We shall see examples of stories from the traditional news domain about sexual behaviour, but also from finance and business. I was unable to speak to any sources in this instance, due either to their refusal, or my own unwillingness to approach people who would certainly not add anything to what they had already said. In these case studies we will see the following features of the news encounter:

- Sources of information about scandals are often hidden, for obvious reasons, but where they can be identified, their motives and the techniques they use for placing information will be shown.
- The nature of scandal is such that in any scandal of substantial duration, sources with very different relationships to the scandalous material are involved, and this provides the opportunity to analyse features of different types of source motive and tactics. In particular, we can look at the features of source activities which come to light in conflict situations.
- Scandals deriving from different domains of behaviour will demonstrate different patterns of source and journalist behaviour. In the case of the sexual scandals analysed, it will be clear that the circulation of information between different types of media, each using their own news criteria, played a crucial role in the structure of the events.

- Scandal is a long-term news value in its own right, in the sense that the denunciation of any substantial breach of consensual morality makes frequent appearances in news output. In Chapter 2 we saw the relationship between the 'universal' or 'textbook' news values and the 'local' contexts in which they are manifested, which are interpretations of events.
- It is often thought that scandal is particularly associated with tabloid reporting, especially perhaps where sexual scandal is concerned. Some attention will be given to the differences between types of reporting of scandal, and particularly to the element of decorum involved in editorial calculations in this respect.

The second case study is the sequence of events surrounding Greenpeace's occupation of Shell's Brent Spar oil storage facility in the spring and early summer of 1995. In this instance, the 'zero-sum game' that arose as result of the direct opposition between two antagonists produced a situation in which countervailing attempts at event definition via the mass media are particularly clear. In this case study we shall see the following features of news encounters:

- The tactics that were used by both sides in this conflict can be analysed in detail, and this will tell us more about the relationship between source motives and tactics, in other words more about source strategies.
- The role of silence in the structuring of event profiles is amenable to analysis because of the particular sequence of events. This reveals a feature of source strategies that is frequently not amenable to analysis since silence is rarely observable.
- The sequence of events in the spring and summer of 1995 was self-contained in the sense that it was dominated by a single issue; this makes it easier than usual to see the main features of the event profile. This shows us how 'universal' news values were embodied in the 'local' news values of event interpretation. This will make it possible to analyse the relationship between news values and source strategies on a well-developed empirical basis.
- Some attention will be paid to the relationship between regional, national and international information flows, a feature of both news and source behaviour which is traditionally less studied than those elements which are national.

In the conclusion to Part II (pp. 119–36), we will look again at what these case studies can tell us about the news encounter; the contents of the case study chapters are primarily oriented to the internal characteristics of each case.

CHAPTER 4

Scandal

_____

Scandal is a staple ingredient of popular journalism, and examples of
press denunciations of improper conduct on the part of those who
ought to behave properly are not difficult to find at all periods in the
short history of the popular press, even though it is commonplace to
denounce current press conduct by reference to an earlier period
where such 'sensationalism' was less prevalent (see e.g. Leapman,
1992: 14–15).[2] The extent to which scandal is – or has been – a staple of
broadsheet journalism is less well discussed, and was the subject of
controversy in the wake of the death of Diana, Princess of Wales.
Arguments about the role of freelance photographers in bringing
about her death rapidly became linked to arguments about sensationalism in journalism in general.[3] Recent UK history has been marked by
a rich crop of scandals: two-thirds of _Great Parliamentary Scandals_
(Parris, 1996), out of a total of forty for the whole of British history,
occurred during the last two decades; while this is no doubt partly due
to editorial choice, the availability of the topics is indicative. 'Reviews
of the Year' for 1998 placed the Clinton/Lewinsky scandal as the major
news story of the year.[4] Political scandals since the 1997 UK elections
are documented in Jones (1999).

Stories categorized in the contemporary press as 'scandal' refer to
events ranging from sexual 'misconduct' to financial impropriety,
political corruption, and negligence or other misconduct which
produces danger for the public.[5] Commentaries on the frequency of
such stories usually refer to the cultural framework within which they
occur in order to understand them. Such framing elements range from
a supposed 'anti-business bias' in journalism (Tumber, 1993: 347–9) to
postmodern theories of 'semiotic subversion', or the 'carnivalesque'
mockery of social norms (Mellencamp, 1992: 209; Fiske, 1989: 87;
1989b: 168–70). Other frequently cited cultural frames (for sexual

scandal) are the supposedly puritanical nature of British culture (see e.g. *Financial Times, Guardian,* 22.3.95, *Independent on Sunday,* 7.9.97), which produces an obsessive interest in other people's sexual peccadilloes; and the sociological function of the media (and gossip in general) in containing deviance by giving it negative publicity (e.g. Markovits and Silverstein, 1988: 2–3; Pearce, 1973; Mellencamp, 1992: 168–71). Central to public understanding is also the 'Fourth Estate' theory of the press, according to which one of its central functions is the watchdog role of denunciation (Siebert *et al.,* 1963: 41–57, 74; Curran and Seaton, 1985: 284–301). These traditional themes in the explanation of the frequency of scandal in news reporting are also markers of the 'local' news values of scandals: they indicate the reasons why scandal provides something which is of interest and/or import-ance. But we should add immediately that these operate in conjunc-tion with even more local news values deriving from the identity of the participants.

I will review relevant theories below, but I can say immediately that they omit one important element: the structure of the information flow which produces the public representation of the events in question (see Lowi, 1988). Any adequate analysis of scandal must be able both to account for the information flows in question (which derive from source strategies) and to speak to the wider framework within which they occur, in other words the news values of scandal.

We start by reviewing an analysis of news which makes 'scandal' one of its main components, and which pays central attention to the role of news sources: Molotch and Lester's 'News as Purposive Behaviour' (1981). The authors start from the distinction between 'occurrence' and 'event'. An 'occurrence' is anything which happens, an integral part of which is the meaning or meanings attached to it by participants. 'Event' refers to the same happening transmuted into something with a public profile which has become fixed in the process of becoming public, primarily via the mass media.

There are various roles in event production, primarily their 'effector' (the person responsible for the original occurrence) and their 'promoter' (the person who makes information about it publicly available). Molotch and Lester then outline a typology of categories of events, distinguished on the basis of two variables: Was the original occurrence intended or unintended? Was the public profiling brought about by the effector or the promoter?

The interaction of these variables produces four categories of events (see Table 4).

Table 4.1 Categories of events

Event promoted by	Occurrence accomplished	
	Intentionally	*Unintentionally*
Effector	Routine	Serendipity
Promoter	Scandal	Accident

Typical examples of a 'routine event' are a press conference and a demonstration; however, for Molotch and Lester the products of investigative journalism are also routine events, but routine events where the promoter is the same person as the 'news assembler' – by 'digging', the reporter creates an event (but not an occurrence) and promotes it by publishing the results (1981: 129). An accident is an event whose original occurrence was not the intended result of purposive activity, but which gets promoted and therefore publicly defined by someone else; whereas 'serendipity' is similarly not the intended result of purposive activity but is promoted by the person responsible. In this schema, 'scandal' is defined in terms of the split between the person who intentionally accomplishes the occurrence and the person who 'promotes' the event by giving it a public profile; there is no further element in the definition.

This schema is not entirely consistent. First, the role of the 'effector' of the occurrence is ambiguous. Effectors are responsible for the occurrence, which has the meanings attached to it by participants, but they play no part in event definition unless they are also the promoters, responsible for event definition. Yet in the case of investigative journalism, the effector disappears: the promotion of the event is the same as the 'effecting' of an occurrence – or rather, the occurrence has entirely disappeared from the scheme of things. However, two features of investigative journalism fit badly with this model. Investigative journalism is most satisfactorily defined in terms of the bypassing of routine sourcing of stories in favour of some other access to information sources (Murphy, 1991: 9–19, 43–50), which implies an important role for sources – in other words someone other than the news assembler. It is also commonly understood to involve the undermining of some set of meanings already established in the public domain: an 'exposé' uncovering facts to establish a set of connections between events not previously established;[6] this implies some concordance of values between the denunciation and a set of publicly recognized meanings, which have no place in Molotch and Lester's schema. Second, in this analysis 'scandal' is not necessarily anything shameful: a modest man who did not blow his own trumpet, and who was discovered and 'promoted' by someone else would be 'scandalous'; at the very least, this runs counter to common-sense understanding of the term. Third, although 'news assemblers' are said to be central to the process of event creation, they have no part to play in the typology of events, which are differentiated entirely by reference to the divergent roles of effectors and promoters. This omission allows no role for news values in the process. All of these weaknesses derive ultimately from the same source: the argument that events have no intrinsic meanings, only the meanings that are attached to them in the act of labelling them (Molotch and Lester, 1981: 119–21); this allows no role for culture, in which events may be assigned to predefined places in accordance with commonplace meanings.

At the same time, the strength of Molotch and Lester's analysis is clear: one of the central elements of a scandal is certainly the fact that the person responsible for the scandalous conduct loses control of the information flow about the events in question. To this extent, defining scandal in terms of the divergent roles of effectors and promoters makes sense. This strength derives from the same source as the weakness noted above: events do indeed have to be defined in some act of labelling them. To put the schema in the terms already used, the role of news sources is central: in the absence of someone prepared to denounce someone else, scandal would arguably never arise (for current purposes, we may ignore guilty self-denunciation). Thus the basic structure of a scandal consists of a denunciation that is picked up by the news media and publicized: a scandal which is only known to a small group of involved people scarcely fits the usual definition of the term, in which the element of public knowledge is central (Lull and Hinerman, 1997: 11–13). If scandal implicitly involves publicity, then what is important here is the centrality of news judgement in establishing the profile of an event which is potentially 'scandalous'; but this is inseparable from the judgement that what has occurred does indeed plausibly have the negative meaning 'scandalous'. A good example is the case of Mary Ellen Synon and Rupert Pennant-Rea (March, 1995). She denounced him as an adulterer, but had considerable difficulty in finding a newspaper willing to publish, not because anyone doubted the reliability of her information but rather its value; despite his public position (Deputy Governor of the Bank of England) there were doubts about the public importance of his behaviour. Eventually the *Sunday Mirror* accepted her story, and he was forced to resign.[7] To this should be added the salacious details Pennant-Rea's mistress supplied about their meetings in his office at the Bank which inevitably attracted puns about the 'Bonk of England' (she subsequently claimed on RTE radio, reported in *The Times*, 22.3.95, that some of these details had been invented by journalists). The salaciousness refers to a news value: sexual explicitness, which is distinct from both fame and deviance (or may be considered a variety of deviance, depending upon the moral framework used to evaluate the information). It is the combination of these elements which brought about the news judgement that this story was worth printing. Here disagreements over the meaning of the event illustrate the point about the interaction between news sources and cultural definitions of events, and the central role of journalistic judgement.

The discussion of the structure of scandals needs more case study material, and recent press history furnishes a rich crop of examples. My chosen focus is the series of sexual and other scandals that involved various members of the Tory Government from 1992 to 1994. The extent to which these can be seen as typical will be examined later, as will the relevance of the various theories referred to above. In keeping with the focus of this book, my initial concern will be the structure of the information flows.

On 20 July 1992 the *People* newspaper revealed an affair between David Mellor, the Minister for National Heritage, and Antonia de Sancha. On the previous evening, Mellor had offered to resign in order to avoid embarrassing the Government; the offer was refused, on the grounds that the affair was a personal matter which did not affect the conduct of his duties. There followed a week of intense media attention, which then rapidly waned; however, early in September it was rekindled by new 'revelations' about the affair – mostly consisting of salacious details – which, in conjunction with further revelations about Mellor's behaviour unconnected with his affair with de Sancha, produced sufficient pressure to cause his resignation.

References to these events continued for an extended period – indeed still occurred occasionally at the time of writing in 1997–98 – and were particularly frequent during the first months of 1994 as the media connected them with a series of other scandals, mostly sexual in nature, involving Ministers and other members of the Conservative Party. Some time in the opening days of December 1993 the *News of the World* learnt from 'sources close to Julia Stent' about the child she had had with Timothy Yeo, then a junior minister. They published the story on Boxing Day, a time when the absence of much hard news ensured that the story would have maximum prominence in the public domain, at least on the day that it broke. The publication was followed by intensive further reporting which lasted until Yeo resigned, on 5 January, following well-publicized lack of support from his constituency party. In the following weeks, a series of other scandals followed: the death of Stephen Milligan MP (a Tory) during an auto-erotic experiment; the revelation that another Tory MP, Alan Duncan, had acquired a council house in Westminster by using the right-to-buy legislation in a way that was arguably not in accordance with its purpose; the suicide of Lady Caithness followed immediately by the revelation that her husband – a Minister in the Lords – had been having an affair with another woman. The sequence of scandals rapidly gave rise to the charge, in both Tory and anti-Tory papers, that the Government was 'mired in sleaze'.

Chronology of 'Back to Basics' scandals

20.7.92	The *People* publishes details of the relationship between Antonia de Sancha and David Mellor
15.9.92	The Bauwenses' libel case opens
24.9.92	Mellor resigns as Minister
26.12.93	The *News of the World* publishes details of the relationship between Timothy Yeo and Julia Stent
5.1.94	Yeo resigns as Junior Minister
January 1994	Three more scandals involving Conservative politicians
March 1995	Synon/Pennant-Rea scandal

'Players' in the 'Back to Basics' scandals

John Major, Conservative Prime Minister, 1990–97
David Mellor, Minister for Culture in the Conservative Government, 1992
Timothy Yeo, Junior Minister in the Conservative Government, 1993
Antonia de Sancha, actress, Mellor's lover
Mona Bauwens, family friend of the Mellors
Julia Stent, Yeo's lover and mother of his child
Mrs Aldine Horrigan, Conservative mayor of Haverhill, Suffolk
Norman Fowler, Chairman of the Conservative Party
Max Clifford, publicist
Rupert Pennant-Rea, Deputy Chairman of the Bank of England
Mary Ellen Synon, journalist, Pennant-Rea's lover

In all of these scandals it is obvious that the person denounced had lost control over information flows. However, the obvious point about loss of control is not the central point: other people suffered similar loss of control, without a scandal developing, by reasserting control over information flows and thus avoiding protracted media attention. For instance, when the leader of the Liberal Democrats, Paddy Ashdown, was found to have had an affair with his secretary, he gave a press conference in advance of the story breaking in the national media. He stated that the information was correct, that the affair was in the past, that his family stood by him, and asked for their privacy to be respected; little more was heard of the incident. In this case, control was reasserted rapidly – indeed, it is quoted as a classic example of successful damage limitation:[8] why did this not happen in the other cases? In general, the pattern of media attention conformed to a common model: an original revelation followed by further information, or reactions of others with a stake in the matter, followed by further reactions and information. This common model is significant because it directs our attention to the distribution of the flow of information across time, which is indeed central to the way in which a story builds. However, it says nothing about the details of how, in each instance, these information flows occurred, and it is in answering this question that we shall gain an understanding of scandal. The answers lie partly in the nature of journalistic enterprise, and partly in the behaviour of the news sources: in short in the interaction between sources and journalists, mediated by news values. As a result, the answers are not identical in each.

In the case of Mellor's affair with de Sancha, the way in which the information became public was a major focus of journalistic interest because of the possibility that it breached the Press Commission Code of Conduct and because Mellor, as the relevant Minister, had publicly discussed the possibility of an inquiry into whether a law to restrict press intrusion into private lives was necessary. De Sancha told a friend she was having an affair with an important man, and the friend scented the possibility of selling the details; he offered the use of his flat and bugged the telephone; it was these tapes that provided the original material. The original story was immediately followed up by pictures in the *Daily Mirror* of the flat where they met, and by a story in the *Sun* in which a former boyfriend of de Sancha gave various salacious details about her sexual habits which produced a punning headline ('toe job'), referred to on many later occasions. Salacious information about de Sancha's career followed, and some days later she gave an interview to the *Independent*. Mellor's wife's parents entered the story with an interview in which they claimed never to have liked their son-in-law, and a second interview in which they alleged he had threatened them with retaliation if they continued to speak to the press; this was followed by a well-trailed 'photo opportunity' of a family reconciliation. At the same time, the legitimate 'public interest' angle of the story allowed broadsheet newspapers, which might not normally give the same level or type of attention to such events, to cover it: because Mellor was the Minister responsible for any official inquiries or future legislation into the conduct of the press, the question of a conflict of interest arose. By the same token of public interest, the question of his possible resignation, the depth of the Prime Minister's commitment to him, and backbench attitudes towards his position were also reported. Tories complained about this harassment of a Minster and charged that the *People*'s argument of public interest in his behaviour was inadequate if not hypocritical. This argument was countered by the editor of the *Sun* stating on radio that during the election a Tory Minister had telephoned him with a series of false revelations about the sexual habits of leading Opposition politicians, a charge which the Government felt obliged to rebut.

Attention rapidly waned and little was said during August.[9] However, two warning signs were in the air: de Sancha was taken on as a client by the top publicity agent, Max Clifford; and it was noted, some days after the original story, that Mellor had been subpoenaed to appear in an unrelated libel case in September. The combination of these two circumstances bore fruit: in early September the tabloids were given a series of salacious revelations by 'a friend of de Sancha', which were in fact placed by Clifford. Carefully calculated to appeal to tabloid news values, they redirected public attention to Mellor at exactly the time he was due to go into the witness-box to speak about a holiday his family had taken with their friend Mona Bauwens and which she had paid for. The tabloid 'revelations' (some of which were later admitted to be pure fabrication) lasted from 7 to 10 September and the Bauwens libel case started on 15 September. Eventually the pressure on Mellor became irresistible and he resigned his ministerial post on 24 September.

In this instance, the protracted information flow that constituted the scandal was the result of a real campaign by news sources, motivated by gain.[10] However, this gain could only be realized by appeal to news values. The values in question are tabloid oriented, and the appeal was successful, as we have seen; however, the appeal had to be constantly renewed, on a daily basis, and there is little doubt that during the first week of the story it was the constant circulation of information between different media categories (tabloid/broadsheet, press/broadcast) that fuelled its growth;[11] the extent to which information was offered unsolicited to newspapers by sources and the extent to which it was unearthed by journalistic enterprise is unclear. During the subsequent phase it was the previous history of the story, plus the well-calculated appeal to tabloid news values, plus the linkage to the forthcoming Bauwens libel case that, in combination, gave the story legs.

The series of scandals unleashed by the *News of the World*'s exposure of Yeo is somewhat more complicated, both for contextual reasons and because of the behaviour of news sources linked to the context. The central element in the context is the Tory Party's decision to adopt the slogan 'Back to Basics' as the unifying theme for a series of policy initiatives debated at their 1993 conference. While many of these policy initiatives had no link to sexual behaviour, one did: the proposal to make it more difficult for single mothers to claim a range of welfare benefits, a proposal which attracted widespread comment. Although Yeo himself scarcely addressed the issue, his junior ministerial post placed him in the frame of association with the policy. The conflicting behaviour of a range of news sources derived fundamentally from ambiguities attached to the 'Back to Basics' formulation. While some Tories interpreted it as no more than a catchy phrase linking a set of policies, others saw it as the prelude to an attempt to roll back the frontiers of the permissive society. In this they were encouraged by the media briefing at the Tory conference which preceded the Prime Minister's launch of the slogan: the briefing included the reference to the frontiers of permissiveness which featured in media reporting.[12] The outline of the disagreement that emerged was that the Prime Minister defended Yeo on the grounds that – as he had said apropos Mellor – it was a private matter; others, however, insisted that such impropriety was a public matter and he should resign. This distinction became embroiled in the 'Back to Basics' policy initiative because it was argued that its fundamental thrust was to show that personal morality was indeed a public matter. When the Prime Minister said on television (6.1.94) that in his opinion 'Back to Basics' was not about personal sexual morality, this brought immediate ripostes from the Tory Right to the effect that the personal moral dimension was integral to grass-roots understanding of the slogan (*Evening Standard*, 7.1.94).[13] Placing this contextual framework around the events does not prejudge what their main dynamic was, nor whether the story was primarily a tabloid-driven sexual scandal or a political story.

The details of the timing of the *News of the World* investigation are significant because they focus attention on the reactions of participants who had ample time to rehearse their roles as potential news sources. Yeo knew by the middle of December that his secret was out and even though he may have hesitated to tell anyone in the hope that it would not be published, no one has claimed that he kept it a secret from the Tory Party hierarchy until the day it was public knowledge. There was some foreknowledge of the publicity, although when the information was available to the Tory leadership is subject to different accounts, as is the extent of their knowledge. According to the *Sunday Express* (9.1.94) neither Ryder (Tory Chief Whip) nor No. 10 knew about the child until shortly before the story broke. One senior Westminster broadcast journalist said the PM knew about the relationship but not about the baby, and as a result was prepared to support Yeo on what he subsequently saw as false grounds. Another broadcaster told me that on 12 January the Tory Whips' Office confirmed to him that Yeo had told the Party hierarchy about the affair, but not about the baby, and that on the same day the PM's office had said they realized that in future they would have to tighten up procedures in order to avoid the PM being misled in this away again.

According to the BBC's Nick Jones, writing in the *Guardian* (17.1.94), the No. 10 Press Office was 'directionless' on the night that the story broke, perhaps because the Director of Information was on holiday at the time. They had a pre-prepared statement from the Prime Minister supporting Yeo on the grounds that it was a private matter, but were unable to say anything meaningful about the relationship to 'Back to Basics' and whether other Tories would take the same line as the Prime Minister; it was not even clear whether the Prime Minister had been consulted about the story in the recent past. Every journalist to whom I spoke and who was working on Boxing Day evening sought further clarification and reactions from a variety of political figures in order to develop the story – although one tabloid reporter said that his paper thought the story would die quickly and down-graded it. Only two papers sought to exploit the angle offered by the MP's relationship to his local party organization: the *Daily Mail* and the *Daily Telegraph*. The Tory Party constitution gives a central role to the local party organization, and the *Daily Mail*, by dint of very protracted enquiries, managed to find a group of local party activists who were in favour of Yeo's resignation. The newsroom had assigned some twenty reporters to the task for a period of roughly six hours; by contrast another tabloid, which had downgraded the story, had assigned one reporter who had made roughly half-a-dozen phone calls.[14] Similarly, the next morning BBC *World at One* staff had started looking for Tories who were prepared to speak out against Yeo; they had guessed that some would oppose the Prime Minister's interpretation of the event,[15] perhaps on the basis of a statement put out on Boxing Day itself by the Conservative Family Campaign condemning Yeo's behaviour. Eventually they found the right-wing MP David Evans who said on air that he thought Yeo should resign, a statement that was widely reported and commented on the grounds that the divergence of opinion from the Prime Minister's was politically significant (e.g. *Daily Telegraph*, 28.12.93 and 29.12.93, and *Evening Standard*, 29.12.93). One broadsheet political reporter to whom I spoke said that he had tried to persuade his colleagues that Evans was too marginal a figure to be worth such attention, but they disagreed on the grounds that every other newspaper would cover it and therefore they had to too. In the days between Christmas and the New Year both sides pushed their interpretations of the events: aside from the above-mentioned condemnations, friends of Yeo were very proactive during this period, phoning Tory newspapers to offer support; Sir Norman Fowler, then Chairman of the Party, was publicly supportive of Yeo in a radio broadcast.[16] These attempts to support him had the effect of provoking even more condemnations from his opponents.

In these details of the beginning of the protracted story we can see some fundamental features of the growth of a scandal. First, the role of losing control of information flows: not only did Yeo lose control, but the Tory Government as an organization also did; whether centralized control would have been possible under different circumstances, given the Party's factionalization over moral issues, is impossible to know. Here we should note that the relationship between 'effector' and 'promoter' – to use Molotch and Lester's terminology – is more complex than their model allows: if Yeo is the effector and his secret denouncer the promoter, what role does the Tory Party play? Second, the role of journalistic enterprise in the pursuit of news values: in the absence of this pursuit, the Conservative Family Campaign press release might well have sunk without a trace (it was only very briefly reported) but it was a clear hint that looking for divergence would bring it to light. The more divergence came to light, the more it encouraged journalists to look for it and the more interpreters made themselves available for interview: journalists will continue to look for evidence of a new angle if they think it is likely to be found.[17] Third, within days the journalistic momentum was such that suppositions about other journalists' behaviour was dictating editorial policy – suppositions supported by the constant circulation of news agency copy, radio, TV, the evening papers, etc. Every journalist with whom I discussed this feature of news recognized its centrality – in newsroom jargon it is often called 'theme of the week' – and all were somewhat mystified by the modality of its operation. All saw it as a process which was not subject to any individual's control, and many had anecdotal stories of trying to go against the flow and failing. Although no attempt has been made to quantify such reactions, it was clear from the way in which journalists discussed this phenomenon that it was very well known to them and occupied a significant place in their understanding of their job (see pp. 131–3).

Subsequently, the local dimension of the scandal came to occupy centre stage, and the process by which local activists came to the decision not to support Yeo is a crucial element in our understanding of the role of information flows in the nature of these events. Yeo had failed to tell anyone in the local party about his relationship, the baby, or the fact that the story was about to break.[18] This ensured that when local activists were contacted by reporters they had no idea what to say, or at best repeated the Prime Minister's statement. However, within twenty-four hours of the story breaking they could read in the *Daily Mail* that some of their number did not support the Prime Minister's interpretation. By the following weekend it was known that Mrs Horrigan, mayor of Haverhill and a prominent local Tory, had written to the Prime Minister saying that Yeo should resign; the letter was printed in the *Haverhill Echo*, and was followed up in the *East Anglian Daily Times* by an interview with another prominent local Tory who estimated that 50 per cent of local party members would not support Yeo. The local circuit of information was crucial in organizing support for a move to oppose Yeo, and at the same time national media were providing proof that the local party was not alone in its evaluation of the situation. By coincidence, Yeo was scheduled to return from a pre-arranged family holiday (in the Seychelles) on the day that Horrigan's letter reached Downing Street (after its local publication). Arriving in a taxi at the airport on the way back he made a fundamental mistake: confronted with photographers he tried to hide his face in his wife's lap. This photograph made the front pages of most national newspapers the following day, and was universally interpreted in the accompanying text as a sign of guilt. Local activists who saw the photograph were horrified, and local impressions were that there was an immediate stiffening of opposition to Yeo.[19] Yeo had clearly failed to appreciate the news value of his story and presumably was unprepared to perform his role as a news source: another element in the story spun out of control. On the following day, Mrs Horrigan gave an interview on ITN demanding Yeo's resignation; it was her willingness to speak out in public that convinced TV newsrooms that the story was worth TV news time, as it clearly indicated that the story was no longer a piece of personal sensationalism, but an important political event.[20] We can now give some answers to the earlier question about the role of the Tory Party as either effector or promoter or both: they – or rather, the different elements within the Party – were promoters in the sense that they made public interpretations of events which they offered to journalists, but effectors in the sense that these interpretations became themselves the events which were the focus of news reporting. The passage of time radically reorients the relationship between effectors and promoters.

The story ran until Yeo resigned, with ever-increasing amounts of coverage. It was rapidly followed by the other scandals referred to above. In these subsequent cases we can see elements of information flows that compare and contrast with what happened in the Yeo case. In the case of Alan Duncan's house purchase, the story failed to maintain any momentum because after a very short time journalists failed to find any new information, despite sending teams to interview Duncan on holiday in Switzerland. In the case of Lady Caithness' suicide, it is clear that attempts were made to limit potential damage. Lady Caithness committed suicide on a Saturday afternoon, and the police and medical personnel were called the same day. However, the first public announcement was made late on the Saturday evening, by the Government, and in this announcement the event was defined as a personal tragedy and – by implication – nothing more. The timing of the announcement was forced by a freelance journalist's tip-off from a police source and was no doubt calculated to give journalists time to process the information for the Sunday news bulletins and Monday's newspapers, but not enough time to pursue investigations into the background (*Scotland on Sunday*, 16.1.94). However, within twenty-four hours journalists had discovered (or been informed) that Lord Caithness had been having an affair with another woman, and the story acquired a new and greatly enhanced profile. In each case, information was made publicly available by mechanisms that have remained hidden, but where – because of the concatenation of events – the common ground was stressed and led to levels of attention that each event individually might have failed to generate in the absence of this linkage. Essentially the same structure of information flow marks them all: an initial loss of control, followed by attempts to reassert control, which were successful where no further information was forthcoming (in the case of Alan Duncan's house purchase) but were unsuccessful where new angles were either offered or found, and gave the story legs.

To what extent can such instances be said to be typical of scandal stories in general? We have seen that the other categories of action commonly labelled scandalous are financial impropriety, political corruption, and public negligence and abuse of power. While an examination of the structure of scandals in all of these domains is beyond the scope of this analysis, a brief examination of relevant features of one of these categories of scandal will show us to what extent sexual scandals are typical or untypical. We will look at two major financial scandals: the closing down of the Bank of Credit and Commerce International and the investigation of share dealings during the Guinness–Distillers take-over.

Certain features of business communication form an essential background for understanding the role of press reporting in financial scandals. Commercial confidentiality – which is increasingly enforced through 'gagging' clauses in employment contracts[21] – as well as regulatory constraints on the revelation of price-sensitive information both place restrictions upon what can be publicly said about business matters. At the same time companies are obliged by law to make public statements about their business activities at specified intervals; this public information is a prime source for business page journalism, usually in combination with comments from informed people, such as market analysts. With some few exceptions – such as tax, birth, marriage and divorce – there are no obligations to disclose personal conduct of the variety discussed above, and no restrictions on what one can say about one's own conduct if one chooses; to this extent, financial communication takes place in a fundamentally different context to communication about personal life. It is also the case that information about the business dealings of corporations (or individuals) has directly commercial value in its own right, in a way that is not true of other categories of information. Business affairs have a specialist press and special pages in most broadsheet media, read by a limited, professionally interested public with a relatively high degree of expertise in that subject matter. The majority of reports about business and financial matters do not transfer from the business pages (or specialist broadcast programmes) to general news pages or bulletins, and those that do are propelled by the news criteria of news pages: the majority of the stories which do cross this threshold appear to be concerned with changes in employment opportunities, major financial impropriety and dramatic new product development. In general, newsroom practices make protracted investigation of (potential) financial malpractice a low priority: news values are ambiguous in this respect, the cost of investigative journalism is high, and the outcomes are rarely certain in advance. At the same time, the risk of litigation is high since any revelations are likely to be damaging to the individual or organization on the receiving end, and the cost of even the threat of litigation is high enough to act as a deterrent (since a defence against a writ for libel has to be produced even if the case never goes to court).[22]

Also important is the nature of the business – and in particular the financial – community: a relatively small and relatively homogeneous group of people, with many links between them, and many channels of communication which are of crucial importance in decision-making and whose primary characteristic is their restricted access: the relationship between information flows in these channels and information flows in mass media channels is not necessarily the same as in other domains of activity. Instructive in this respect is the analysis of information flows in cases of 'ramping' – spreading rumours about matters likely to affect share prices in order to manipulate them for personal gain. Because this is illegal, evidence of what has happened sometimes surfaces in law reports. On occasion, newspapers are used to spread the rumour in question, but it is equally probable that the rumour may be an entirely face-to-face matter, in which case evidence of its existence will only come to light if someone brings it to public attention. For example, in a case reported in the *Guardian*, someone had offered unsolicited information about a potential take-over bid which, if published and believed, would push up the price of the shares in question; the *Guardian* checked the story and concluded that it was false, but it was published in another paper, and eventually a complaint was made that the false rumour had had the effect of pushing the share price up substantially. Here the role of the media was the crucial element in the 'ramp': spreading the rumour in this way, via the media, gave apparent authority to the false information; it may be assumed that the rumour-monger had already bought the shares in question (or was 'selling short'). In another case, a broker persuaded a company, bidding for a large block of stock in another company, that there were competing bids in place, which encouraged the bidders to increase their bid; in fact there were no other bidders. The defrauded bidders sued for damages, which brought the original incident to light. Here, the media are irrelevant to the 'ramp' tactics. It has recently been shown that interactive information systems such as TOPIC, websites and private newsletters published via the Internet are being used to post similar information, whose origins are difficult to trace.[23]

At the same time, there is a dearth of authoritative bodies that would act as alternative sources of information for journalists. The pressure groups which abound in the areas of social policy and criminal justice, and which regularly act as news sources,[24] are largely absent from the business and especially the financial community. It is possible that regulatory authorities – who are responsible for 'policing' the financial community – do not have the same status as information sources as apparently comparable organizations such as the police.[25] For example, when the DTI finally published its inspectors' report into the Guinness affair (27.11.97), although its conclusions were published as authoritative, several accounts of the publication also quoted the rejection of the DTI version of events by Ernest Saunders, the convicted ex-Managing Director of Guinness whose conduct was at the centre of the events in question; the implication is that Saunders was regarded as an equally authoritative source as the DTI (*Evening Standard* 27.11.97; *Independent* and *Guardian*, 28.11.97, for example).

In the two cases to be examined, it has been well documented since the events in question that things were done which were arguably improper – and in some cases criminal – and which were not publicly reported until well after the sequence of events had been closed off by changed circumstances. Information which became available to law enforcement and regulatory authorities resulted in actions which – had they been carried out earlier – would have prevented the sequences of events reaching the closure that in fact occurred (Kochan and Pym, 1987; Pugh, 1987; Adams and Frantz, 1991; Truell and Gurwin, 1992; *Financial Times*, 1991). In other words, the two financial scandals in question also resulted from a loss of control over information flows by the perpetrators, but the mechanisms involved in this loss of control are substantially different from the ones involved in the case of sexual scandal.

The ability of the Guinness Chairman Ernest Saunders to place material in the press favourable to the corporate plans he was pursuing is well documented in accounts of the Guinness affair. In both the take-over bid for Bell's Whisky and the Distillers Company he was able to use business-page news values to place stories concerning various elements of the situation in order to discredit rivals and persuade shareholders that the Guinness offer was the one to accept. At the same time he was able to circulate information through private channels that did not become accessible to journalists until after the intervention of inspectors from the DTI. The information related to the 'share-price support' exercise he organized in order to make possible Guinness' acquisition of a majority shareholding in Distillers. This was possible because of the confidentiality of the relationships. Within these circles, information circulates very easily once participants are persuaded that it is in their interests to pass this information on. For example, in October 1985 a Guinness director let it be known at a lunch that they would be interested in helping Distillers beat off a hostile take-over bid by the Argyll group; word of this remark quickly reached the Managing Director of the Argyll group, who immediately approached Saunders to see if the rumour was true. Saunders denied the truth of the rumour, but a few months later a story was leaked to *The Times* (4.1.86) to the same effect, and was followed up by other stories in the press, including the speculation that Saunders was being pushed by City institutions to make a bid for Distillers, an interpretation of events that Saunders himself publicly favoured. This suggests that the source of the leak was inside Guinness itself. Argyll again contacted Guinness to enquire about the truth of the story and was again reassured that it was untrue. However, further press stories convinced them that Guinness were lying and they sent someone round to the Distillers headquarters building to see whose cars were parked outside on a Sunday afternoon. The presence of the cars showed them their suspicions were correct: the small scale of the social group involved meant that the ownership of the cars was well known to participants (Kochan and Pym, 1987: 84–5, 94, 100–1, 123–4). At a later stage in the Guinness/Distillers affair, an American journalist working on a story about the take-over was given information about the share-support information by a merchant banker working for the rival bidder, Argyll; the purpose of the gift of the information was clearly in Argyll's interest – to discredit Guinness and thwart the take-over. However, the journalist could not persuade his (American) editor of the interest of the topic, and shortly afterwards the DTI inspectors made the details public (Pugh, 1987: 124–5).

Similarly, in the case of BCCI, London financial circles had clear evidence that something strange was going on at BCCI five years before the scandal became public in the UK (on 5 July 1991), but nobody in the know made the information public; instead they used it to make a profit from the circumstances (*Financial Times*, 1991: 17). The Treasury section of BCCI was incurring huge losses on ill-advised speculation which were disguised by various accountancy devices. In 1986 the bank's UK auditors, PriceWaterhouse, penetrated the disguise and confronted management; however, the information was not revealed to wider circles as the auditors assumed it was the result of incompetence rather than fraud. The auditors of the Luxembourg-based section of BCCI, Ernst and Whinney (now Ernst and Young) resigned in 1987; if the resignation was publicly noted, its significance was not (Adams and Frantz, 1991: 98–9; Truell and Gurwin, 1992: 201–6). In 1989, PriceWaterhouse realized that what their investigations were revealing was a form of malpractice, and refused to sign off the bank's annual accounts. If this had been publicly known, it would have been a clear indication of something fundamentally wrong; however, the auditors were satisfied by a fresh injection of capital which apparently restored the bank's finances to a healthy state and the annual report was duly signed and published (Truell and Gurwin, 1992: 203, 292).

At the same time, attempts at investigation by journalists met with considerable difficulties: as reports of their enquiries reached sensitive ears, lawyers were instructed to hinder the enquiries. Even when reports were published in authoritative publications (May 1990) few journalists followed them up for some time and BCCI was able to counter the negative publicity with its own interpretation of events. An article published in the UK (*Observer*, 21.1.90), based on BCCI's guilty plea to money-laundering charges in the US courts, fell on deaf ears (Truell and Gurwin, 1992: 293–6, 357; see also Leapman, 1992: 275–9). In these circumstances, we can see both how permeable the barriers to information flows are in such closed circles, and yet at the same time how easy it is to maintain the barrier between those closed circles and the wider public whose access is limited to the mass media, due to the various institutional factors cited above.

In both the cases reviewed, extensive negative journalistic activity followed public revelations by regulatory and/or criminal authorities: 'scandal' was produced by officialdom, and reflected in journalism. In the terms used in this book, what is revealed here is the extent to which differences in information flow between various groups who are potential news sources vary considerably, due (in this instance) to clear differences between their institutional positions. Of course, the extent to which revelations about scandalous behaviour also fit the interests of the revealer is something which must be taken into account. In the case of BCCI, it seems clear from published accounts that the Bank of England – which launched the public career of the scandal in the UK by deciding to close down the bank – did so unwillingly and as a last resort, since it feared severe knock-on effects on the banking system as a whole, and would have preferred an unpublicized rescue of the bank (*Financial Times*, 1991: 3). Subsequently, the Bank was criticized for not acting sooner, a charge which its officers refused to accept (Truell and Gurwin, 1992: 356–7). The Bank was effectively forced to act by the mounting scale of the revelations emerging from auditors' accounts, and criminal and regulatory investigations in the US. In the case of the Guinness 'share support' affair the regulatory body was 'tight-lipped' on the nature of their enquiries, but journalists were able to use indications already in the public domain, plus information from organizations which had acted for Guinness and were now ready to speak about events (Pugh, 1987: 126–8). In each case, the public existence of official enquiries meant that the factors inhibiting journalistic enterprise ceased to operate. The official nature of the enquiries made litigation much less likely, and the fact that enquiries were being made meant that the story ceased to be investigative and became a routine breaking story: even if the enquiries came to nothing, the fact that they existed made a story. The existence of the official enquiry not only breaks a story but also changes all the news values and the meaning of newsroom practices by the same token.

At the same time, we have seen how various factors deriving from the nature of the financial community impact upon journalistic ability and willingness to report the activities of this community. In almost every respect, the structure of information flows in the case of financial matters is significantly different from that involved in sexual matters, and as a result even if scandals in these two domains share the feature of loss of control over information flows by the person who has most to lose by revelation, the mechanisms by which information flows eventually reach the mass media are very different.

All the scandals in these categories of action share the common feature of a loss of control over information flows by the perpetrator. However, since many of them involve actions which are either criminal or in breach of a regulatory framework, what constitutes a loss of control over information for one party is the exercise of such control for another: if the police, or some other body in authority over possible breaches of public norms, release information saying that X is under investigation, or being charged with such-and-such an offence, they do so for their own reasons. Of course, this is also true of the sources of sexual scandal – as is particularly clear in the case of Mary

Ellen Synon and Rupert Pennant-Rea – but it is often difficult to establish who they are or why they acted as they did. Therefore we should beware of theorizations of the role of the mass media in scandal which assert that its fundamental structure is the revelation of secrets 'whose form generates an investigative, adversarial search for the content – called truth or reality ... [where] TV ... manufactures events ... through sheer repetition, piquing audience interest, creating experiences and affects which can then be transformed into commodities' (Mellencamp, 1992: 239).

For example, the famous interview that Princess Diana gave to BBC TV *Panorama* (broadcast 20.11.95), in which she frankly discussed both her married life with Prince Charles and one of her extra-marital liaisons, no doubt fascinated millions – it had one of the largest audiences in the history of television. However, the opportunity that this predictable interest gave the Princess by no means explains her motives for doing so, which must have been linked to her separation and likely divorce. In particular, the decision to give the interview to *Panorama* rather than to a more 'down-market' outlet must be explained by the Princess' desire to make the Royal Family appreciate how serious she was in her attempt to continue to maintain her public profile and demand what she thought she was entitled to.[26] She was far from averse to using down-market outlets when it suited her strategic purposes, as can be seen in the incident where she tipped off a photographer from the *News of the World* that she would be found visiting a hospital late at night, which produced the headline 'Di: my secret nights as an angel' (3.12.95). The editorial policy of the *News of the World* made it unlikely that the coverage would analyse her motives for the incident, whatever individual journalists' estimation of them might have been; indeed, on the following day both the *Guardian* and the London *Evening Standard* published accounts of the event understood as a PR stunt. By the same token, it is an over-simplification to see scandal revelation as a form of investigation: all too often the revelation is entirely due to someone with prior knowledge deciding to offer the information to the media, for their own reasons. Under these circumstances, even if the appearance of hard investigative labour is maintained in the reporting, or if investigative journalism is needed to reveal the full ramifications of what happened, and even if the appearance of the adversarial relationship contributes to the fascination, it does not necessarily explain the process by which the information becomes public.

CHAPTER 5

Scandal and Theory

At this point we can return to our review of framing theories. They are:

- sexual scandal about public figures excites readers' prurient interest for reasons to do with (variously) human nature or British culture;
- the ideological containment of deviance;
- the 'anti-business bias' of news journalism;
- the watchdog or 'Fourth Estate' role of the mass media;
- delight in subversive mockery.

Also commonly alleged is the hunt for sensational stories due to inter-title competition, especially among the tabloids who are more dependent upon sales income than the broadsheets (see for example *Guardian*, 25.7.92). This argument depends for its force on an acceptance that sensational stories have high news value, and while no one doubts the truth of this proposition, in the present context it is what needs to be explained rather than the explanation. This fits a more general theory to the effect that newspapers are increasingly driven by market research which shows that readers consistently prefer human interest stories to coverage of public affairs (Curran and Seaton, 1985: 112–17).

We have already seen that these theories presuppose the existence of news values and therefore the process by which news values are put into practice in the interactions between journalists and sources. This is particularly significant because an explanation of scandal framed solely in terms of some universal human interest would be unable to explain why – or more exactly, how – some scandalous behaviour by famous people is prominently featured in the media over extended periods of time, whereas other instances receive brief, even cursory attention. The analyses above suggest that it is the constant renewal of appeals to news values that is responsible for the difference between cursory and extended attention, a renewal located in the interaction between source interests and journalists' commitment to news values. However, it is equally true that descriptions of these processes also imply the wider cultural framework within which they operate: we have seen that there are two sorts of news value – the 'universal' ones that are to be found in journalism textbooks, and which operate within all stories, in some combination or other (and which include such elements as the constant renewal of information); and those values which are mobilized in individual stories, in other words those elements of concrete individual situations which incarnate the universal news values and attract journalistic interest. Where scandals are concerned, and perhaps especially sexual scandals, the features of the individual events which make them newsworthy derive from elements of our culture such as those referred to in the framing theories.

The 'prurient interest' explanation essentially relies on a combination of various explanatory features: interest in other people's lives, curiosity about famous people, interest in deviation from cultural norms, perhaps especially with respect to sexuality, which will be the focus of this chapter. Commonly, such interest and curiosity are thought to be universal, a theme to which we shall return. However, it is often alleged that specific features of our society are responsible, especially the supposed puritanical repression of sexuality; this allegation seems implausible in light of the rapid increase of media attention to such events over the same time period as a universally recognized relaxation of repressive norms. International comparisons are sometimes made, to the effect that other supposedly 'less repressed' societies (e.g. France) give less media attention to sexual scandal; however, legal variations in the status of privacy, and related editorial norms, make such comparisons ambiguous (see e.g. Brenda Maddox, *Daily Telegraph*, 22.7.92). A more plausible historical explanation has been advanced by Tillyard (1994): the growing emphasis placed on 'sensibility' after the middle of the eighteenth century gave public importance to private emotions, and therefore both brought about and legitimated public attention to what would otherwise be a 'purely private' matter; such concerns were rapidly used to provide material for the new household magazines such as *Town and Country Magazine*. At the same time, the norms of aristocratic behaviour – or at least male aristocratic behaviour – which included adultery were incompatible with the values of the new middle class for whom sensibility was a central element in their conception of what a rightly organized world should be. Although this explanation refers to a long-distant time, the modern notion of the family is still dependent upon this world-view, for it is here that the role of emotional satisfaction in the structure of the family has its origins (Stone, 1977). During the nineteenth century, the middle-class definition of the family came to dominate British culture in the sense that alternative definitions of sex, marriage and child-rearing became marginalized. Deviations from this norm were condemned more and more forcibly, a situation which only changed with the liberalization of the post-World War Two period (Weekes, 1981; Hobsbawm, 1975: 230-1). It is arguable that mass-mediated scandal played a role in this process. In the early century, adultery could easily be ignored as a charge against a political leader: both Wellington and Palmerston shrugged it off. Subsequently, moralists argued that immorality made men unsuitable for public life and two famous Victorian divorce cases – Dilke and Parnell – brought on grounds of adultery, were heavily politicized as the co-respondents' right to political position was attacked by the moral reformers. Here the public moral evaluation of their behaviour played a part in delineating the value system used to judge such events (Fisher, 1995: 91, 96, 105–7, 131–2).

Such values continued to dominate public life until after the Second World War. Gaster (1988) explains the Profumo scandal of 1963 partly in terms of changing sexual values. The public value system that dominated the sexual mores of late Victorian Britain had broken down in the post-war period, but had not been replaced by any new consensus on what could be considered normally permissible. The revelations about sexual behaviour on the part of both the political and social elite, as well as other members of society, were shocking because they revealed the lack of fit between what were still widely accepted as appropriate moral guidelines and actual behaviour about which the people in question apparently felt no guilt. In other words the denunciation of Profumo in terms deriving from the Victorian reformers' conviction that immoral men should not hold public office sounded hollow to many people, but at the same time no other conviction replaced it. Onto this uncertainty was grafted a series of other worrying facts to do with Profumo's honesty and the possible security implications.

It seems unlikely that any such explanation could be made of the recent sexual scandals. Divorce is a commonplace, and it is widely recognized that little or no shame attaches to the breakdown of relationships, which causes a re-evaluation of 'adultery'. It is unlikely that many people seriously believe that such failings in personal life make anyone unfit for public office. To that extent our public value system has changed fundamentally since the Second World War. Yet at the same time there is little in our public value system that would generate a positive account of such behaviour: the breakdown of relationships and the accompanying behaviour may have become morally neutral, but it has not acquired the public profile of an unequivocal good. Monogamy has not been replaced by its opposite in our public value system, but by 'serial monogamy', a lesser and ambiguous modification. Between unmarried consenting adults little is regarded as impermissible, but as soon as infidelity is involved the equation changes and even though universal condemnation regardless of circumstances is unlikely, the only common source of a positive account is a narrative in which a previous relationship has already broken down and the new relationship will be a valued and (at least implicitly) stable element in personal life. The plausibility of such a narrative is greater if no conflicting narrative is publicly available. The presence or absence of countervailing narratives clearly depends in large measure on the nature of information flows concerning the events in question, and in particular on the question of who controls the information flows.[1]

Thus the historical version of the 'human interest' explanation has a limited applicability in recent contexts: the history of the family accounts for the limited plausibility of favourable accounts of extra-marital sex, but at the same time the prevalence of accounts of scandal has been accompanied by a reduction in real public censoriousness.

Theories according to which the denunciation of deviancy has the function of policing the boundaries of the normal presuppose that the denunciation does indeed bring about a negative judgement upon those denounced. This presupposition is grounded in a consensual conception of deviancy, according to which the boundaries between the normal and the deviant are clearly defined and commonly agreed; under these circumstances, recognition and condemnation of an act as deviant both reinforces the norms according to which it is defined as deviant and reinforces the community which has concurred in the application of these norms; this sociological commonplace has been applied to the analysis of political scandal by Markovits and Silverstein (1988: 2). In this process, the mass media simultaneously depend upon the existence of this boundary and reinforce it by implicit reference to its norms. It seems unlikely that this function (apropos sexuality) could survive unmodified in a period of history when consensus over the boundary between acceptable and unacceptable behaviour, especially sexual behaviour, was subject to rapid change.[2] Moreover, this function is based upon the presupposition that media representation of the actions in question will faithfully reproduce the terms in which the major value institutions of the society, and especially the law, refer to the actions in question. Where scandal in the media consisted primarily of court reporting and it was guaranteed that the moral profile of the representation would be similar to the moral profile of the legally defined situation, it was reasonable to suppose that media representations would in fact have the function described. But it is impossible to see the representation of many prominent recent scandals in this light: as Lull and Hinerman point out, the 'not guilty' verdict on O. J. Simpson (accused of murdering his wife and a friend) did not exonerate him in the eyes of many Americans, and although Lorena Bobbitt (who cut off her unfaithful husband's penis) could have been found guilty in a court of law, it is unlikely that public opinion would have universally supported such a verdict (1997: 27). It is impossible to understand the Mellor affair or the 'Back to Basics' scandals in the light of a theory of moral transgression alone: even though the section of the population which still adheres to 'traditional' conceptions of sexual morality might well have read the texts in the light of this morality and have reacted entirely in terms of a traditional moral condemnation, much of the textuality in question would make it difficult to do so. Tabloid puns about the 'Bonk of England' or the headlines the *Sun* gave to the Mellor affair clearly invited a humorous, perhaps mocking response, and although other papers' coverage was less overtly comic there can be little doubt that the definition that dominated news coverage was far from unequivocal outrage at immoral behaviour.[3]

As we have seen, the analysis of political scandals in Markovits and Silverstein in part depends on the functionalist theory of the denunciation of deviance (1988: 2). The explanation of the Profumo affair that is given here is cast in terms of three elements of British society at the time. Firstly, the changing sexual mores of the post-Second World War period, where partial abandonment of traditional inhibitions had led to widespread public uncertainty about what constituted moral normality; this gave particular resonance to the behaviour revealed. Secondly, the British political system did not give a central place to money as a source of political success, which meant that money as the source of scandal was not very likely. Thirdly, the absence of money as a prime motivating force in British politics was the source of ideological homogeneity in the British political class, not where policy is concerned but where political propriety is concerned: Profumo breached this unwritten code by trying to cover up what he had done. These features of the Profumo scandal are related to the fundamental structure of scandals in liberal democracies, according to the authors, since it is in the nature of these systems that the boundaries between the public and the private overlap in a conflicting way: the basic pull of liberalism is towards individual privacy, whereas the basic pull of democracy is towards the use of the polity to create a unified public good; this conflict is reconciled through the practice of 'due process' (1988: 3–5). Scandals thus tend to occur at points where 'due process' (in this case, political propriety in Parliament) is unable to contain the conflict in question. In the Foreword, Lowi makes the point that scandals can be either 'substantive' (i.e. derive from a gross breach of morality) or 'procedural', where the scandal derives less from the original act than from attempts to hide it which breach due process in some form or other (1988: viii). The Profumo case was therefore both, but perhaps primarily 'procedural' due to his lie to Parliament. This subtle theory of political scandal fits with the range of examples studied, but is difficult to reconcile cases such as the Yeo or Mellor affairs, let alone largely non-political instances such as Pennant-Rea.[4]

Thus neither the historical version of the 'prurient interest' nor the 'denunciation of deviance' model seems to give a sufficiently robust explanation of the nature and prominence of scandal in recent years. Commonly, 'human interest' is posited as a universal, a feature of 'human nature'. While this may indeed be so, it is arguable that the role of the mass media in satisfying this curiosity in modern society changes the relationship between the curiosity and its satisfaction. In mass-mediated gossip or scandal, as opposed to the face-to-face gossip of pre-industrial communities, 'personal knowledge is no longer a pre-requisite for either gossiper or audience – resulting in an imaginary, shared intimacy, a familiarity with a persona neither public nor private' (Mellencamp, 1992: 169).

In mass-mediated interactions knowledge of the personalities of those seen in the media 'cannot be refined or controverted by the ... dialogical interaction characteristic of face-to-face interaction' (Thompson, 1995: 99); for Thompson, this situation is typical of the shift in public visibility, and therefore in the boundary between the public and the private that is typical of modernity. As a result, the nature of the attention given to the famous and the deviant (separately or in combination) is significantly different in a modern society in so far as the information about them reaches the audience via the mass media rather than via any other information transmission chain.

Mass-mediated information has the characteristics of proximity and distance in a mixture which is unique. Distance is given by the social space separating viewer from spectacle, but mediated access to the person represented bridges this gap. The resulting 'proximity' is both chronological and – especially in the form of TV and photography – spatial: in print, the person interviewed or reported may say what their feelings are; photography provides us with a form of proximity given by the nature of the camera, a form of intimacy in which we are allowed access to the feelings of the person photographed.[5] By the same token, the intimacy is non-reciprocal, and therefore carries none of the usual possibilities or obligations of intimacy. The authenticity of this access may be doubted, as photographs commonly need verbal interpretation in order to 'reveal' the feelings of the person upon whose face such feelings are supposedly clearly visible (Hall, 1973: 177–8). The fact that this 'para-social interaction' produces 'intimacy at a distance' does not reduce its emotional impact and may even increase it (Horton and Wohl, 1956): witness the public expressions of grief about the death of Diana, Princess of Wales, on the part of many whose knowledge of and contact with her was exclusively through the mass media.[6] Such one-way intimacy may be critically interpreted as 'voyeuristic' and therefore inauthentic, but whether evaluated negatively or positively, the 'proximate distance' which is constitutive of the experience is a product of mass mediation.

This clear-cut distinction is probably an over-simplification, in that the relationship between face-to-face communication and mass-mediated communication is more complex and variable than this admits – as we have seen in the case of financial scandals. In this respect, earlier studies of rumour are revealing: for example, the finding that 90 per cent of the US population had heard of President Kennedy's assassination within forty-five minutes of its occurrence, and of these 50 per cent heard of it by word of mouth (Rosnow and Fine, 1976: 32); in a parallel instance, 'Within 3 hours after the death of President Roosevelt was announced, the *New York Times* had received 4,968 telephone calls asking for verification' (Shibutani, 1966: 42–3). I learned of Princess Diana's death from a mechanic in a garage in northern Italy about twenty-four hours after her death. None the less, despite such reservations about the nature of information flows, the underlying principle of 'intimacy at a distance' is not in doubt. Thus at the very least we would have to say that the nature of 'human interest' is different in a mass-mediated society than in non-mass-mediated societies. Here may lie the explanation of the vulnerability of people and institutions to shifts in allegiance brought about by media revelations. In a mediated relationship, the (pseudo) intimacy made available by intense public scrutiny is one-dimensional, while still being potentially emotionally intense. When information which contradicts the coherent emotional appeal of the public persona reaches the public arena, there is no countervailing and ongoing dialogical interaction which can counteract the newly negative impression, and no sense of obligation to the person. The resulting sense of deception may be all the deeper for having been grounded in a 'depthless' intimacy. This is not a question of the amount of information available about a person, and deficits in the quantity of information cannot be made up by increasing it – for example, by 'contextualisation' or interviews with intimates. It is a question of the different types of emotional commitment involved in the different information chains. This also suggests the limitation of thinking of promotion of political personalities as akin to 'brand equity' in marketing. Brands are very trusted guides to consumer behaviour, but this is because people have direct experience of incorporating them into their everyday lives, whereas this can never be true of public personae.[7]

Secondly, it is arguable that 'fame', at least in the form which is typical of our society, is itself a product of the mass media. In part, this is a necessary consequence of the previous point: in so far as segregation produces dependence upon mass-mediated information flows, fame – and any other attribute dependent upon widespread public knowledge – derives from the media. However, the proposition that fame derives from the media also implies that it is the forms of activity which correspond to news values that produce fame, and that forms of activity which do not conform to them will pass relatively unnoticed. This situation creates a circle of causality in which the media representation of activities produces fame, and the resultant fame creates a high news value for the activities of the person in question, no matter how trivial they are, and regardless of whether the same activities on the part of another person would have the same news value. For example, as has often been noted, Princess Anne's patronage of charities relatively rarely attracts media attention, whereas Princess Diana's had a very high media profile. In particular, the 'intimacy' that is promoted by news attention and the fame that is also its result combine to produce a special public profile for those who are its object, in which they are simultaneously very distant from those who know their activities only through the media – fame isolates the famous – and very close in so far as the illusion of intimacy is created. Under these circumstances, the activities of the rich and famous have a status which is productive of the news value which also caused it in the first place, and which singles them out for potential media attention.

The presupposition of the 'watchdog' theory is that media organizations and their readers or viewers share a concern for public affairs in which a rational assessment of the value of actions in a democratic society defines what is found to be worthy of presentation in the media. This rational concern would override, or at least be independent of, any prurience, human interest, or fascination with the sensational. This theory is probably incompatible with the 'human interest' explanation of scandalous stories, which postulate exactly the opposite of a rational concern with public affairs. At best – if the human interest theory is right – we could say that the media are helped to play their watchdog role by the fact that human interest stories maintain media publics and thus provide the financial underpinning for the other activities that do fulfil the watchdog purpose. As a refinement, one might add that even if the audience's motive is largely prurient, it is none the less true that the possibility of denunciation operates to control potential immoral behaviour, or that at least some of the behaviour that gets denounced is indicative of character defects that are legitimately a matter of public concern: for example, David Mellor's choice of a sexual partner was said to reveal lack of judgement. In truth, it is difficult to see how these arguments can actually justify the type of reporting of celebrities' behaviour which has been typical of the tabloid press for many years: the reason is undoubtedly public curiosity, even if the exposés can sometimes be justified on the grounds that they give rise to real matters of public concern such as the debate over the meaning of 'Back to Basics'. Where sexual scandal is concerned, the watchdog theory seems to act chiefly as a guideline for newspapers which want to distinguish themselves from the tabloids in making decisions about what stories to cover, or – when the decision to cover the same stories as the tabloids is made – how to cover the stories in question; we have already seen examples of such decisions in our analysis of the scandals analysed above. It is also important, by implication, in regulatory adjudications, since the Press Complaints Commission Code of Conduct balances the 'right to privacy' with 'public interest'.[8] Where sexual scandal is concerned, the watchdog theory is primarily ethical rather than sociologically descriptive – or rather its descriptive value depends upon its ethical role.

If the watchdog theory is only a partially plausible one for the analysis of sexual scandal in the media, it is far more plausible in the case of scandals concerned with financial impropriety, fraud, misman-agement, the abuse of power or public negligence. Clearly, the theory of an 'anti-business bias' in the press is closely related to the watchdog theory: they are obverse and reverse where reporting of business activities is concerned. The alleged anti-business bias consists primarily in the fact that business affairs are not regularly reported on news pages, and only make the transition to those pages when events conform to general news values; as a result, 'When business news is confined to the business pages, corporations maintain the upper hand. However, when big business becomes big news, moves to the front page, and becomes the lead story on network news, corporate news management techniques are severely weakened' (Berkman and Kitch, quoted in Tumber, 1993: 355). By implication, the 'breakdown of corporate news management techniques' allows events to be profiled in a way that is inconsistent with the interests in question, which gives rise to the allegation of anti-business bias. Frequently, this involves scandalous misdeeds, or negative stories of a less scandalous nature such as corporate losses, product liability, 'downsizing', etc. However, an analysis of the balance between negative and positive coverage of business matters in 1992 by *Presswatch* indicated that roughly one-third of the UK national press consistently favoured positive over negative coverage in the period surveyed, and another third of national titles only marginally favoured negative coverage (Tumber, 1993: 354).

The collapse of BCCI, the trial of Ernest Saunders on charges relating to share dealings during a contested take-over, the Matrix Churchill trial and the subsequent investigations into breaches of guidelines for ministerial conduct – all of these clearly fit conventional definitions of matters of public importance.[9] Moreover, even if such stories are not entirely devoid of human interest elements, it is clear that the focus on publicly defined obligations can be used to characterize the coverage in a way that is consonant with the watchdog theory. It is also the case that in each of these instances the moral profile of the events and the actions of those denounced may be less clear than is the case in sexual scandal. Commonly, in sexual scandal the question is not whether the actions in question were morally justifiable or not, but whether lapses from 'personal' morality were publicly important. In the instances of the Guinness share-support operation, and recent political scandals, the meaning of the events was ambiguous. If some reporting was clearly based in the supposition – or even outright statement – that the activities in question were wrong (for example, the *Guardian* reporting of former Minister Jonathan Aitken's stay at the Paris Ritz), the profile of the 'Arms for Iraq' affair was never completely unambiguous: the politicians involved mostly argued – and appeared to be convinced – that what they had done was perfectly justifiable.[10] Similarly, in the Guinness affair, some protagonists never ceased to argue that what had been done was perfectly legitimate business practice, and that either the law was out of touch with normality, or that there were grey areas involved where legality and morality were only ambiguous guides to action. Here we must distinguish between a moral argument which turns upon whether the alleged facts occurred, and one where the facts are agreed, but their moral status is subject to different assessments. In the 'Arms for Iraq' affair, the latter was the case; in the Aitken affair, it was the factual base that was primarily at issue.[11] Under these circumstances, the role of reporting in bringing conduct to light which may be the subject of divergent interpretations is both the motive and the justification of the reporting.

Lastly, we can turn to the theory according to which the representations in question are a form of semiotic subversion of social norms. Against arguments based on the rationality of the role of the media, this theory insists on their emotional role for the audience, on which commercial strategies are built (Mellencamp, 1992: 230–43; cf. Lull and Hinerman, 1997: 28–9). In particular, a Freudian-based theory of curiosity is advanced as the explanation of the appeal of gossip and scandal, which contradicts both a functionalist account of scandal as the containment of deviance and a rationalist account of the press as a public watchdog. These last two accounts insist on the role of investigations in getting to the truth of the matter; but the gossip audience is indifferent to truth in the traditional, factual sense – which operates only as a constraint on the production side, because of the threat of libel, or regulatory action, or the withdrawal of source cooperation. In mass-mediated gossip and scandal we never make contact with the 'real person' in question – since the real person who is the object of gossip is simultaneously available and non-available – but deal with a new persona which is half-public, half-private. This produces an 'imaginary, shared intimacy' which is grounded in the act of denial (in the Freudian sense: i.e. the simultaneous recognition that there is no intimacy and the repressed disavowal of this recognition). Extreme versions of this produce the behaviour of some soap opera fans, who act as if the characters had a real existence (e.g. trying to take holidays in the hotels used as a setting), or the psychotic behaviour of the fictitious female fan in Scorsese's *King of Comedy*.[12] Indeed, the attraction of gossip depends less on access to a person than on the performance of participation in the chain of gossiping (Mellencamp, 1992: 169; Thompson, 1995: 99). At the same time, the promise of 'secrets', which will supposedly be revealed in the scandal process, is both an incentive to attend to it and a constant thwarting of the desire for this satisfaction, since as soon as the secret is revealed it ceases to be a secret and the process must be renewed: it is thus both a 'tease' in the popular sense and also a commercial strategy for media which feed on gossip as a source of income (Mellencamp, 1992: 156–8).

At the base of this theory Mellencamp places Freud's analysis of 'epistemophilia', the desire for knowing, an appetite analogous to voyeurism. In each of these cases, the pleasure of seeing or the pleasure of knowing becomes an end in itself instead of a means to an end:

> The thought process itself becomes sexualised, for the sexual pleasure which is normally attached to the content of thought becomes shifted onto the act of thinking itself, and the satisfaction derived from reaching the conclusion of a line of thought is experienced as a sexual satisfaction. (Freud, 1979: 124)

For Freud, this process is a hangover from normal childhood curiosity, but one where the repression of various drives in the formation of the adult personality has produced neurotic compulsions to obsessive behaviour. In particular, the emotional satisfaction of the thought process described above is a part of the process of neurotic doubt, the deliberate inability to take decisions to act, which accompanies more obvious obsessive symptoms such as irrational fears and anxieties (Freud, 1979: 116–25). In this process, curiosity – the desire for knowledge – is always in practice a projection of a fantasy onto the world about which the curious person is apparently seeking knowledge. Freud makes it clear that the role of conscious, rational thought in this neurotic process is to disguise the reality of the psychic process which underpins it, namely the obsessive compulsion, just as in dreams the appearance of coherence in the dream's content is always a disguise for the real wish-fulfilment fantasy underlying it (Freud, 1979: 102–5).

Thus it is clear how curiosity can be said not to seek some truth about a person (or event) but rather to use the existence of that person as a focus for the projection of a fantasy: it is in this sense that gossip never aims at the 'real person'. Yet at the same time, the person certainly must be believed to be real, for gossip about a person known to be fictional makes little sense.[13] Does the gossiper need to believe in the truth of what is being said? Certainly some gossip is malicious lies and known to be such; but this activity is probably psychologically different from gossip where there is some belief in its truth. However, in the Freudian account, the truth and the belief in it are primarily supports for the fantasy projection, not ends in themselves. In this account may lie the outline of an explanation of the role of the personalization of issues in news reporting:[14] while personalization may well make issues more comprehensible, it is also the case that it makes them more interesting because it provides a focus for emotional investment.

In what sense can gossip and scandal, analysed in this fashion, be said to have a subversive potential? Essentially by promoting accounts of the world around us which are incompatible with the types of account of the world which in combination make up the dominant culture of our society. For example, it is claimed that the constant revelation of secrets has a subversive potential, not because this reveals the reality behind the image (the 'watchdog' justification of scandal), but because 'Gossip's assertions exist for their own sake, referring to nothing beneath the apparent. [It] delights by an aesthetic of surfaces.' This has 'subversive implications' as a 'resource for the subordinated': this delight makes the difficult task of assessment of the accuracy of information unnecessary (Spack quoted in Mellencamp, 1992: 178–9). By the same token, the characteristics of US tabloid newspapers and related TV shows make them into 'primary sites of rupture in the ideological fabric of bourgeois culture' by challenging 'normalisation'. The characteristics are excessive representations of deviancy which invite the 'undisciplined pleasures of the tasteless and the *hoi polloi*', which 'disfigure and defamiliarize' the normal in ways which leave the spectator 'uncomfortably but pleasurably' suspended between the normal and the abnormal, and are attended to by readers and viewers in a sceptical or cynical manner (Glynn, 1990: 28, 26, 30–1). In each case the subversion derives from the avoidance of concerns such as truthfulness, verification, plausibility, consistency and coherence which are part of the mental apparatus, or the culture, associated with the dominant order of society, and said therefore to be intrinsic to its continued maintenance.[15] However, an analysis of audience response to scandal stories suggests that members take this material seriously, using it as the starting point for moral speculation about the reported behaviour (Bird, 1997). In general, the dialogic properties of scandal reporting are little explored.

The theory which sees scandal as a form of gossip has the strength that it both grounds the appeal of scandal in a universal feature of the human mind and yet at the same time gives an account of the role of the mass media which is culture-specific. However, we may doubt whether the Freudian theory of epistemophilia is adequate as an account of mass-mediated gossip precisely in so far as it is an account of pathological behaviour, whose mark is the fact that the person who behaves in this way suffers psychic pain as a result of the combination of symptoms in question: obsessive doubt, superstitious fears, phobic anxieties, etc. It is clear in Freud's analysis that the normal desire to know manifested in childhood sexuality is not characterized by the sexualization of the thought process, as Mellencamp suggests: the 'sexualized' version occurs at points where severe anxiety accompanies a marked regression from acting to thinking – the characteristic indecisiveness of the obsessional neurotic; it is specifically the mark of neurosis and suffering (Mahoney, 1986: 162–3). Regardless of whether we evaluate gossip positively or negatively as a social activity, it is difficult to see it as a pathology, as suffering.

How useful is the set of explanations advanced here?

The explanation based in inter-title competition is simultaneously true and useless for our purposes since it assumes what we need to know: why does scandal have news value? The usual reference point is delight in prurience, and we have seen that this is a partial explanation because of the historical circumstances (at least where sexual deviance is concerned). By the same token, the watchdog theory and the containment theory are of little value today where sexual scandal is concerned (even though they were no doubt relevant a hundred years ago, in a period when condemnation of non-marital sexuality had a more solid institutional foundation) but are clearly central to the news value of financial and non-sexual political scandal. In this historical analysis lies the dismissal of both the traditional 'cultural forces' explanation of sexual scandal, as well as of the relevance of gossip as a permanent feature of human society: while this may be so, the nature of the behaviour likely to attract censorious gossip has probably changed, and it is probable that the role of the mass media changes the nature of gossip anyway. We are left with explanations formulated in terms of the role of the mass media, considered both as a conduit for motivated information flows and as the incarnation of mediated curiosity.

Freudian explanations would suggest a link between gossip in everyday life and mass-mediated gossip, but they suffer from the restriction of pathology: 'epistemophilia', in the sense in which Freud outlines it, is an unlikely candidate for an ordinary everyday, non-pathological activity. The role of the mass media must be seen to change the nature of gossip fundamentally, in the form of 'intimacy at a distance'. Thus curiosity – in so far as it is an explanation for the passage of scandalous information through the mass media – is an explanation only because it refers to a particular version of curiosity, the mass-mediated version, where the lack of genuine intimacy (i.e. reciprocal intimacy) is what allows the satisfaction of curiosity to be what it is. However, we should remember that audience curiosity is only one element in the explanation of scandal in the media. Certainly, where 'confessional' talk shows are concerned, media competition and the low cost of such programmes are central elements: they are, as Mellencamp shows, integral parts of a commercial strategy.[16] However, this does not explain the motives of those who reveal scandalous information to the media. We have seen just how complex and varied these may be.[17]

Finally we can return to the concerns with which this case study opened, and which have dictated their overall analysis: the implication of centring the analysis of scandals on the nature of the information flows that allows them to come into being. We have seen a central problem in the Molotch and Lester analysis of scandal: it is that in fact 'occurrences' (as they call 'unpromoted' events) are assigned to classificatory slots, or categories, according to schemata which are already present in culture. But at the same time 'scandal' only truly conforms to the common-sense definition which underpins media usage (or abuse through over-use) of the term when it has in fact become an event present to public attention through the mass media. It thus acquires its characteristic profile through conformity to news values. In this process, it is clear that some features of the event are selected for public focus and others are left in the shadows: the event becomes profiled through the process of selection in accordance with news criteria. In particular, its profile fundamentally depends on the event's capacity to maintain a presence in news media through the constant renewal of information. Certainly the moral profile of an event does not depend upon its presence in the media, let alone its continued presence; arguably, even brief appearances in the media under the heading 'scandal' are no less scandalous than extended appearances. But it is certainly the case that prominence depends on continued presence and it is arguable that moral deviance only becomes 'scandal' at the point when a certain level of public importance is attached to the event. This level of importance may depend upon protracted media attention. At the same time, continued prominence is clearly dependent upon the nature of information flows, and – crucially but not exclusively – upon the motives of news sources.

With this in mind, we may ask one final question concerning the Clinton/Lewinsky scandal. It became a banality of reporting that the profile of the event was in large measure due to the role of Special Prosecutor Kenneth Starr as a news source. His constant feeding of newsworthy information to the US media was a central element in the development of the entire event.[18] Presumably his tactics were based upon the supposition that these revelations would discredit President Clinton. The opposite occurred: Clinton's standing in opinion polls about his competence as President continued to rise as the event unfolded. This suggests that the US population did not judge the event to conform to the profile of it presented in the media. Whether they enjoyed the revelations in question is unknown – though the circulation of jokes based on them makes it likely – but clearly they did not collectively translate any such pleasure into judgements against the President. The British political commentator Hugo Young, writing in the *Guardian* in the aftermath of the November Congressional elections which saw a modest increase in Democrat votes, concluded: 'In this age, we gorge on intimacies. The secrets of the power elite have never been more lubriciously exposed ... Yet we may be on the verge of discovering that this gorging, this raging torrent of supply, rests on a premise that is fundamentally false' (cf. Jones, 1999: 185–98, on the handling of Robin Cook's divorce and remarriage).

The false premise is that scandal necessarily undermines public opinion about the worth of the scandalous person. Although this does not necessarily suggest that the public appetite for such revelations is any less, it certainly implies – although Young does not explore this possibility – that it may modify news' sources willingness to provide information: after all, if the effort to discredit someone is going to fail, why bother?

CHAPTER 6

Brent Spar

On 16 February 1995 the UK Government announced that it had given permission to Shell to dispose of the Brent Spar storage buoy by sinking it in the Atlantic. The decision was reported in the national broadsheets and the Scottish press, but not on the national broadcast media; the Scottish fishing industry and environmental groups recorded their disapproval. The decision appears not to have been mentioned in other nations' media at all. Little more was heard of the Brent Spar in the UK media until Sunday 30 April when Greenpeace announced that they had occupied it to highlight the environmental danger. The occupation was immediately and widely reported. Also widely reported were their later eviction by Shell security men, protests organized in Germany and other European countries (especially a boycott of Shell petrol stations), and the reoccupation of the Spar and confrontations on the high seas around it. Opposition to its disposal occupied a significant place on the agenda of the inter-governmental conference about the North Sea at Esbjerg in late May and even found its way onto the agenda of the G7 summit some weeks later. At both, representatives of European Union states voiced strong opposition to Shell's plans and to the UK Government's role in allowing the disposal. Shell announced its intention on 20 June to abandon its deep-sea disposal option and seek an alternative. The final disposal method was announced in January 1998.

Shell changed their disposal plans on 20 June 1995 because 'The European companies of the Royal Dutch Shell Group find themselves in an untenable position and feel that it is not possible to continue without wider support from the governments participating in the Oslo-Paris Convention' (Shell, 1995a).

Shell ascribe this lack of support to opposition to deep-sea disposal; yet none of these governments had raised any objection during the consultation phase of the disposal process. A combination of the media portrayal of the events and public protest against Shell's plans must have been responsible for the opposition shown at the two inter-governmental conferences. In March 1997, the Shell group of companies announced that it was publishing a revised edition of its *Statement of General Business Principles* which would guide its commercial operations with due sensitivity towards human rights and environmental concerns. The statement was prepared in consulta-tion with 'a range of outside bodies in various countries – including church, environmental and human-rights organisations' (Herkstroter, 1997: 6). According to John Jennings (*Financial Times*, 17.3.97) it had 'learnt from those ... events that [Shell] had not been listening enough'.[1]

It is not the purpose of this chapter to try to discover the extent of the media's influence in the articulation of opposition. None the less, the Brent Spar coverage, and Shell's subsequent decision to change their disposal plans, provide us with a case study in which the passage of information through the news media appears, at first sight at least, to have contributed to the events being reported. The profile that the event acquired became the context in which decisions were taken, and we may assess the role of the media by describing the profile of events found in news reporting. This involves consideration of media coverage in the countries most directly involved: Britain, Germany and the Netherlands.[2] It will also involve analysis of how the media portrayal of events came to assume the form that it did in the UK and Germany, analysis – that is to say – of how source strategies influence media output.

We can start with a media analysis conducted on Shell's behalf by Computerised Media Associates, carried out in the aftermath of the decision to abandon deep-sea disposal, and summarized in an August 1995 press release. According to this study, UK media coverage of the Brent Spar in the period leading up to Shell's change of plan was not on balance markedly unfavourable to Shell, nor markedly favourable to Greenpeace: 'Across all media, averaging over the 9 weeks from May 1st ... until 30th June ... the Shell and Greenpeace impact is far more balanced than some have suggested: 55% positive for Greenpeace/ 45% positive for Shell' (Shell, 1995b). The method used by CMA was based on counting the number of mentions of themes which were favourable/unfavourable to either side and weighting them by the amount of emphasis they were given and by the circulation or audience of the title or programme in question. Neutral, or purely factual information was excluded from the analysis as published by Shell.[3] The balance between the weighted number of mentions of these overtly partisan themes constitutes the basis of the assertion about the extent of media favour towards one side or the other. No doubt this enumeration and calculation is correct. However, if that is so, we must also accept that the media coverage in the UK made no substantial contribution to the difficulties that Shell encountered, to their decision to change their disposal plans, nor to their decision to modify the ethical content of their code of business practice.

It also runs counter to the cries of *mea culpa* from TV newsroom editors at the Edinburgh International Television Festival seminar on Brent Spar (August 1995). Richard Sambrook (editor, BBC News-gathering) said that Greenpeace's ability to address news agendas allowed them to 'pull us by the nose through too much of the campaign ... in some sense we were had over Brent Spar, it was our own, the media's, fault'. David Lloyd of Channel 4 News said, 'We were bounced' by Greenpeace, and that even though they had tried to counteract the pressure group's dominance of interpretation of events, they had failed because by that time the story 'had long since been spun far, far into Greenpeace's direction'.[4] Sambrook mentioned the Shell/CMA media evaluation and commented that it ignored the power of dramatic video footage.

The purpose of the media evaluation commissioned by Shell was to measure the impact of messages, not to assess the impact of all news. Information that was not part of a message was omitted. However, the publication of factual information can favour or disfavour people: that is why one of the defining features of a scandal is the loss of control over information flows when the mechanism policing spaces breaks down. As a result, the content analysis devised for this chapter includes all information that passed through the media, without distinction between factual and polemical statements, on the grounds that degrees of emphasis on different aspects or dimensions of an event are crucial to the profile that an event assumes in the public domain despite the fact that the information may be entirely factual. The publication of any information is potentially to someone's advantage and by the same token may well be to someone else's disadvantage: however, although there is no such thing as neutral information, it may still be perfectly possible to distinguish between factual and non-factual information, and between truth and untruth: the 'interestedness' of information has no necessary connection with its truth or untruth, a distinction which exists in a different epistemological dimension.[5]

The calendar of significant events in the period analysed in 1995 is shown in Table 6.1.

When Government plans for North Sea oil installations were announced on 16 February, UK press reports treated the topic overwhelmingly as a normal consultation-based procedure.[6] Media reports referred briefly to objections from Greenpeace and the

Table 6.1 Significant events, February–June 1995

16/2	Government announces Brent Spar disposal.
30/4	Greenpeace occupy Brent Spar.
22–23/5	Shell security men evict Greenpeace from Brent Spar; first calls for a consumer boycott of Shell in Germany.
7/6	Esbjerg conference of North Sea states opens. Greenpeace occupy again. Clashes at sea for several days.
12/6	Shell start moving Brent Spar towards scuttling site, followed by Greenpeace boat.
16/6	G7 Heads of State meeting in Halifax, Nova Scotia. Chancellor Kohl criticizes the Shell/UK Government plan. Greenpeace occupy Brent Spar using a helicopter.
20/6	Shell announce change of plan.

Scottish fishing industry, with the exception of the Glasgow *Herald* which emphasized the objections. I have found no reports in national broadcast or European media at this time, nor in the London-based tabloids. It was covered by business-page or political staff reporting a routine business-political interaction where cost considerations were of central importance because of the tax implications. According to an undated Greenpeace news release at the end of June 1995, it had been difficult to get the DTI even to accept and note their documented objections. We may speculate that if Greenpeace had not done anything about it, that is the way things would have continued. Business-page and Westminster journalists used routine sources to report a routine event and would no doubt have continued to do so.

The occupation on 30 April was widely reported in UK media. It was a Sunday, more or less ensuring broadcast coverage in the evening, which in its turn made national daily coverage the next morning more likely. Press attention continued, albeit at a lower level, throughout the week: there was some mention of it every day, but coverage was far from common in the nationals. Unsurprisingly, coverage was more frequent in Scottish papers than in London-based ones; only the Scottish papers covered it on Sunday 7 May. It figured rarely in national broadcast media during the first two weeks of the occupation.[7] It would appear that the news value of the story was insufficient at this stage to warrant extensive, let alone continuous national broadcast attention despite a continuing high level of print media interest and continuous Scottish local radio interest.

The nature of the first week's coverage is crucial to the way in which the subsequent media coverage developed. Two things are especially important. First, the way in which the event was understood, in other words the features of the event that were deemed newsworthy by media personnel; second, the fact that the event was of greater regional than national (let alone international) importance at this stage.

The event was overwhelmingly defined as an action undertaken by Greenpeace in protest at the (perceived) mistreatment of the environment. Shell's actions received approximately half the attention that Greenpeace's received, and Shell's preferred definition of the event – which had dominated the February reporting of the plan's announcement – was a distinctly subordinate theme in the reporting. Further subordinate themes included the question of whether the disposal of the Spar would set a precedent for other installations, the possibility that Scottish police would evict the protesters, and the cost of different methods of disposal (in February deep-sea sinking was said to be the cheapest, and this factor was highlighted in the Government's analysis of the plans). That is to say, in news terms the event was seen as significant in so far as it was something done by Greenpeace for reasons to do with Greenpeace's purposes and with the environment; all other features of the event were of subordinate importance in news terms. This is especially significant because the content analysis of both national and international coverage of the subsequent sequence of events reveals that news values continued to define the story predominantly in these terms. In other words, a media agenda was set in the opening days of a protracted sequence of events. Of course, it was always in theory possible that this news agenda could have been changed by the actions of news sources, but for reasons that will need to be explored this did not occur.

Analysis of the role of regional news is more speculative. Broadcast coverage was nearly exclusively Scottish during the first occupation (ended 23 May). If we separate the total number of UK press reports each week by region (Scotland/London-based UK nationals) we can see the extent to which early coverage was divided by area (Table 6.2).

Table 6.2 Total number of UK newspaper reports by week and by national/regional titles

Week	1 (1–7/May)	2 (8–14/May)	3 (15–21/May)	4 (22–28/May)
UK nationals	15	7	9	31
Scottish	20	3	11	14

While these indications are hardly conclusive of anything, they show the extent to which Scottish attention was aroused by this event in Scottish waters. Given that the Scottish media system is relatively small in comparison with the UK national one (but remarkably large given the population), the extent of reporting suggests a relatively high degree of attention. But what is far more important is the extent to which reporting of the event – both in the first phase and throughout the whole sequence of events – involved newsmen and women based in Scotland. Except for those journalists sent north by London-based media, information flows about events at the Spar to the national press depended heavily on information deriving from two Scottish news sources: the North Scotland News Agency, based in Aberdeen, and the Press Association office in Glasgow (some of whose reporters were temporarily assigned to Aberdeen and to the Shetlands). The North Scotland News Agency on-line files show that their stories were sent to a substantial number of national newspapers and Scottish regional papers on the following days: 1, 2, 3, 4 May, 18 May, 22 and 23 May. For example, a story in the *Daily Mail* on 4.5.95, by-lined Paul Riddel and giving nothing but the Greenpeace side of the story, comes direct from this agency which Riddel worked for at the time; in total the agency generated 144 reports on the Brent Spar during the period up to 20 June. A reporter from this agency was the only reporter on board the Shell vessel *Stadive* when it was used to expel the Greenpeace team from the Spar on 22–23 May.[8] According to Steve Smith, who covered the story for this agency (both from Aberdeen in the early stages and from the Greenpeace boats during the final stages of the confrontation) all the UK press reporters on the Greenpeace boats were Scots-based. Much of the Press Association reporting which gave details of what was happening in Scotland or at sea came from the Glasgow office. BBC Radio news reporters who covered the Brent Spar affair were mainly Scotland-based.[9] As we shall see, Shell information during May derived primarily from Aberdeen because Shell UK decided to leave responsibility for information with the Shell Expro office there. Of course, other information derived from national sources: the Greenpeace office in London, Shell UK in London and to a lesser extent Government sources. However, in a story where a lot depended upon live footage, live radio interviews and location-oriented information (photographs, quotes from Greenpeace activists, etc.), the role of locally based reporters was much greater than might be the case in other events where this angle was less important. This is less true of media outside the UK who relied heavily upon their London correspondents, sent reporters to the Spar with Greenpeace boats, or – in the case of Deutsche Press Agentur (the main German language news agency) – sent a reporter to Scotland to cover events. Radio stations in all interested countries were in direct contact with Greenpeace activists via satellite telephones.

While it is difficult to draw any firm conclusions from the facts about the role of Scots-based journalists in the information flows about Brent

Table 6.3

	Scots press	*National press*	*All titles (incl. PA)*
Shell	9.3	26.9	23.8
Greenpeace	52.1	39.1	45.3

Spar, some factors are probably relevant. The role of North Sea oil in the Scottish economy is controversial in Scotland, where there are arguments about whether Scotland receives its 'fair share' of the oil revenue. Certainly our content analysis suggests that Scottish newspapers were more likely than the national average to give prominence to the Greenpeace side of events. Table 6.3 shows the percentage of mentions in which the two main actors figure as the initiators of events compared by region of press publication (other actors account for the missing figures).

While there is no reason to suggest that Scottish journalists are any less (or more) objective than their London-based counterparts, the type of attention given to the activities of the main actors in the Brent Spar affair in the Scottish media suggests that they were more likely to see Greenpeace as the leaders of events than were their national counterparts.[10] Importantly, these journalists tend to see only – or mainly – the Scottish editions of UK national newspapers, as well as of course the regional press.[11] Thus there is a circuit of information in which Scottish journalists are seeing Scottish media reports of events and are also reporting the same sequence of events for London-based national media. The supposition which we may tentatively draw from this evidence is that the Scottish dimension of events may have operated to reinforce the Greenpeace definition of what happened despite the undoubted commitment to objectivity in the normal journalistic sense.

In discussing the Scottish dimension of events we have moved away from analysis of Week 1 of the confrontation and generalized about the entire period. In fact, the definition established in the first week of coverage continued to dominate press coverage. More specifically, what the press content analysis shows is that the event was defined as predominantly a confrontation between Shell and Greenpeace, in which Greenpeace maintained the initiative and in which the confrontation was seen chiefly as a protest about the environment. It also shows that this is true regardless of whether we analyse the coverage on a week-by-week basis or simply for the period as a whole: in other words, the news agenda did not vary substantially throughout the period of the confrontation. To be sure, once governments became involved – at the time of the two inter-governmental conferences – attention was directed towards political decision-making, thus reducing the hitherto exclusive focus on the chief protagonists. At this time the focus on the environmental protest dimension of events could have been somewhat diluted by a focus on what major political actors were saying, because the British Government continued to support the Shell plan right to the end. However, the dilution was limited because much of the reporting focused on the conflict element of the Brent Spar affair: it was already high on news agendas in the three main countries involved and non-British political actors ensured that its environmental dimension stayed there. UK headlines on the Esbjerg conference sometimes emphasized political action about the North Sea in general but since much of the political activity did in fact focus on the Brent Spar, reports of political activity inevitably also referred to environmental protest even when political actors such as the UK Government were trying to move the agenda elsewhere. Of course, other actors were interested in keeping the environment at the top of the agenda, notably Chancellor Kohl at the G7 summit.[12]

In a sense, this argument states the obvious: the events in question arose unequivocally from Greenpeace's protest. However, this transparency is misleading. We have only to think of the way in which the original plan for disposal was reported in February to see that another definition of events could have prevailed: for both Shell and the UK government what was happening was that (in my words, not theirs) a group of misguided idealists undertook an illegal act which disrupted the normal functioning of industrial-political decision-making. While no one used the phrase 'misguided idealists', Shell said in a statement immediately after the first occupation that Greenpeace should behave responsibly and leave the Spar now that they had made their protest (*The Times*, 1.5.97). Indeed, whenever journalists asked Shell for a statement about events, the reply focused on the normality of Shell's actions.

The focus on the themes of 'protest' and 'environment' is not neutral ground. Shell consistently pointed out (with support from Government) that it had fulfilled all national and international obligations in respect of finding the environmentally best solution to the problem of disposal. But when we compare what Shell said and what Greenpeace said, it is clear that whenever 'environment' is the dominant theme in news coverage Shell is forced on the defensive. Shell press releases and briefing documents in February stress the normality of the negotiating process between government and the company, and mention environmental factors in passing; clearly, for Shell, the environment was only one on a list of relevant considerations, of which the chief others were economic efficiency, health and safety of employees, and technical feasibility. Greenpeace's actions ensured that the environment was singled out as the overwhelmingly most important of these considerations, which distorted Shell's agenda. Subsequent Shell press releases and briefing documents move environmental considerations to the head of the text, in what is clearly a response to the change in the public agenda created by Greenpeace's actions and the way in which they were reported. When statements about the disposal represent it as unproblematic – which corresponds to Shell's preferred definition of the event – they appear in the content analysis under the heading of 'engineering'; whenever statements about the disposal are premised upon the supposition that it might be problematic, they appear in the content analysis as 'environment'. The number of 'engineering' statements and the degree of emphasis placed upon them is far outstripped by the number and emphasis of 'environment' mentions; in other words, the disposal process is far more likely to appear as something problematic than as something unproblematic (with the exception of reports of the original February announcement).[13]

This finding is consistent with the Vrije Universiteit comparative analysis. The authors show that across all media in all three countries Shell received more attention than Greenpeace and was consistently the subject of negative mentions whereas Greenpeace was consistently the subject of positive ones (De Haan and Van Leur, 1996: section 6.5).[14] When press coverage alone is analysed the story is not essentially different: there are variations in the degree of favour shown to Greenpeace, but the conclusion is always the same (section 5.2). In one respect alone is the British press significantly different from the press in the other countries analysed: the amount of attention given to Shell and Greenpeace is more approximately equal than in Germany and the Netherlands, and at the same time the balance between negative and positive mentions of Greenpeace is less favourable to Greenpeace than in the Continental countries; the negativity of evaluations of Shell is not essentially different in the three countries. This corresponds to the CMA analysis which was also based on a comparison of the two sides' success in placing favourable and unfavourable messages.

Moreover, other features of the event which might have dominated interpretation were silenced, sometimes to Greenpeace's benefit, sometimes to Shell's. Of these possible themes the most important is the potential illegality of Greenpeace's activities. Immediately after the occupation of the Spar on 30 April, Shell announced that they were in consultation with Grampian police to see if eviction could be organized under criminal law procedures. After some days, Grampian police announced that they would not be taking action against the

Greenpeace team. The decision not to proceed was taken by the Crown Office in Edinburgh because 'there were complex legal questions relating to matters of jurisdiction and evidence and it was not appropriate to bring a prosecution'. Shell was therefore obliged to seek a civil court order against Greenpeace which allowed them to use 'sheriff's officers', or bailiffs, and their own security men to evict the protesters. The effect of this situation on news coverage should not be underestimated. Since the police would not take action under criminal law procedures,[15] Shell had to face a considerable delay before they were able to enforce a court order – the eviction eventually occurred on 23 May – which gave Greenpeace further opportunities to pursue their media relations efforts and other purposes. Also, the fact that it was a civil process meant that in legal terms it was a conflict between two partners of equal legal standing, whereas if the process had used criminal law procedures, it is probable that the event would have had a different legal and arguably moral profile. Police are conventionally regarded as highly credible news sources by journalists, and if the Grampian police had gone into action against Greenpeace there is little doubt that the event would have been portrayed as much in terms deriving from police sources as in terms deriving from Greenpeace.[16]

A second theme was an ambiguous one – the question of cost. The original Government announcement on 16 February had stressed that the deep-sea solution was favourable for the taxpayer because the reduction in costs meant a reduction in the expenses Shell could claim against tax. The emphasis on cost-effectiveness was used by Greenpeace to suggest that Shell was sacrificing the environment to save money ('Shell is going for the cheapest disposal method. The Government must stop the dumping', Greenpeace spokeswoman, quoted *Daily Mail*, 1.5.95). Potentially, this was a strong anti-Shell message, but in practice it was not very prominent in UK news agendas: after the first week it was scarcely visible except during the final two days of the confrontation. Similarly with the question of whether Brent Spar would set a precedent for the disposal of other redundant North Sea installations: the original announcement was taken to imply that Brent Spar would be a precedent in the sense that the disposal methods would be settled on a case-by-case basis (*Financial Times, Daily Telegraph, The Times*, 17.2.95), but Greenpeace argued that it would serve as a precedent in a wider sense, allowing firms to scuttle derelict rigs without counting the environmental cost. Again this was potentially a strong anti-Shell message which in practice did not get as much prominence as it might have done. As can be seen from the content analysis tables, rarely was it the main focus of a report, and mentions of it never constituted a substantial proportion of the themes of coverage.

Objections from the fishing industry are another case of a row that never happened. At the original announcement in February, the Scottish Fishermen's Federation recorded its objections, and references to dangers to fishing from abandoned rigs continued to appear sporadically throughout the coverage of the confrontation (for example, the Federation was quoted extensively about objections to disposal plans in the Glasgow *Herald* on 4.5.95). Given that the fishing industry has a well-organized industrial association which is well able to make its interests known in the public domain, it is at first sight surprising that more was not said on this subject. However, the Federation had in fact been in talks with Shell about methods of disposal for eighteen months before the confrontation over the Brent Spar began, and were far more worried about the remains of installations being left in shallower waters where they would be a danger to fishing vessels than they were about any possible pollution that might derive from the deep-sea disposal of the Spar. Specifically, they had 'reluctantly agreed' to the deepwater disposal of the Spar despite the risks involved because they were persuaded that in- or on-shore disposal would present even greater dangers to fishermen. Their tactic was to put pressure on Shell to clean up the shallow-water seabed, but not to be so antagonistic as to jeopardize the long-term negotiating relationship they had built up with Shell over the years and which would have to continue after the Brent Spar affair was over. For example, they refused to agree to a Greenpeace proposal to organize a flotilla of fishing boats to demonstrate against the sinking, but used their 'critical support' for deepwater disposal to lean on Shell to clean up other bits of the seabed.[17]

The significant silences help to reveal the extent to which the reporting of events established a defined public profile. Two further features of the reporting lend support to this theory. Firstly, the frequent use of the word 'dumping' in news reports of the events. Shell and UK Government statements prefer neutral terms such as 'deep-sea disposal' or even 'sinking', but many headlines and broadcast reports use the emotive and negative term 'dumping', which seems to have been introduced into the discussion by Greenpeace's statements. Secondly, as TV news editors said at the Edinburgh seminar referred to above, the sheer drama of the video footage (in large measure made available by Greenpeace) outweighed any discussion of the merits of the disposal options: this is at the centre of broadcast editorial criticism of Greenpeace's 'media manipulation'. This analysis is born out by the Vrije Universiteit comparative international media analysis which includes sample analysis of TV coverage in Germany and the Netherlands (but not the UK); the authors found the following:

- Of all shots showing the main participants in the events 75% were given over to Shell and Greenpeace; 40% of these shots were devoted to confrontations around the Brent Spar (i.e., 30% of all shots of the main participants were 'action shots' at the Spar).
- Of all TV shots, 41% were of Greenpeace and 81% of those were of action (i.e., 37.5% of all TV shots were of Greenpeace actions).
- German TV gave 49% of its pictorial attention to Greenpeace and only 23% to Shell (De Haan and Van Leur, 1996: section 6.4).
- Levels of attention to Shell and Greenpeace were very different on the audio and video tracks of TV coverage: on the audio track, Shell received most attention, on the video track Greenpeace scored highest (section 6.5).

The drama of the video footage is also to be seen in newspaper coverage: for example, the German tabloid *Bild am Sonntag* ran a two-page spread on 18 June under the headline 'The Heroes Of The North Sea' superimposed on a photograph of Greenpeace boats under water cannon spray. Harmsen (1996) found that approximately 50 per cent of all UK, Dutch and German press photographs related to the events were taken at sea and, of this 50 per cent, half were of Brent Spar itself and most of the rest were of Greenpeace activists; where Shell was shown pictorially it was mostly through objects rather than people and mostly through images of failure – e.g. damaged petrol stations in Germany.

Thus far our analysis has focused largely on the UK press coverage of the event. However, it is unlikely that this coverage by itself had a significant impact upon the course of events: it was the international orchestration of the campaign and perhaps especially the dramatic TV coverage which is likely to have been responsible for the impact. Moreover, the UK press coverage was significantly less unfavourable to Shell than German or Dutch press coverage: the Vrije Universiteit analysis makes this clear. Even cursory investigation of the coverage makes it obvious: UK press coverage is objective in the usual journalistic sense of seeking and giving quotes from both sides and sticking as closely to established facts as possible. Moreover, many articles in the UK press go out of their way to stress the Shell version of events.

In the sample of German press I examined in detail (two national broadsheet dailies and one tabloid) it was very difficult to find a single article that was overall in favour of Shell; even business-page articles in the conservative daily *Die Welt* were largely antagonistic to the Shell proposal;[18] the negative nature of German media coverage was reported by UK German correspondents (e.g. *Independent*, 20.6.95). Even the *Handelsblatt* (the German equivalent of the *Financial Times*) gives as much emphasis to a negative account of the situation as to a totally objective account of Shell's intentions (22.5.95; reproduced in

Table 6.4 Paragraph order in PA and DPA accounts

PA	DPA (as published)
Greenpeace occupy – details	Greenpeace occupy – details
Police and Shell monitor situation	Greenpeace quote
More Greenpeace details	Greenpeace intentions: (four paragraphs)
Greenpeace claims	• precedent for North Sea
Shell statement	• poisonous content
Context – North Sea installations	Shell and police; Shell quote
Greenpeace quote	Greenpeace details
Shell quote	Government permission for sinking

Mantow and Podeus, 1995: 32). As an indication of the differences in tone, we can compare two press agency reports of the original occupation, the British PA and the German DPA. In the PA report, a balance is struck between Greenpeace actions and claims, and Shell actions and claims; in the DPA version only Greenpeace is quoted. In the first published version of the DPA report that I have located, there is some attempt to balance the accounts, but it is very different to what is found in the PA report. The paragraph order in the two accounts is shown in Table 6.4.

Although the information is very similar, the DPA-based report gives more attention to Greenpeace's activities, both in terms of the amount of space and in the running order of the material. It uses more quotes from Greenpeace and it uses Greenpeace's own terminology in factual reporting.[19] The content analysis commissioned by Deutsche Shell concludes that during the first week German coverage spoke Greenpeace's language; included in this version of events is a more prominent emphasis on the role of the cost factor in Shell's decision, implying that Shell cared more for profit than for the environment (Mantow and Podeus, 1995: 22).

The event was not initially significant national news in Germany. According to the Deutsche Shell media analysis:

> Public interest and the linked media coverage was initially restricted exclusively to the area of Hamburg and the coastal regions ... At first Brent Spar was not a nationally dominant theme – with the understandable exception of the news reports of the eviction on 23 May. At the most it was dealt with in news bulletins. Exceptions: ARD broadcast 'Panorama' and reports about the Greenpeace actions in the magazines *Spiegel*, *Focus* and *Stern*. (Mantow and Podeus, 1995: 7–8)[20]

On the other hand , the events were instantly news in German regional media in the north-west of the country, around Hamburg and on the

North Sea coast; Hamburg is also the location of both Deutsche Shell's main office and of Greenpeace Germany.[21]

Special attention should be given to a report on the NDR/ARD national current affairs programme *Panorama*, broadcast on 4 May. NDR's Jochen Graibert (and a reporter from the Munich-based news weekly *Focus*) accompanied the original Greenpeace team to the Brent Spar at the end of April; they filmed the Greenpeace team boarding the Spar and shot extensive location footage. These were the only journalists from any country who accompanied the Greenpeace occupation team on the first day.[22] Their coverage was entirely given over to the Greenpeace version of events, as Deutsche Shell did not participate in the programme. It is likely that this report played an influential part in giving the event the public profile that it acquired, both because of its national prominence and because it was so pro-Greenpeace.

All participants I have interviewed agreed that the story became national with the Shell eviction of Greenpeace activists on 23 May, because these were the 'first pictures from a war' (Jochen Graibert). However, television coverage dropped again after this moment. But at the same time as the eviction other developments occurred which in the long run transformed the German coverage. Firstly, the North Rhine-Westphalian, Thuringian and Bavarian branches of the Junge Union – the youth wing of the ruling German Christian Democrat Party – called for a boycott of Shell (reported in e.g., *Die Welt,* 24.5.95). Greenpeace says they had no contact with the Junge Union prior to this call.[23] Secondly, Environment Minister Angela Merkel (who had already condemned the Shell plan on 9 May) on 23 May repeated her call at a conference in Hamburg on 'Current Environmental Problems in the Seas'; on 31 May the Bundestag Environment Committee condemned the Shell plan and asked the Federal Government to put pressure on the UK Government to change it. This political action transformed the scene in Germany and ensured that the boycott would be considered respectable as well as newsworthy. At the same time it ensured that Greenpeace lobbying at the Esbjerg conference in early June would take place in a context where the German delegation would have a predisposition to accept the Greenpeace line.

It seems clear that the situation in the two countries was fundamentally different, and that media played a slightly different role in the two as a result. In both cases the media focus was somewhat skewed towards a predominantly regional interest. On the other hand, the balance between regional and national interest was different: in the UK, national press interest was present from the beginning, whereas in Germany it was a late arrival. In both countries, national broadcast interest was late on the scene; but the difference in its scope is striking: in Britain, the interest grew in a relatively gradual fashion, whereas in

Germany the swing from a restricted interest to a major 'newswave' was quite rapid. In Germany, the late move to a national level meant that the story was already well defined by the time this occurred.

Moreover, according to participants, the nature of national media interest in both print and broadcast media in Germany had a special quality. According to Jochen Graibert, the debate in the German media was oriented towards the theme of a 'new communitarianism' in which participation in the boycott was seen as a breakthrough in participation-based politics. According to Wolfgang Mantow (a Shell PR consultant) the level of antagonism towards Shell was so great that he himself experienced it among his own circle of friends. Radio stations overtly campaigned for Greenpeace by encouraging the boycott, going live to petrol station forecourts, and inviting listeners to phone in and talk about their own changed consumer behaviour. According to both Jochen Graibert and Thomas Schreiber, radio presenters made it very difficult for correspondents to present information about the events in an objective way – the terminology was emotional and pro-Greenpeace.[24] The Greenpeace activist Christian Bussau, who was on board the Brent Spar for the second occupation, said in interview that he was amazed at the level of sympathy for Greenpeace implied by the way in which he was interviewed live on radio on a more or less daily basis: many of the questions were purely personal ones ('What's the weather like', for example) which were clearly aimed to provide a human face for the story. While this evidence is anecdotal, it fits with the universally recognized negativity of German news coverage in respect of the Shell plan.

It is likely that political lobbying in Germany was responsible for the role that political organizations played. Greenpeace had started lobbying opposition politicians involved in the preparation of the Esbjerg conference as soon as they had the occupation of the Spar secured, but were surprised when Merkel – who was not known for her support of Greenpeace – spoke in favour of their position in the weeks before the conference. Ritt Bjerregaard, the EU environment minister, had spoken against the sinking in the second weekend in May (Vorfelder, 1995: 125, 131). According to Remi Parmentier, head of the political section of Greenpeace International, no special effort went into political lobbying of German or European Union politicians in the preparation for the Esbjerg Conference, although Greenpeace certainly used the contacts they had already established in the European Commission and elsewhere to try to call attention to the arguments they were putting forward. At a preparation meeting in late March for the ministerial conference (attended by senior civil servants but not ministers) there was so little interest in the subject of offshore installations in the North Sea and discharges from them that Greenpeace failed to obtain an answer put under 'any other business' to the UK delegation and no national delegations supported them despite prior prompting from the Greenpeace people. Clearly, once the Brent Spar occupation was under way, attempts to focus ministerial minds on these issues were easier, and Parmentier said that in his opinion the normal routine of ministerial attention to inter-governmental conferences would lead ministers to settle on a line to pursue which would justify their presence and define why they were there, about a month in advance of the meeting.[25]

Lastly, we must consider the media strategies of the protagonists, Greenpeace and Shell. The UK Government might potentially have played a substantial role, but Government media relations were restricted until John Gummer, Minister of Agriculture, attended the Esbjerg Conference; subsequently the Prime Minister became directly involved at the time of his confrontation with Chancellor Kohl of Germany at the G7 summit on 16 June. According to David Robinson, Information Officer at the DTI, the relative paucity was because Shell was the lead organization involved.[26] Shell media personnel did not think that the relative shortage of Government statements about Brent Spar had any effect on the course of events, since they repeatedly made clear that they were committed to the Shell disposal plan and never wavered in their support of it.

Greenpeace built their media strategy into the planning of the event; they also realized at this stage that Shell's plans gave them an ideal opportunity because of the coincidence of the Esbjerg Conference (Vorfelder, 1995: 51–2). As was made clear at the Edinburgh seminar, Greenpeace's communications links – satellite links and willingness to provide video footage – were a significant information subsidy to broadcast news organizations; they also supplied the camera crew that provided footage for the German *Panorama* report, and guaranteed exclusive coverage.[27] The information subsidy also included photographs and a steady stream of press releases, interview opportunities by satellite phone from the Spar, and background briefing. According to the Greenpeace website (http://www.brentspar.com:80/), UK press releases were issued on a close to daily basis, with the exception of a gap between 24 May and 7 June; German Greenpeace also issued press releases on a more or less daily basis.[28] However, it is clear from information from Greenpeace personnel that this considerably understates the amount of media relations they undertook. Firstly, in addition to the national Greenpeace press offices, Greenpeace International Communications in London acted as a clearing-house and resource centre for photographic and video material. The shooting of this material was done by hired-in camera crews, who decided themselves what to film; decisions about when to have camera crews available and when to release the footage were taken by the campaign office in the Shetlands and by Greenpeace International Communications in London. Greenpeace camera crews are encouraged, in general, to shoot as much footage as possible in order to have a public record of events, for security purposes. While no detailed records were made available, Cindy Baxter (press officer at Greenpeace International Communications at the time) testified in interview to the exceptionally high volume of enquiries that were handled. In particular, she reported that television companies were voracious in their need for constantly fresh video footage, even if what was shown was probably indistinguishable to the audience from what had been shown the day before: in the absence of direct confrontation all video footage showed essentially the same scene day after day. Secondly, Greenpeace facilitated visits by journalists to Brent Spar while they were in occupation, and places on Greenpeace boats shadowing the towing of the Spar. In general, the press personnel were in majority German and UK, although during the last few days of the occupation, Greenpeace made an effort to get Dutch journalists out to the confrontation point since they knew that the regular international coordination meeting of the Shell group of companies would take place in the Netherlands shortly before the scuttling was scheduled and they wanted to use the Dutch media to put on pressure at this point.

According to Cindy Baxter, although Greenpeace had built media relations into their advance planning they had no 'master plan' which guided their communications throughout the whole sequence of events. The planning for the whole campaign was done between 11 and 30 April, and this did not give time for any detailed planning of communications contingencies, including police eviction; the relationship between campaign activities and communications tactics was in fact very chaotic, and often press releases were issued too late (after 4.00 p.m.) to be much use that day. In their analysis, it was uncertain at the outset whether the occupation would be sustainable for a long period and whether or not there would be sustained media interest.[29]

Shell's communications strategy was premised upon an initial misreading of the situation.[30] In their planning, they had estimated that the stakeholders involved in the disposal operation were all local to Scotland, and that media interest was likely to be primarily regional. The decision was taken to locate communications management in the Shell Expro communications department in Aberdeen. The combination of these two decisions was to weight all Shell communications towards a restricted and relatively routine interest oriented around regional media; the type of information prepared for release reflected this planning. In retrospect it was clear that this definition created problems of tactics and late in May they relocated communications planning to the London office of Shell UK. In addition, they had entirely failed to spot the possible international dimension of events, to the extent that the managing director of Shell Germany learnt of the disposal plan from television (interview with *Der Spiegel,* 16.6.95: 33); according to Rainer Winzenried, head of media relations at Deutsche Shell, the German office had been told during the previous winter that decommissioning was going to take place, but had failed to understand the implications since they had no experience of offshore operations and no knowledge of what was involved.[31] Deutsche Shell media personnel were thus at a disadvantage when trying to respond to local media enquiries or brief journalists.

The fact that Deutsche Shell was 'out of the loop' had additional unfavourable consequences. When contacted by German journalists their reply to enquiries was that they knew nothing and that the journalists should seek information from Shell Expro in Aberdeen; the impression in Deutsche Shell was that the Aberdeen office was unable to handle a public relations matter of such complexity. Furthermore they had difficulties themselves in 'optimising their communications with Aberdeen'. They received a technical folder about the nature of the Brent Spar disposal, but it was not suitable for public relations purposes and required lengthy adaptation as well as translation before it could be released to German media. During May, Deutsche Shell asked Shell UK to send over a German-speaking director, Heinz Rothermund, for a press conference but this was not possible. Another failure was to make no contact with German media personnel working in London, who were extensively used for this story, and some of whom claimed (to Deutsche Shell) that they had had difficulty in getting local access to Shell material.[32] By the time Deutsche Shell were in a position to give authoritative information to journalists, the story had already acquired a clear profile, which the eviction of Greenpeace on 23 May confirmed and made into a genuinely nation-wide story for the first time in Germany. At no time did Deutsche Shell attempt to brief the specialist journalists who might have had an understanding of Shell operations that would have produced a more sympathetic attitude. On the other hand, the lack of expertise about offshore operations was as true of German journalists as it was of Shell personnel. Deutsche Shell personnel, German journalists and activists said in interview that they had never seen an oil platform, nor even a photograph of one in the German media, before the Brent Spar events.

Deutsche Shell also suffered from long-term features of the Shell culture: the national operating company took responsibility for everything to do with their operations and global thinking did not extend to public relations. It was this tradition that underpinned the difficulties referred to above, and produced as well a feeling that at the end of the day it was not their responsibility: Deutsche Shell had a different culture, which would not allow sea dumping, and 'their' public would realize the difference between the two Shells; in the event, the German public did not see it that way. While Deutsche Shell continued publicly to defend the UK company, 'on the working level' they were not happy about the disposal. Differences such as these within the Shell group finally surfaced in a comment on Dutch TV by Mr Slecht of Shell Netherlands, which suggested that the Shell Group as a whole might rethink their strategy (reported by Press Association, 16.6.95).

A diary of Shell UK media activities shows that they released material to the press at a comparable rate to Greenpeace: with the exception of two gaps (1 May to 12 May; 31 May to 7 June), press releases were virtually daily, and on occasion more frequently. However, until late in the sequence of events Shell personnel made relatively few broadcast appearances and most output took the form of press releases rather than more personalized information flows such as interviews and background briefings. They only briefed on request, did no specialist briefings for the science correspondents who might have been considered their natural allies in this endeavour, and only proactively arranged briefings on three occasions: in Aberdeen (for local media) a week before the end of May, on 31 May in London (for news editors and environment correspondents), and on Friday 16 June in London again. They did far less press facilitation in the North Sea than Greenpeace: the only journalists who were present on Shell installations were a freelance camera crew whose output was little used, and a reporter from the North Scotland agency who was on the *Stadive* at the time of the eviction of the activists on 22 to 23 May. According to a Scots-based news agency reporter with whom I discussed this, it was difficult to get anything other than routine press releases from Shell Expro, and on occasions the only response was 'no comment'.

Footage of the 23 May eviction shot by the Shell camera crew was used by the BBC and Grampian TV,[33] and some footage used on ITN was clearly shot from the Shell 'side of the fence', but is credited in the ITN index to ITN itself. At the same event, several journalists, including a camera crew, were still on the Spar itself, and extensive use was made of Greenpeace-originating video footage of the eviction (e.g. ITN, 23.5.95). All UK broadcast video footage of confrontation during the towing seems to have originated from Greenpeace or from journalists facilitated by them. For example, on 10 June during a clash around the Spar during the towing a couple of Greenpeace activists ended up in the water and were picked up by a Shell boat. According to Greenpeace, who made a photographic record of the incident available, Shell deliberately rammed their boat and threw the protesters into the water; according to Shell, the Greenpeace boat

115

sank itself by scraping razor wire and the Shell boat came to their rescue. Both sides had photographic records available, but it was the Greenpeace photograph which made the front pages; the Shell video was only shown retrospectively, in a BBC TV documentary shown on 3 June (*The Battle for Brent Spar*, BBC2); ITN coverage on 10 September used old stock footage of the site credited to Greenpeace, but had no video footage of the actual confrontation.[34]

The availability of dramatic video footage probably only played a significant role at the time of the eviction and the final confrontation – although foreknowledge that it would be available may have played a role in TV editorial calculations. Even when video was either not available or not used, still photographs were available and contributed to a pro-Greenpeace profile of events. Shell only made still photographs available on request, and they appear to have consisted of non-event-specific stock shots of installations, whereas Greenpeace made available a large number of stills of the events as they unfolded.[35]

We have already seen that content analysis reveals that the profile of events was fundamentally more favourable to Greenpeace than to Shell. Is it possible to account for this disparity on the basis of their communications strategies?

Certainly the availability of Greenpeace originating video material and the facilitation of journalists on Greenpeace 'territory' at the most dramatic moments helped towards that definition. More important perhaps is the facilitation of reporters at an early stage in the sequence of events at a time when the profile of events was still open to reinterpretation. Within days of the original occupation the number of journalists on Brent Spar had increased as Dutch, German and UK reporters joined the original invited journalists; the trace of their presence is clearly visible in the first week's reports of events in the UK press. There is no parallel trace of the presence of reporters on Shell facilities in the neighbourhood of the Spar. Greenpeace deliberately treated journalists on the Spar 'like everybody else', getting them to 'muck in' and share their way of life, a point repeated by two German reporters with whom I discussed this matter and who spent some days on Greenpeace facilities. This 'assimilation into beat culture' helped to produce definitions of events that were favourable to Greenpeace's case (e.g. *Independent*, 25.5.95). One reporter also said that access to the radio room on Greenpeace ships was fairly limited, and that Greenpeace tended to tell journalists what had happened after the event rather than inviting them in advance to witness events, perhaps in order to avoid endangering security; both journalists commented on the extent to which Greenpeace PR personnel tried to control access to other Greenpeace personnel and were (by professional standards) more than averagely ideologically motivated.

This analysis, in combination with the content analysis, shows how the public profile of events as it was articulated in the media was more favourable to the actions of one side than the other. Since Shell rescinded their original decision on 20 June 1995, the public profile of events to do with the Brent Spar has been very different, again for reasons linked to the management of information flows into the public domain.

Shortly before 20 June, Greenpeace announced that their laboratory analysis of samples taken from the Brent Spar showed that the amount of polluting residues in the buoy were far in excess of what Shell claimed; this claim was reported in the media, although not very prominently, and so late in the sequence of events that it probably had little impact on the course of events before 20 June. Some weeks after Shell rescinded their scuttling decision (4 September), Greenpeace announced that its analysis of the sample was mistaken (the sample had been mistakenly taken from the wrong place) and publicly apologized to Shell. Shell seized on this admission and claimed that it demonstrated that Greenpeace's attacks on Shell had been factually incorrect. In general, in the summer of 1995, Shell argued that the events of the spring had been premised on emotion rather than fact. A year later, a long article in *Die Zeit* (6.9.96: 9–14) claimed that the Greenpeace 'sampling error' was not a mistake but a deliberate misinterpretation of what they always knew was an inappropriate sample.[36] Shell did not attempt to make any capital out of the new claims, to avoid disruption to their long-term programme of consultation about the Brent Spar. Greenpeace during the same period has claimed that the mistaken sampling did not affect the claim they were making, that sea dumping was morally wrong and that Brent Spar would have set a precedent.[37]

What can be deduced from this sequence of events depends a lot on the chronological cut-off point chosen. If we close the sequence of events on 20 June 1995, we are likely to conclude that Greenpeace won a significant victory over Shell, thanks to the commitment of their activists, well-organized campaigning and astute media relations. However, the revelation of their mistake and the well-orchestrated campaign against their factual credibility that followed certainly made life difficult for Greenpeace during the following year,[38] and subsequent Greenpeace campaign materials about Brent Spar show a less polemical tone and an attempt to regain public trust by presenting a mass of background factual material: 'This book … is not a self-representation by Greenpeace, nor a polemic against Shell, nor an indictment against the destruction of the North Sea. Rather it is a contribution to a public debate and the affirmation of the offer of dialogue' (Greenpeace, 1997: 7).

What has been shown about source strategies and news values in this case study? The news values that dominated the period of the conflict between Shell and Greenpeace before the 20 June decision are clearly revealed in the content analysis of UK press coverage and largely confirmed by the Dutch and German analyses. All point to journalistic decisions to report the event as being primarily about an environmental protest, in which Greenpeace maintained the initiative, as opposed to any of the other interpretations that could have obtained. This definition was clearly in accordance with Greenpeace's priorities, not with Shell's. This analysis shows how this definition of the event was achieved by Greenpeace and how attempts to achieve a different event profile failed.

One last point remains to be made: to what extent did the international circulation of information affect the course of events? The story was certainly international from the outset. Greenpeace ensured this by taking German journalists with them in the occupation of a UK-owned facility. At the same time, as we have seen, Shell wrongly concluded that the event was of primarily regional significance. The disparity between the two potential arenas of action and representation immediately played into Greenpeace's hands – or at least against Shell's interests. This was compounded by Shell's slowness in mobilizing its own internal international communications facilities. By the same token, the immediate internationalization of the affair probably had the effect of bypassing the nation state during the crucial first weeks of the story, during which event definition was achieved. The UK Government was by no means sidelined in this affair, since it supported Shell consistently, and the Scottish police were involved – albeit in the end fruitlessly – in the actual confrontations themselves. However, the UK government involvement appears to have been relatively distant, and there are no public indications that it made any approaches to the German government. Indeed, it seems as though the German government was not in any way involved for some time; Greenpeace personnel testified how surprised they were to get support from Angela Merkel, Minister for the Environment, in the run-up to the Esbjerg conference. What we see here is a situation in which the simultaneous profiling of an event in different national media systems results in a sequence of events which make purely national organizations somewhat marginal. No doubt in theory it would have been possible for the various governments in question to have coordinated a response: but in any time frame that was plausible it would arguably have been too late, since the event definition moved so quickly. We may conclude that the international news dimension was absolutely crucial to the course of events.

Conclusion

In the introduction to Part II, I gave an outline of what the case studies would show: various features of source–journalist interactions were highlighted as implied in these events. A brief review shows the ways in which the case studies have illustrated the themes listed there. We will also (pp. 133–5) revisit a methodological question.

Source motives

These have appeared at many points in the narratives of the case studies, and are as varied as their determinants would suggest. De Sancha's obliging friend, who lent her a flat to enjoy her lover's company, was motivated by gain; Max Clifford has been very candid about his motives for his involvement in the Mellor scandal. Tory Party sources who responded to or were dragged into the 'Back to Basics' scandals were motivated by their understanding of the threats to and opportunities for particular political positions that the scandals created. In the case of Brent Spar, we may assume that in the main source motives were to further the aims of the organizations to which they belonged.

Source techniques

The commonest technique to be seen in the case studies – or the common denominator of techniques – is the appeal to news values. This consists primarily of either creating events that conform to them – such as the occupation of Brent Spar – or interpreting events to journalists in such a way as to give them the desired profile. Greenpeace were hugely successful in this respect – they created a highly visible event, gave maximum facilitation to the media and provided constant updating. The updating derived from their initiative in the creation of events, in which they were helped by the timing of the Esbjerg Conference and the G7 meeting. Shell were unable to counter this form of publicity directly, partly because the Scottish police refused to evict Greenpeace, and were forced to rely on refutations of the Greenpeace case, which were unlikely to match Greenpeace's activities for newsworthiness. Whatever credibility these refutations had, they were somewhat dull in comparison with Greenpeace's activities.

The sexual scandal cases appealed directly to tabloid news values. This appeal was used both to launch and to maintain the media lives of events by those who wanted publicity for them. The techniques of other sources – notably of those unwillingly implicated – consisted in the main of trying to limit the damage by showing that they had support from friends, family and colleagues, or by maintaining that the events were lacking in any important public dimension. Success was varied. On one occasion they backfired hopelessly, when David Mellor tried to control his in-laws' press statements: coordination between different sources is essential. The difference in news values between the tabloid and the broadsheet press played a significant role; participants used different types of outlet to place different types of interpretation of events. This in turn led to the circulation of information between different media outlets, contributing to the prolongation of the sequence of events. In the financial scandals, different patterns are to be seen. Where scandals involve court proceedings, the role of institutional sources is paramount.

Source strategies

The combination of motives and techniques constitutes a strategy. A classic example is Max Clifford's handling of the Mellor affair. Although he only became involved after the story was launched by its original source, his understanding of its potential is clearly shown in his use of tabloid news values, in combination with an appreciation of the importance of Mellor's court appearance in the Bauwenses' libel case. In the Brent Spar affair, both Greenpeace and Shell had a strategy. For Shell, it was to maintain their long-term reputation for credibility as information sources, and to minimize the damage done by the publicity. For Greenpeace, it was to prolong the event so that their media facilitation would create a high profile.

We can see several examples of how fundamental source calculations about the strategy to be pursued played out over a period of time and resulted in an event profile that became uncontrollably bad from several source points of view. In each case, we have seen what the source motives were, and looked – in as much detail as possible – at the tactics used on the various occasions. In each case another factor came into play: namely the analysis of the situation which led to a particular strategy being chosen. In the case of the 'Back to Basics' scandals, the Downing Street Press Office was briefed to say that Yeo's baby was a personal matter, in the Prime Minister's opinion; the press office was therefore directionless when confronted with the fact of a division in Tory ranks over precisely this issue. The Downing Street response exemplifies the failure of the strategic dimension: either because of misinformation or because of incompetence, there was no strategy in place for dealing with the damaging divergence of interpretations; it was the failure to kill the politicization of the story that allowed it to spiral out of control. Perhaps Tory factionalism made this impossible. In a similar fashion, Shell's erroneous stakeholder analysis of the situation when the Brent Spar was first occupied led them to assume that it was a regional story; by the time they realized this was not true the event definition was out of their control.

News values

We have seen that news values always consist of an interpretation of events filtered through the 'universal' values of timeliness, interest, importance, etc. In the analyses of the case studies, the news value of sexual scandal was assumed: the role of elite persons plus sexual 'misbehaviour' so obviously fit these criteria that little need be said. However, the differences between broadsheet, tabloid and broadcast news values are significant. Clearly also the impact of the stories was bound up with the fact of political importance. In this respect, the most interesting cases are those where a scandal does not occur, or is restricted in its scope. Our attention was therefore directed to the larger question of why sexual misdemeanour has its present cultural profile, and to the role of the media in it. In the case of the Brent Spar – as well as two other stories, Louise Betts and Louise Woodward, analysed in Part I – the news values of events were analysed by looking at the recurrent and cumulative patterns of meaning to be found in media coverage. These were taken to correspond to the news values. But we should remember that such analyses are always retrospective, and care must be taken to establish at which point a cumulative pattern of meaning – which is by definition not in existence at the beginning of a story – is in fact a reliable indicator. We saw how this was a relevant consideration in the case of journalists' own understanding of the Yeo scandal, and we shall return to this matter below.

These considerations indicate how the case studies illustrate the themes listed earlier, and which derive directly from the focus on the 'news encounter' illustrated with smaller-scale examples in Chapter 1. However, the case studies have implications which relate to the wider framework of recent analyses of news.

Credibility and the ethics of media relations

Ethics are indeed a central part of the news process because they are a central feature of source–journalist interactions; therefore they must figure in source strategies. The central value involved in such negotiations is credibility, since it dictates the value placed on source information by the journalist. In the words of Sir Bernard Ingham:

> Fairness [in dealings with the media] does not … run to helping reporters on a subject when it is not policy to do so. No.10 press office is entitled to make judgments about what best serves the Prime Minister and his or her office. … trying to provide accurate information … does not preclude presenting that information in the light most favourable to the Government, *consistent with its credibility*. (1991: 343–4; my emphasis)[1]

This is well documented in previous literature on the subject, and the examples found in our case studies substantiate and expand the point.[2]

In the Brent Spar case study we have seen that Greenpeace was clearly regarded by at least some journalists as a credible source; it is also the case that the mistake which they admitted in the aftermath of their victory over Shell dented their credibility in journalists' eyes, at least in the short term. Shell's credibility varied nationally. In the UK, the Shell version of events was widely reported, especially by broadsheets. My analysis of German media was too unsystematic to allow a firmly based comparison, but Shell's own media evaluation clearly concluded that they had failed to get their message across.[3]

An interesting case is the Pennant-Rea/Synon scandal analysed in Chapter 4. Synon's difficulty in persuading editors to publish her account of events derived not from doubts about its accuracy (in that respect she was entirely credible) but from doubts about other matters: the ethical validity of her motivation and by extension of journalistic collusion in her efforts, and the public importance of the events. While this does not deny the centrality of credibility in the factual sense, it suggests that credibility may be an ethical issue in a wider sense as well. The role of largely invented information in the scandal surrounding David Mellor's relationship with Antonia de Sancha is interesting: in a televised interview with Andrew Neil (former editor of the *Sunday Times*), Max Clifford, de Sancha's publicity agent at the time, admitted fabricating some of the details which figured in tabloid reporting of events. Yet journalists continue to regard him as a credible source of information.[4] Perhaps his claim in the same interview that such inventions did not affect the fundamentals of the matter, and just added amusing spice to it, has been accepted by journalists, or at least some of them. It must be said that this claim is disingenuous, as the added spice was calculated as a function of news values, and clearly had the effect of extending the life of the story at a time which was crucial from Mellor's point of view.

Truth and credibility

Clearly this also implies that we should be careful to distinguish the different elements that constitute credibility: 'truthfulness' is utterly different from 'timeliness', where credibility is established by a source's 'productivity' – although clearly a 'productive' source who was also a liar would in the end not be productive. 'Consistency' may be ambiguously related to truthfulness, since different departments (Ingham's example) may see the same events very differently.

The distinction between the truth or untruth of statements is analytically distinct from the question of the strategic purposes they serve. Shell and Greenpeace made conflicting claims about the value of scuttling the Brent Spar as a precedent: Shell said it was a unique case which would set no precedents, Greenpeace claimed that it would in fact be used as a precedent, and that it was clearly seen in that light by the oil industry.[5] Both statements were perfectly credible, and no final judgement between them has been made, to the best of my knowledge. It is difficult to see how both could be true. Both – regardless of their truth, but not regardless of their credibility – served strategic purposes. From the point of view of source strategies, what is at issue is not ultimately truth but credibility, although truth and untruth are also crucial since being caught out in an untruth is a disaster, as Greenpeace found out: it was a disaster even if publicly believed to be 'untruth' in the scientific sense (a mistake) rather than the legal sense (a lie).

The distinction between 'credibility' and 'truth' is central to journalism, because the objective method of news reporting asserts (implicitly) that it is credibility that establishes the regime of truth in question. The production of accurate information is guaranteed by the choice of sources used to acquire the information: 'Normal news coverage uses the choice of news sources to resolve the need ... *to establish the validity of stories*' (my emphasis); in other words, institutional spokespersons are accepted as purveying truth for all practical purposes as far as their institutions are concerned: 'When the spokesman is speaking within the competence of his institutionally determined role an accurate account of this is normally accepted as true for all practical purposes' (Murphy, 1991: 12).[6] This does not imply a criticism of journalists' subjective commitment to truth-seeking.

'Local' and 'universal' news values

The 'universal' news values of timeliness, proximity, human interest, etc., only operate in conjunction with particular features of the events in question: it is feature X of the events which – at any given time – makes them novel, interesting, important, etc. In the case of Brent Spar, the routine engineering procedure to dispose of a redundant installation was not especially interesting or important; it was only when a protest redefined it as a threat to the environment that it acquired the capacity to dominate news agendas, and that news value needed constant renewal. Similarly, the fact that *someone* has a baby out of wedlock is publicly insignificant (nowadays); the fact that a married cabinet minister does so and the fact that someone influential then says he should resign redefines the event in accordance with a wider set of news criteria. In these instances we can see how the capacity to act in such a way as to (re)define an event as newsworthy is a key element in source strategies. Of course, this is also true of one-shot stories, but the process is more visible in the case of protracted events. This is because the process of updating, or looking for new developments to give the story legs clearly shows how event profiles are built up: the continuity involved in updating indicates what features of an event are being selected for news value.

The relevant features of events always derive from, and link them to, some aspect or aspects of the cultural environment. For instance, in Chapter 2 we saw the difficulties posed to reporters by the 'milk-drinking statues' story of September 1995: the supernatural is only partially consonant with the cultural values of Western society. Reports of witchcraft are a normal feature of the Indonesian press since this element of the supernatural is entirely consonant with the culture of the country.[7] On the other hand, tabloids may be more willing than broadsheets to run stories on scarcely believable things – in other words, events that are only partially believable in our culture – due to differences in news values. Stories about UFOs, for instance, are likely to be more cautiously evaluated by broadsheets. Because the links between events and the values that dictate our understanding of them are deeply rooted in culture, it may be difficult to analyse how they function; multiple theories may exist, as we saw in the case of scandal. In this instance, there clearly is some relationship between 'local' news values and the surrounding culture, but it is so deep-rooted that it is not clear what it is.

Story duration and news agendas

The prolongation of a story is likely to produce a definition of an event which is difficult to turn around, as we saw in the case of Brent Spar: Shell did not succeed in changing the definition of the event established by Greenpeace until after they abandoned their option of deep-sea disposal and Greenpeace admitted their mistake in measuring the toxic waste in Brent Spar. However, this development is also significant for another reason: it indicates how a prolonged media life means that potentially any details will become relevant, as we saw in the case of the death of Leah Betts in Chapter 1. Now this is equally likely to lead to a destabilization of the profile of the events as to their continued stability of meaning.

This point can also be illustrated by another sequence of events. Although the analysis needed to establish this point far exceeds the scope of this book, it seems likely that the development of the Lewinsky scandal fits this pattern: here the meaning of events was destabilized by the interaction between source strategies and news values in a long-running story. The association of the special prosecutor with the fundamentalist Christian right wing of the Republican Party in the long run gave credibility to the Clinton administration's claim that his efforts were part of a right-wing conspiracy to discredit the Democratic presidency; this characterization of events appeared to resonate with voters, at least on the evidence of the Congressional elections of autumn 1998. The special investigator's office had used the obvious news value of sexual revelations to reinvigorate an already long-running investigation into alleged financial irregularities; however, there was some confusion over whether what was being investigated was sexual misconduct or the President's truthfulness. Here it seems likely that the news value of sexual revelations, so powerfully used by the investigators, may have detracted from their capacity to insist on the question of truthfulness, and this ambiguity allowed a reinterpretation of what was being done and why. In the absence of the protracted news value of the investigation into President Clinton's personal life, it may be doubted whether Starr's religious convictions would have been significant; the context of the protracted media life of a sexual scandal made it potentially relevant, and therefore available as part of a source strategy.[8]

News agendas and power

It is clear to what extent source capacity to dominate news agendas derives from the capacity to produce events that conform to news values. Greenpeace were able to dominate news agendas to a greater extent than Shell because of their ability to constantly produce new events – more specifically, to produce new events at points in time where the themes of 'their' events connected to other events, in this case pre-scheduled ones (North Sea Inter-governmental conference, G7 meeting). As we saw, it is legitimate to hypothesize about what might have happened if Grampian police had been willing to evict Greenpeace under criminal law procedures: this would potentially have produced an event, or series of events, equal in stature to Greenpeace's event-production, and we may suppose that this would have inflected news agendas in a different way from what in fact happened. The relationship between event-production and news agendas in general benefits the powerful, since it is obvious that they have a differential capacity to exploit it. Brent Spar clearly demonstrate that it is not inevitably so. Scandal demonstrates the same point: the Conservative Government was entirely unable to control the meaning of the events labelled the 'Back to Basics' scandals (see pp. 127–8, 132 for some further implications of this example). We should also add that event production does not necessarily coincide with event definition, as the American radicals found to their cost in the 1960s: reporting often ignored their issue definition in demonstrations, preferring police and national politician definitions of the events as simply violent disruption. One of the reasons for 'kite-flying' is to check out in a low-risk fashion what the relationship between event-production and issue definition will be (see pp. 49–50).[9]

Governments are regularly accused nowadays of 'media manipulation' or 'news management'. Governments – and the state in general – by definition are a prime location of the production of significant and newsworthy events. When the accusation of media manipulation is made, what is effectively being said is that the state machine is using this privilege to excess. But the dividing line between what is normal and legitimate on the part of the state, and what is reprehensible, is a delicate and negotiable one. For example, in February 1999, two girls were kidnapped in a small coastal town in England; police found them some days later. Journalists were given access to the children, including a photo-opportunity. At the same time, the police announced that 'a man was helping them with their enquiries', the usual formula used in the period between arrest and charging or releasing the suspect. In this instance, it is clear that the man was caught red-handed and there was not a lot of doubt about guilt, which was admitted. However, charges were not brought, and the suspect identified, until twenty-four hours later. We may suspect that the purpose of the delay was what its result was: two days of headlines reporting a major police success rather than one day. In a discussion of these events on Radio

4's *Getting the Message*, contributors appeared to think the situation was not abnormal or reprehensible. On the other hand, in the *Evening Standard* on 14.5.99, Max Hastings denounced Government attempts to disguise the failure of their policy towards Serbia and Kosovo by portraying British soldiers' role in Macedonia as refugee relief. He clearly thought that this was a cynical abuse of definitional power.[10]

Disunity in source organizations

As we saw above, the 'Back to Basics' scandals had the explosive force that they had because they revealed, and were fuelled by, ideological disagreements within the Conservative Party. Of course, any antagonism is likely to add fuel to the flames of information circulation. While antagonism between political or ideological opposites is scarcely unexpected, and in itself scarcely newsworthy, the details of how the opposition plays itself out in individual instances may well be. In his memoirs, Sir Bernard Ingham discusses various occasions on which journalists given advance access to Government information used it to invite responses from the Opposition or from potentially dissident members of the Government, a process he calls leaking 'to anyone who might usefully express a destructively newsworthy view on [it]' (1991: 303).[11] However, when the antagonism is between members or factions of the same organization, the process of making the disagreements public may in itself add to the antagonism, thus provoking a further round of negative information release.[12] The process thus inevitably produces a prolongation of the information flow by adding new – and thus potentially newsworthy – elements to the situation by causing it to change in the process of information release.

This situation is a particular version of the process in which an agent loses control over information flows. In this respect, the events discussed above are not typical of all events, since in many events or event sequences there is no loss of control over the information flow. As was suggested earlier, in events where control is successfully maintained, the process involved is relatively invisible: one of the purposes of such control is to achieve a presentation of information in which the act of presentation is itself invisible, so that the information is seamlessly transparent in its capacity to refer to the event in question. However, as soon as control is lost, features of information control that were relatively invisible become visible: the processes are not in fact very different, except in so far as the visibility itself is concerned.

This situation is more obviously visible in environments where there are antagonistic organizations permanently at play in the same arena, such as politics or environmental matters; where internal splits occur, visibility rapidly increases. In arenas where this is not the case we may expect that the types of process outlined above will not commonly be observed. For example, in financial and more generally business circles, we have seen that there is no direct equivalent of the police in criminal matters or political opposition in governmental matters – or even of environmental groups in situations such as Brent Spar. There is little in the way of credible 'oppositional' groups to counter the weight of financial public relations, and it is commonly only when something goes wrong that the type of breakdown of control over information flows that we have seen occurs: perhaps it is the involvement of the police, or hostility between two business organizations, or business failure on such a scale that investigative journalism goes into operation.

Media silences

Famously, Sherlock Holmes solved a case by paying attention to a silence – the dog that did not bark. Silences in the media are indeed significant, although it is by definition difficult to know that they exist, and equally to know what they mean in the absence of alternative information sources. In the case of the Brent Spar affair we saw how the Scottish Fishermen's Federation decided that near-silence was the best policy for dealing with the situation, given their need to maintain an ongoing relationship with the offshore oil industry. A similar crashing silence during the Brent Spar affair was from Esso, partner-owners and -operators of the Brent Spar. The existence of a media silence may be inferred from a knowledge of the circumstances in question, if for example one knows that such-and-such a person or organization was in fact involved and is not saying anything. As a very obvious instance: for some days after his release by the Los Angeles police (see Chapter 2) Hugh Grant succeeded in disappearing from public view, presumably to allow things to cool down. But in the absence of such knowledge, silence may not be visible, and therefore no one will be able to work out why or how it occurred. In March 1999, the entire European Commission was forced to resign in the fall-out from a corruption scandal; this was only a matter of weeks after the launch of the single currency; not only did the resignation not affect the exchange rate of the euro, hardly anyone even thought to discuss whether it might do so. Various journalists commented briefly on the possibility of a link, but within days total silence reigned again.[13] Was this because there genuinely was no link between the two things? Because no one saw that there was? Or was it the result of careful briefing? *Die Welt*, the *Daily Telegraph* and the *Guardian* refer to analysts' fears and briefing by the European Central Bank; in the absence of information from 'inside the loop' it is impossible to say anything more detailed.

Story duration and source communication strategies

Comments have already been made about various elements of source strategies; central under the circumstances of protracted stories is the question of facilitation. Providing media facilities is the necessary starting point for any communications strategy which involves the media. Of course, by itself it does not necessarily achieve anything: the facilities must give access to something that attracts media interest. And it is not necessarily the case that the media interest will produce the event definition sought. However, all other things being equal, facilitation tends to inflect event definition by exposing journalists to a particular point of view. An example can be seen in this report in the Scottish *Daily Record* on 20 June 1995:

Battle of the Atlantic

By BOB DOW on board the *Solo* in the
North Atlantic.

Greenpeace have just hours to halt Brent Spar sinking. The battle of the Brent Spar is heading towards its final showdown tomorrow. Greenpeace activists have brought in their big guns in a last bid to halt the dumping of the oil platform.

Early this morning, their flagship *Solo* – a converted North Sea tanker – caught up with the convoy towing the Spar in the North Atlantic. And the 14,500-tonne platform will reach its final resting place, 150 miles off the Hebrides, tomorrow afternoon.

As protests continued in Britain, Germany and elsewhere, owners Shell remained defiant. They are expected to storm the Spar to seize two activists on board since Friday.

The protesters – one British and one German – have been drenched continually

> with gallons of freezing water hosed from fire pumps on oil boats towing the Spar.
>
> At one stage, one of the two men was almost blasted off the heli-deck by the powerful jets and was only saved by grabbing a wire.
>
> The fire pumps have smashed every window on the Spar, leaving the protesters exposed to the elements.

Here the relationship between press facilitation and event profile is worth analysis. The reporter is on a Greenpeace ship, and the report is predominantly written from the Greenpeace point of view (although I have only quoted the opening third of the report, the marginalization of Shell's point of view continues throughout). But it is not necessarily the case that the adoption of Greenpeace's point of view is caused by the facilitation: it is equally likely that the editorial decision to accept the facilitation derived from acceptance of their point of view – perhaps in conjunction with Shell's lack of facilitation. But whatever the exact nature of the editorial process in this instance it is clear that the facilitation has produced results: the emphasis on Greenpeace's side of things is supported by telling details, in an apparently eye-witness account.

Under routine circumstances, facilitation may be well-nigh invisible. The example of Bush's visit to his troops before the Gulf War is a good example: if one did not see the photo-opportunity diagram (Figure 1.1, p. 8), the event would seem completely natural; the diagram makes clear how carefully constructed it is. In circumstances such as the Brent Spar confrontation, where the site is physically remote, facilitation becomes an obvious issue, and the decision to engage in it may entirely define the event profile as all journalists see the event from one side or the other. Third World disasters and conflicts are sometimes reported by international aid agencies facilitating journalists' visits to areas which may be remote and dangerous; the agencies may even supply video tapes made by their own camera crew.[14] The nature of the facilitation may well influence what the journalist is able to find out about the events in question. However, the example of the Vietnam War – in which the US media benefited from massive facilitation by the American armed forces – demonstrates that facilitation is by no means the same as control over event definition (Hallin, 1986). This process is well known. However, it has an implication that is less well analysed: the continuity of facilitation through time is a key element in the way in which a protracted event acquires its profile; it is the continued capacity to ensure that journalists witness events from a particular vantage point that plays – or may play – a central role in the kind of process whereby a protracted event, or event sequence, comes to acquire a profile which takes on a life of its own and becomes the theme of the week. Journalists with whom I discussed this process professed to being baffled by it. Its essential components are probably these: an event is 'promoted' by a source and journalists estimate how much promotional capacity the source has; this includes an estimate about the likelihood of other agents or sources intervening, as well as a judgement about their likely capacity for generating newsworthy items. Central to this is intuition about the likelihood that events will produce as yet unforeseen ramifications. If intuition indicates this is likely, journalists are more likely to start looking, especially if tantalizing hints have been dropped about its possibility by someone in a position to know. The intuition needs to be backed with editorial allocation of resources to produce an effective investigation. Source judgement that cooperation with journalists is likely to be fruitful will affect their willingness to suggest the possibility of future developments, or indeed to keep material in reserve for timely future use.

Media relays

Some attention was paid in the case studies to the way in which information circulates between media at different points in the news cycle: journalists watching real-time TV as in the case of the Woodward trial; the role of Internet sites in the Clinton/Lewinsky scandal; German local radio overtly campaigning for Greenpeace during the Brent Spar affair; the circuit between local media and national media during the Yeo affair. Many other examples could be found.

It seems likely that this is one essential feature of the way in which protracted media events acquire a momentum of their own. Each channel in the media system is both in competition with other channels and occupies a particular position within the system, a position which is defined in part by its place in the twenty-four-hour cycle of news publication. For example, something said in an interview on early morning radio may be taken up by the afternoon papers and subsequent TV news bulletins; a trajectory like this may lead journalists working on morning papers to seek some updated information to use in the next days' papers; and so the cycle is launched. Skilled public relations practitioners build this cycle into their calculations.[15]

Similarly, specialist media which deal with particular areas of activity may well pick up stories in advance of general interest media, which subsequently recycle them for general consumption. For example, the relatively obscure *Pesticides Review* carried a report on pesticide residues in carrot skins which – several months later – resurfaced in the *Guardian* via a journalist who specialized in food stories, and was briefly carried by many other papers as well (Collins, 1999). The *Wall Street Journal* carried brief stories about concerns over the Bank of Credit and Commerce International which were eventually picked up by less-specialized media (Truell and Gurwin, 1992: 203).

Under this heading we can also consider the relationship between medium- and title-specific news values, and in particular the relationship between broadsheet and tabloid news values.

In the case of sexual scandal, there is little doubt that matters were tabloid-led in the sense that it was tabloids that broke the stories in question, and that the initial definition of events was therefore achieved in accordance with their values. However, it is unlikely that the events would have achieved the stature that they did solely on the basis of tabloid coverage. It is the circulation between different media, and in the press between tabloid and broadsheet outlets, that is responsible for the overall impact of these stories; their explosive growth both causes and allows the constant redefinition of events achieved in the process. In the case of the financial scandals, they were largely broadsheet led, and – as we have seen – the role of journalism was subordinate in the sense that the scandals were broken by investigative agencies. In this instance, one news source is largely credible and the potentially opposing news source figures only as the object of suspicion or condemnation.

Brent Spar is far more complex. We have seen how the circulation of information between press, radio and TV was central to the impact of events, but little was said about the relationship between tabloids and broadsheets. Although the content analysis did not distinguish between these categories (largely due to lack of online access to tabloid titles), it was clear that most of the UK reportage was broadsheet, with less-regular and less-developed coverage from the tabloids until relatively late in the sequence of events. None the less, it is likely that tabloid emphasis on photographic qualities and the dramatic nature of events contributed to the event profile, even if the basic news understanding was largely shared across all sectors of the media.

This system of relays is significant for many reasons. First, it creates competing spaces for those interested in event interpretation, allowing them to maximize exposure. Second, it also gives them the possibility of using the multiplicity of outlets in order to place particular bits of information by playing to known identity features of the channel in question: salacious titbits for tabloids, live interviews for radio, good video facilitation for TV. Third, it makes a significant contribution to the rhythm of event interpretation by structuring the flow of information through time. We saw how in the 'Back to Basics' scandals the hint of the possibility of a split in Tory ranks over this issue led to a radio interview in the morning which launched a wave of subsequent reports and fuelled local divisions. Finally, the increasingly intense division of time – due to the pressure of inter-channel and inter-title competition – accelerates the rhythm of updating news, which we have seen is the basic technique used in prolonging the media life of an event. Perhaps in the contemporary media system it is no longer yesterday's news that is out of date, but this morning's. No doubt this is an exaggeration: anyone who relies on multiple news channels can observe how something reported during the day on radio or TV is still being reported in the following morning's papers, even without any significant addition. However, the ever-increasing speed with which news can be made publicly available and the ever-increasing number of places and times during the day at which the availability occurs leads to a situation where updates can be and are accelerated. It is difficult to know to what extent this is changing the fundamental twenty-four-hour rhythm of news, but it certainly creates a pressure which plays into this rhythm.[16]

News values and content analysis

Finally, a methodological point. Content analysis is a technique for assessing the presence or absence of specified thematic material in a body of text. The thematic material is specified by the researcher for any reason deriving from the purpose of the research. It is particularly apt for capturing cumulative patterns of meaning that arise in extended bodies of text with multiple authorship and no single focus in time or space. To this extent it is an obvious tool in the analysis of news.

However, the purpose of its use here is to capture the operation of news values, and it is not obvious that a pattern of cumulative meaning found in an extended body of news texts is the same thing as the news values of the events reported there. In the case of Leah Betts, the news value of the original event did not figure prominently in news coverage after the first few days of the story: it was replaced by updating material and subsequently by other similar stories which were linked to hers. This implies that the cumulative pattern of meaning established across time would not be the equivalent of the news value of the story, since the sequence of events produced several different patterns of meaning. On the other hand, in the instance of Brent Spar, the claim was made that the two were the same thing: the cumulative pattern of meaning which stressed the thematic material associated with 'environment' and 'protest' – rather than Shell's preferred definition of the event as a normal engineering procedure – was stated also to be the news value of the sequence of events in question.

Content analysis does indeed do what it is designed to do – reveal cumulative patterns of meaning. The question is whether and how it is possible to develop relevant units of meaning which capture news values within cumulative patterns of meaning.

In the case of Brent Spar, it is reasonable to suppose that the cumulative pattern and the news values were closely related to each other because the nature of the events made it so: the sequence of events was a relatively self-contained and unified set, opened by two clearly defined incidents (Government permission, Greenpeace's occupation) and closed by a similarly clearly defined event (Shell's change of plan). However, it could legitimately be asked: why close the sequence of events at that time? My justification is that by closing it at the point I chose, I was able to focus on a sequence of events which had a defined consequence and in which the interrelation between news values and source strategies was particularly clear. Moreover, the sequence of events was essentially repetitive: a confrontation between two parties, with no third party centrally involved, followed by repeats of the same confrontation and extensions into other events (Esbjerg, G7) where the links to Brent Spar were clearly distinguished from the other elements of the events. Under these circumstances, the relationship between news values and the cumulative pattern of meaning was relatively simple to establish: what made the events newsworthy was always essentially the same. As noted, if third parties (e.g. the Scottish police) had become more centrally involved the course of events would have been very different and the relationship between news values and the pattern of meaning would no doubt also have been very different.

In the case of Leah Betts, a different pattern emerges, and this despite the fact that in a sense her funeral provided a natural closure. The original news value given by the circumstances of her death and the perception of her as a non-stereotypical drug user probably referred to an unstated principle: she was the crystallization of parental fears. This principle – in conjunction with source determination to use the news value of her story – resulted in the extension of her story into domains beyond her own life and death. In this case, the pattern of meaning that accumulates through time does not provide direct evidence of news values. However, informal assessment of the news coverage plus some interview-derived indications provided the basis for content analysis to reveal various patterns of meaning which were indicators of news values. Content analysis did indeed tell us something about news values, but not in the same way as in the case of Brent Spar, because the event sequences were so different.

In any instance we have to demonstrate the pertinence of the units of meaning whose presence or absence we study, and the results of the content analysis can never justify the choice of units of meaning (since they are determined by the choice). How do we derive the list of units of meaning that we choose? In essence the choice derives from two sources: our own sense of what is newsworthy about a given sequence of events, and expert guidance from journalists or other participants – or both. Here we should enter a last caveat. Journalists are no less prone to retrospective understanding of events than anyone else. All the journalists to whom I put the question: 'Why was so much attention paid to Timothy Yeo's baby?' gave an answer couched in terms of his failure to 'square his local party'. No doubt it was true that this was the main reason why events spun out of control over such a long period of time, because under the Tory Party constitution the local party has considerable powers in relation to its MP. However, most journalists with whom I discussed this also said that they did not see the relevance of the local issue until roughly a week after the story broke. Therefore it is unlikely that the local party was the main news value involved at the beginning of the story. I discussed this matter with them some time after the peak of the story, and no doubt the timing of the conversations was a relevant factor in their interpretation of events. However, it is also a question of what questions one asks: had I placed more stress on what they thought, said and did at the beginning of the story, they might have given a different answer.

Summary

To summarize this summary: we have seen the various ways in which the case studies add flesh to the bare bones of the analysis in Chapters 1 to 3, and demonstrate some of the enormously varied ways in which source–journalist interactions, mediated by news values, constitute the news process. Many of them merely illustrate, with new examples, well-known features of this process such as source motives and tactics. However, the central argument of this analysis, in relation to previous academic literature on the subject, is its insistence on the role of time. Exploration of this theme enables us to see two things: the protracted media life of particular events makes well-known features of news more visible than they are in short-lived events, and it allows us to see that some features of news operate in specific ways in the case of prolonged media events.

Central to this analysis has been the assertion that news is only comprehensible if we always simultaneously analyse the role of news values and source strategies, never considering them in isolation from one another. I believe that the empirical analyses carried out here substantiate that assertion. In Part III we will consider some more theoretical matters, using this assertion as a guiding principle in our analysis of some well-known political and social analyses of the role of the media.

PART III

Information Flows, Primary Definition and the Public Sphere

———

Introduction

There are many different ways of relating the concerns that run through the preceding pages to wider frameworks. Clearly, both journalists, and information officers and public relations personnel have eminently practical motives for wanting to understand these processes: they need to be able to intervene in them in a way that allows fulfilment of their professional purposes (see Ingham, 1991, and Bruce, 1992, for discussions from the point of view of 'spin doctors'; see Jones, 1999, for a discussion from the point of view of a journalist). In the academic literature on the mass media, discussions of these processes figure in many different theoretical contexts.

From the earliest days of such discussions, a concern with the 'effects' of the mass media was central: here it was either argued or assumed that the attention given by the mass media to events or event sequences had a direct impact upon audience attitudes or behaviour. While such direct influence was largely discredited from the 1960s onwards, a more subtle version of influence was inferred in various analyses which argued that although the media might not influence beliefs or attitudes (let alone behaviour) in such a direct fashion, they might exercise influence through their capacity to define what elements of the world were worthy of consideration. For example, media reports might cumulatively focus on particular aspects of events, systematically ignoring others. Broadly speaking, this concern became manifest in two different research traditions: in one, the focus was on the process by which aspects of the world became selected for inclusion in media reporting. Since the 1970s this has tended to focus on the study of journalists' relationships with their sources – clearly this book is an example of that approach. Another approach focused more on the relationship between recurrent patterns of media coverage and patterns of understanding of the world to be found elsewhere, particularly in public awareness of the surrounding world, as revealed in opinion polls, laboratory experiments, focus groups and other survey instruments. This tradition is usually called the 'agenda-setting' or 'framing' approach (see Dearing and Rogers, 1996; Scheufele, 1999; McCombs and Bell, 1996 for overviews of this tradition). The commonest conclusion reached in such studies is that public understanding of events corresponds primarily to the way in which they are handled cumulatively in the media, despite many differences of opinion over the extent of such influence and the processes by which it occurs.

Clearly this book has said nothing about the extent to which the cumulative media portrayal of events impacts upon public opinion. However, I will conclude by examining in some detail a series of arguments in recent studies of news reporting and related matters which focus on the type of influence that privileged access to media space – in the form of acting as sources – may bring to those who exercise it.

CHAPTER 7

Event Definition: Some Recent Controversies

The pattern of activity caused by the central elements of news flows has been interpreted by earlier analysts in terms which privilege news as a source of power for the ruling class, in conformity with Marx' famous dictum that 'the ruling ideas are the ideas of the ruling class'. In particular, this pattern of activity gives rise to the 'primary definition' of events by those people whose privileged access to the media, as sources of information, enables them to impose their definitions of the world as publicly valid definitions (Hall *et al.*, 1978: 53–66). Events are interpreted through the grid of common sense dictated by the culture of the population in which the news channel functions, and one of the central elements in such cultural maps of the world is the assumption that there is indeed some consensus about the meaning of events. In the process of assembling and diffusing information about these events, journalists seek information from sources, subject to professional rules about objectivity, impartiality and balance. The application of these rules ensures that journalists privilege information from sources that are accredited as reliable, and such sources tend to be drawn from among the powerful – they are typically representatives of organizations or other power centres within society, and 'The media thus tend, faithfully and impartially, to reproduce symbolically the existing structure of power in society's institutional order' (Hall *et al.*, 1978: 58).

This claim has been much contested in subsequent accounts of the role of news media, based in detailed empirical accounts of information flows between sources and journalists. It is also comparable in some respects with the account of public information flows to be found in the work of Juergen Habermas. This chapter reviews the debates about information flows through the news media related to these bodies of work.

Certainly, according to Hall and his colleagues, the achievement of 'balance' in journalistic accounts of events allows conflict and debate, but the primary institutional definition of events sets the parameters within which debate is conducted:

> This interpretation then 'commands the field' in all subsequent treatment and sets the terms of reference within which all further coverage or debate takes place. Arguments against a primary interpretation are forced to insert themselves into its definition of 'what is at issue' – they must begin from this framework of interpretation as their starting point. This initial interpretative framework ... is extremely difficult to alter fundamentally, once established. (Hall *et al.*, 1978: 58)

It is this 'structured subordination' of the media to primary definers that gives media an ideological role. Of course, news media actively transform the primary definitions of events in a variety of ways determined by professional skills and the acceptability of rhetorical forms, but this variety is contained within the terms of an ideological field.

Such accounts often claim to be the 'voice of public concern' and indeed 'communication skills' involve finding relevant elements in a stock of acceptable imagery to use in constructing the news profile of a given event. This 'objectifies a public issue' (*ibid.*: 62), in the sense of giving it the status of being a valid issue of public concern, since the constructed profile will indeed – assuming the communicator has done his or her job properly – actually fit into some set of publicly available, acceptable images. Typically, the press asserts that the public wants such-and-such, when the 'primary definers' have not proposed this interpretation of events. Here there is 'a spiral of amplification', in which 'this playing back of (assumed) public opinion to the powerful, which is the reverse of the earlier process described of translating dominant definitions into an (assumed) public idiom, takes the public as an important point of reference on both occasions (legitimation), while actually bypassing it' (*ibid.*: 63).

This process is not entirely devoid of conflict: oppositional groups exist and oppositional voices are indeed heard. But usually it is the 'reasonable' versions of these voices that are heard, while other versions are defined away as 'extremist' and the terms of the debate make alternative conceptions difficult because only certain questions get asked (*ibid.*: 64–5).

This account of how news is integrated into the field of ideology has been much criticized in the recent past. For their critics, Hall and his colleagues' account wrongly implies that 'the movement of definitions is uniformly from power centre to media … (where) there is no space to account for occasions on which the media may take the initiative in the definitional process by challenging the so-called primary definers' (Schlesinger, 1990: 67).

As a result, they produce an account which suffers from the more fundamental defect of proposing that 'state organisations … are not internally divided … (that) there is no room for negotiation over definition prior to engagement with the media … that "the structure of access necessarily secures strategic advantages" for official sources' (Miller, 1993: 385–6).

These charges by Schlesinger and Miller are typical of the line of argument pursued in a number of recent studies of news journalism. Of these, the most detailed is Murphy's study of the press coverage of the Stalker affair (Murphy, 1991).

Murphy's argument, in brief, is that the coverage of the Stalker affair demonstrates the inadequacy of the 'primary definers' approach, since Stalker was presented by all sections of the press, regardless of their usual political affiliations, as the victim of an unjustified conspiracy by state personnel (*ibid.*: 2). Murphy distinguishes between what he calls 'routine' news reporting and 'investigative' reporting, a distinction based primarily upon the different costs incurred by news organizations in the two cases, secondarily upon the different relationships involved between journalists and their sources (*ibid.*: 10–13, 17–18). In routine news reporting, production of relevant and accurate information for the assumed readership of the newspaper is guaranteed by the choice of source used to acquire the information: 'Normal news coverage uses the choice of news sources to resolve the need to establish the significance of news … and to establish the validity of stories' (*ibid.*: 12).

In other words, institutional spokespersons are accepted as purveying truth as far as their institutions are concerned: 'when the spokesman is speaking within the competence of his institutionally determined role an accurate account of this is normally accepted as true for all practical purposes' (*ibid.*: 12).

However, it is the distinction between routine and investigative reporting that is central here, for under various circumstances such arrangements cease to hold, and the Stalker affair presented one such set of circumstances. For reasons which have never been made clear, the usual sources of routine information were silent at a crucial moment in the sequence of events; as a result, journalists began to speculate about why there was a mystery, and to approach alternative sources for information in an attempt to resolve it. Such sources were readily available because normal democratic processes produced conflicting versions of what had happened:

because the normal channels were either silent or confused [about Stalker], voices opposed to the established view of matters were able to use the press's routine ... as a way of getting their own alternative versions ... to determine the agenda ... [In these circumstances] even apparently passive reporting produces a version of events that undermines rather than sustains the interests of institutions of authority. (*ibid.*: 46)

For example, the *Manchester Evening News* was able to reveal the central involvement of a local businessman, Kevin Taylor, because he gave them an interview for his own reasons. He revealed that he was being investigated by the police, who refused to say what the ground of the investigation was, but clearly indicated that Stalker was linked to it. This enabled the *Evening News* to pursue an enquiry into the Stalker affair, while allowing Taylor to define the police enquiry into his affairs as dubious (*ibid.*: 59). In this type of reporting, the activities of the journalist are foregrounded, but 'that is not the same as saying that the form of the discourse or issues attended to is decided upon by the journalist' (*ibid.*: 65): both journalists and their sources may be pursuing agendas that are different from those who would normally figure as the 'primary definers' of reality.[1]

These studies use detailed examples to demonstrate how the play of interests and activities that result in the construction of news events cannot be reduced to a single monolithic entity such as 'primary definition'. Specifically, they claim:

- that the state is not sufficiently unified in itself to produce such unified definitions of reality;
- that the outcome of attempts to control journalists' definitions of events are insufficiently predictable to assert that the process of primary definition necessarily secures strategic advantages for the state;
- and that Hall's argument is invalid because 'Although it has the advantage of directing our interest to the question of definitional power, it offers no sociological account of how this is achieved as the outcome of strategies pursued by political actors. They do not need strategies because they have guaranteed access by virtue of their structural position' (Schlesinger, 1990: 69).

However, it is not clear that Hall and his co-authors are in fact guilty of such over-simplification. While it is true that a reading of Chapter 3 of *Policing the Crisis* (from which the above account is taken, and to which these criticisms are directed) does indeed provide a basis for the charges levelled, two caveats are necessary. First, we have seen that the account allows for areas of ambiguity in that opposition occurs, and that the media may provide accounts of events independent of primary definers' activity (although it is true that the examples given are not of any media activity that could be called critical of the established order). Second, this chapter should be placed in the context of the book as a whole and crucially in the context of the theory of the state around which the analysis revolves. Drawn largely from Gramsci, this theory underlines the centrality of the organization of consent as one moment in the exercise of power, not as an autonomous process: 'thus what the consensus really means is that a particular ruling class alliance has managed to secure through the state such a total social authority, such decisive ideological leadership, over its subordinate classes that it shapes the whole direction of social life in its image' (Hall *et al.,* 1978: 216).

However, this form of consensus, they argue, has broken down in the period since the mid-1960s, and there has been a move towards a greater use of coercion where the organization of consent has failed. In the analysis of this process, Hall *et al.* point to the way in which primary definition is problematic:

> Although this is a process which is heavily structured and constrained ... its result is to make the 'reproduction of the dominant ideologies' a problematic and contradictory process and thus to recreate the field of signification as a field of ideological struggle. In analysing the way the post-war crisis came to be signified, then, we shall not expect to find a set of monolithic interpretations, systematically generated by the ruling classes. (1978: 220)

Such definition, in any event – as Hall makes clear in a subsequent essay (1982: 36–44) – does not operate at the level of the actual definitions of actual events, but rather through the framework of understanding in terms of which the (often conflicting) attempts at definition of events are conducted.

This section of their argument then goes on to stress that where the 'crime wave' is concerned, the process of definition was relatively successful, but this too should be seen in the context of the long argument which concludes (Hall *et al.,* 1978: 320) that consensus no longer (at the time of writing) existed and had been replaced by 'managed dissensus'. While it is difficult to give an adequate summary of a long and empirically complex argument about the history of Britain since the Second World War, it is clear that central to their account is this: that the state is never a monolithic block, that it is composed of factions whose coexistence is always in some measure uneasy and which may profoundly disagree on the tactics to be pursued at different times (*ibid.*: 227–38). State success in defining a particular issue may coincide with a much lower degree of success in the overall 'manufacture of consent'. Primary definition works – Hall *et al.* contend – in limited arenas, in this instance the definition of a crime wave, or a moral panic. But this may well go hand in hand with a more general failure to manage consent, which would suggest that the process of primary definition is, in their view, always a tentative achievement which may always be reversed, or may be fragile in its capacity to achieve any effects outside the particular arena in which it is deployed.

It is true that *Policing the Crisis* frequently offers formulations that suggest the success of the process of primary definition, and on many occasions the authors slide between, on the one hand, analysing this process as an aim of the state and a means of its constitution as a unified whole, and on the other implying that the process is uniformly successful. But the entire third section of the book is given over to an analysis of how unsuccessful the overall process of managing consent had been up until the moment of writing (shortly before the 1979 Tory election victory), and when the often-quoted remarks about primary definition are placed in this context, it seems an exaggeration to suggest that the authors' intention is to assert that '... state organisations ... are not internally divided ... [that] there is no room for negotiation over definition prior to engagement with the media ... that "the structure of access necessarily secures strategic advantages" for official sources ...' (Miller, 1993: 385–6).

The point at which there is a potential divergence between the 'primary definition' thesis and the weaknesses of which it is accused is to be found in the distinction between the actual definitions of events – which are achieved (or not achieved, contingently) in given sequences of news management – and the longer-term process manifest in the 'cultural maps' in terms of which the meanings of individual events are negotiated. It is the latter which is constitutive of the field of ideology, i.e., that place where the 'ruling ideas are the ideas of the ruling class'. A brief example based on this distinction will illustrate this argument.

In April 1994 a political row erupted about the public events planned for the fiftieth anniversary of the D-Day landings in Normandy which signalled the end of Nazi domination of Continental Europe. Specifically, the row centred on whether the anniversary should be 'commemorated' (implying a focus on the memory of those who died) or 'celebrated' (implying a focus on joyfulness). The D-Day anniversary has a predefined place in the British map of cultural reality, not in the sense that it is immutably fixed nor in the sense that everyone totally agrees on its meaning, but in the sense that there is clearly a dominant meaning, and not much in the way of any alternative one except the reaction of boredom or indifference. The row about the appropriate form of remembrance arose not because of minor differences of emphasis within this overall dominant definition, but – crucially – because journalists spotted the possibility of this being so. The nature of the proposed ceremonies was fixed during the second half of 1993, and relevant organizations, especially veterans' groups, were involved. At some stage it was suggested in Government circles that because it was the fiftieth anniversary, and because at the time of the Normandy landings such enormous relief was felt throughout the land, it was appropriate to have popular celebrations as well as the more usual solemn military/religious commemorations. The question of the motivation of this innovation then became part of the struggle for political definition of the event.

Given this innovation, PR firms were invited to tender for the contract to organize the popular 'celebrations'. The winner was Lowe Bell Spink, a firm with previous links with the Government. Until mid-April 1994 there seemed to be no controversy involved. On Wednesday, 13 April BBC *Newsnight* broadcast a story, based on interviews with veterans of the landings, that they were upset by the proposed tone of the celebrations and wanted only to be involved in solemn commemoration of the dead. BBC sources say that no one tipped off *Newsnight* journalists, who had scented the possibility of a story and then found it when they looked; alternatively, a PR man who represented both the British Legion and the Labour Party tipped *Newsnight* off that Legion members were opposed to the plan (*Evening Standard*, 21.4.94). In either event, it is clear that journalists found a credible source of a counter-definition of the plans, and bringing this counter-definition into the public realm provoked a controversy about what the meaning ought to be. Part of the row focused on who had taken the decision to give a dimension of jollity to the occasion, and part on the motivation for doing so. According to the pro-Government side of the argument, the celebratory events were the results of local initiatives without any advance coordination from Government, and the motive was to remember the mood of popular celebration. According to the anti-Government version, the celebrations were the result of initiatives taken by Lowe Bell Spink in a circular sent out in March and leaked to the *Guardian* (20.4.94); in this version of events, the Government was cynically exploiting the possibility of reinterpreting the D-Day commemorations in order to create a 'feel-good' factor in advance of the June European elections.

What does this imply for the theory of primary definers? The theory states that there are definitions whose domination of the public realm supports the class that dominates that realm ('The ruling ideas are the ideas of the ruling class') in the form of the state. In this process journalists' recourse to 'credible' sources of information, whose credibility is established by their institutional positions, is a central element in the struggle to maintain definitions of events that do favour the continued dominance of the ruling class via the state. A row such as that over the meaning of D-Day is ambiguous in relationship to this theory. On the one hand, it is certainly true that such rows undermine the credibility of government: they imply that government is out of touch with important elements of public opinion, and out of control of elements of the political process. But 'government' is not the same as 'ruling class' or 'state', and Marxist theory allows that on occasions governments may even cease to represent the fraction of the ruling class whose interests they had previously represented. However, the example also makes it clear that the process of 'primary definition' is not necessarily a unified one – the group of primary definers may well be in deep disagreement about the meaning of many issues. What this suggests is that the unity of the process of primary definition, when achieved, is the result of political organization and not something that occurs solely as the result of the institutional position of 'credible' sources. More importantly, what we see in such disagreements over the meanings of events is the process in which political organizations (and fractions of them) vie for the right to define how a way of life is to be organized. Neither the position of primary definer, nor what the 'primary definition' of an event is, are fixed in stone; both are the place of constant struggle for dominance.

However, the disagreement which we are analysing here in no way displaces the ultimate ground of the meaning of the event in question: D-Day has a more-or-less fixed meaning in our culture, and a disagreement about whether it is to be commemorated or celebrated does not fundamentally affect the basic profile of the event; indeed, without that fundamental profile, the row about celebration vs. commemoration would not have occurred. This fundamental profile is part of the wider meaning of the Second World War as the struggle for social justice against dictatorship and the basis of the 'post-war settlement'. At the time of writing it has not been suggested that this row reflects a more profound disagreement about the meaning of the Second World War or the 'post-war settlement'; however, a recent analysis of another similar minor spat suggests the potential for a deeper row. At the Remembrance Day ceremony in 1981, when Michael Foot as leader of the Labour Party laid a wreath at the Cenotaph, he was dressed in a way that many commentators thought was highly inappropriate: he was wearing an old duffel coat. Patrick Wright (1985: 135–40) has argued that beneath the disagreements about this coat there lurked two versions of what the two World Wars meant: on the one hand national glory, the continuity of a well-established public order, on the other the 'people's war' in which motives were different and the results being celebrated may be at odds with the official version. Especially, the 'people's war' version is inextricably bound up with the post-Second World War settlement centring around the conviction that some measure of economic justice had to be built into the social order. Given the deep divisions within British society in the 1980s and 1990s, and the extent to which the post-war settlement could be seen retrospectively as the basis of a now lost unity, the D-Day row could have had the potential for bringing about a wider questioning of recent politics, along the lines suggested by Wright. Although this did not happen – indeed was unlikely since there was no significant political organization willing to orchestrate such a division – the point is that the potential exists in theory, and this suggests the possibility of conducting the analysis of news coverage of such events on more than one level.

From a short-term, journalistic perspective, the D-Day row shows how split the group of primary definers is; but placed in a wider context, this is a dubious analysis, for the disagreement did not involve a full-blooded ideological crisis in which the whole meaning of the Second World War and the post-war settlement came to be questioned. If that were to happen, this would suggest a really fundamental split in the group of primary definers, beside which the D-Day disagreement would seem insignificant.[2] The point ultimately is that the process of 'primary definition' operates at different levels. At the obvious level of everyday politics, it is frequently the case that there are raucous disagreements about policy and the meaning of events. Indeed, some of these disagreements provoke political crises: the Westland affair under Margaret Thatcher and Maastricht under John Major, are two examples. Either of these could have become a major ideological crisis in which fundamentally divergent views about the long-term nature of our society might have emerged; neither did, although the disabling effects that both had upon the Tory Government should not be underestimated.[3] The fact that neither resulted in such a fundamental political reorientation demonstrates that beneath the noisy disagreements of everyday politics there is a basic layer of fundamental agreement, and it is arguably here that the real process of primary definition operates, in the way that Hall and his colleagues meant this phrase to be understood. The place that Second World War occupies in the 'map of meaning' that is basic to contemporary English culture is sufficiently stable to resist deformation by arguments such as the one reported here.

However, the point about the concept of primary definition as it is advanced in *Policing the Crisis* is that it is intended to express the mediation between these two levels in the political process: the level of everyday negotiations about news coverage and the level of long-term, common-sense cultural meanings. For this task it is perhaps unsuitably simple, for it suggests a process characterized by a certain unity: primary definitions derive from basic cultural maps because primary definers are able to reproduce them as the terms of debate in which smaller-scale events are understood. Yet we have repeatedly seen how problematic this is. But beyond these problems lies a further one: the meaning of the elements of the cultural maps is in its turn only established in the course of the interpretation of current events. What our examples show is that the stability of the maps themselves is always open to disruption, which may arise at any time due to (among other possibilities) divergences in interpretation between different groups of primary definers. What has eluded earlier commentaries is a coherent account of how this process occurs.

We can summarize the problems involved in what is at issue between Hall *et al.* and their critics in these terms:

- Their critics have little to say about how long-term, relatively stable cultural 'maps of meaning' are maintained since their focus is on the relatively short-term processes in which contested, destabilized meanings are produced.
- Hall *et al.* have problems in showing how long-term, relatively stable 'maps of meaning' produce short-term variations in event definition, since their focus is on the functional correlation between long-term maps of meaning and the details of the ongoing political process.

Each approach clearly corresponds to a feature of the social world, and is thus – within limits – valid; the problem is how to reconcile the inconsistencies, or to find another approach which takes account of both processes within a common framework. It is necessary to do this because, as we have seen, news reporting involves both.

Moreover – and crucially – these two approaches share a fundamental feature: in both, source power to create event definitions predominates over the event-defining power that derives from the media themselves. This is so because what differentiates the two approaches is not a disagreement over whether the media have any autonomous power, but a disagreement over the nature of source power over the media. In both cases, the margin of independence attributed to the media as institutions in their own right is relatively narrow.

CHAPTER 8

Communicative Action
and Factual Reference

At this point we may turn to the alternative account of public information flows that has been derived from the work of Juergen Habermas. This account turns on two features of his work: the nature of the 'public sphere' as he describes it in his early work, and the analysis of dialogic interaction and its position within modernity in his later texts.

We can start with his critique of Marx. Habermas largely accepts Marx's account of the human/nature interface, with the crucial proviso that in the form in which Marx puts it, it is inadequate. This is because Marx conceives of the source of all human awareness of the world in terms of the labour process or – as Habermas prefers to call it – 'instrumental action' aimed at technical control of the natural environment (1972: 35-42). However, human interactions with nature are always mediated by a process of social interaction which cannot be analysed using only the concept of instrumental action (1972: 51-3). Thus, within limits, Habermas accepts Marx' analysis of the role of work in establishing the boundary between humanity and its environment. The significance of his critique of Marx, from our point of view, is that it establishes the necessity of his own distinction between instrumental action and communicative action. Communicative action has an entirely different status from instrumental action: it is the modality of all social interaction, it is the simultaneous capacity for and necessity of dialogue between human subjects. Conceived integrally as dialogue and not as expression or as a mode of instrumental action, it plays a central role in both his description of the social structure and his ethical conception of the possibility of emancipation.[1]

Of most importance from our point of view is the role of communicative action in what he calls the 'lifeworld', approximately what is often called 'culture' in modern debates about the media. It is the structure of individual experience embedded in 'a reliable intersubjectivity of mutual understanding' (1972: 173). It is the set of all the normative and meaningful interactions between individuals in a particular bounded, localized collective space, and therefore also the location of the formation of the ego.[2] The norms and the meanings which constitute the framework of these interactions are historically transmitted by being replicated in the interactions in question. Under these circumstances, the meaning of all events and actions is settled within a framework which is, at any given moment in time, fixed. Habermas is accepting – within some carefully defined limits – the analysis of the social world put forward by the interactionist school. Importantly, the lifeworld as defined in these terms is undifferentiated by any form of social stratification or power relations.

Let us recall what is at issue: the analysis of source–journalist interactions shows that definitional power cannot be taken as pre-given on the basis of the position that agents occupy in the social structure. At the same time, those who maintain this are unable to give a consistent account of how stable maps of meaning are maintained – in other words, how the lifeworld (or: ideology) is constituted and transmitted. The inverse is true of the Marxists. Is it possible to use Habermas to give an account which avoids these pitfalls? We can note immediately that earlier attempts to use Habermas – often critically – as the foundation of an account of the mass media have centred on his notion of the 'public sphere'; for reasons which will become clear this is not the line I will follow.

Although in Habermas' analysis the lifeworld is not differentiated by power relations or by social stratification, he of course recognizes that such differentiation is a normal feature of the modern world. The mechanism by which he accounts for this he calls 'system differentiation'.[3] He posits that 'archaic' societies were characterized by a lifeworld in which there was no divergence between participants' consciousness of the world and the social structure within which they lived (1987: 156–60). Any functional differentiation that occurred in such societies – such as division of task by gender – would only lead to permanent segmentation and the creation of fundamentally divergent lifeworlds if there was some mechanism for the institutionalization of power and exchange relationships (1987: 156–64). Thus the concept of 'lifeworld' is adequate by itself to frame an account of a particular type of social formation. The historical evolution of human society, however, created social formations in which systematic differentiation was the norm, and Habermas demonstrates that the concept of the

152

lifeworld is not adequate to deal with such a society: institutions, for example, do not have a reality which is exclusively intersubjective, since their existence is underpinned by the law and their modes of action are constitutive for social action, not derivative from it (1987: 154).

In archaic societies there are mechanisms that may lead to long-term differentiation if they are tied into religion or kinship, for these are the fundamental components of the lifeworld in such societies: the mechanisms are personal prestige and organizational command, i.e. the recognized right to give orders where certain tasks are concerned. Either of these may lead to a separation of some function from others, and the ascription of this function to a particular group or category of person. For Habermas, the motor force behind system-differentiation is the specialization of social functions, and in particular the way in which political control and economic activity become autonomous activities, no longer regulated by the norms of the lifeworld. This process is rooted in an assumption he makes about archaic societies, that here – as indeed in any society – the mutually accepted norms that regulate all social interaction may fail to give adequate guidelines for individual instrumental action (1987: 133, 154). Under these circumstances people withdraw from the normative regulation of the lifeworld and impose their own strategic purposes on others, by whatever means are available. The usual first functional differentiation is political, and therefore it is the birth of the state that launches system differentiation as a fundamental element of social evolution. As social systems evolve, more and more specialized 'sub-systems' are hived off into autonomous spheres of activity (1987: 164–72). One of the most important examples, for Habermas, is the law. In the lifeworld of archaic societies there is no distinction between morality, social obligation and the law, but in societies with a high degree of system specialization certain rules are made binding and enforced using the coercive power of the state; as a result, morality and the law are no longer the same thing and each becomes a specialized sub-system of action-orientation. One of the results of this analysis has a particular significance which we shall return to: like institutions, specialized sub-systems of action – or 'spheres of action' – cannot be reduced to patterns of interaction between independent actors. Indeed, the norms which regulate activity in these specialized spheres of action confront social agents as something external to and independent of their own existence. Of course, all norms are independent of the will of social agents, but in the undifferentiated lifeworld we only experience the world *through* these norms, and therefore do not become aware *of* the norms as a separate entity (1987: 132–3). In the differentiated world, these external norms confront us as a 'second nature': they are object-like to us, because experienced as external and we 'behave toward formally organised action systems, steered via processes of exchange and power, as toward a block of quasi-natural reality; within these ... sub-systems society congeals into a second nature' (1987: 154).

At this point we need to consider another line of argument that Habermas develops, starting from the concept of communicative action. For him communicative action is one of the bases of all forms of sociality; its core is statements made in dialogue and in particular the fact that all statements are also validity claims. In other words, everything that anyone says always includes the tacit presupposition that saying this is a valid activity for that person, under those circumstances. Naturally, other participants in the dialogue may well contest the claim. Interactions of this nature are the foundation of the lifeworld, for it is through them that the norms of which it consists are transmitted.[4] Validity claims are always of three types, which correspond to different forms of social action: they are instrumental action, 'normatively regulated action' and 'dramaturgical action' (1984: 85). Instrumental action is – as we saw above – action defined by the function of control over the environment, judged by its success in relation to a purpose; its validity claim is therefore truth in the empirical sense: does this statement conform to the state of affairs which it purports to represent? Normatively regulated action is action considered from the point of view of its conformity to codes of what is permissible or not permissible under the circumstances in question; its validity therefore consists of establishing such conformity. Dramaturgical action is action considered from the point of view of the presentation of the self in everyday life, and its validity consists of sincerity: does the statement accurately represent the real intentions of the speaker? These forms of action are monologic, but the nature of sociality is such that they are necessarily realized in dialogue, and are brought together in the process to which Habermas gives the name communicative action. The validity claims are necessarily made in all interactions and are indeed their basis; all are potentially contestable by other participants, and the securing of agreement is never pre-ordained.

Validity claims are assessed by participants according to the transmitted norms of the lifeworld. In archaic societies, as we have seen, the lifeworld is undifferentiated; in particular, validity claims do not fall into fundamentally different types (except in so far as the three types of action are a permanent feature of all forms of sociality). For example, the nature of archaic religion implies an understanding of the external world in which nature and culture interpenetrate, and therefore the understanding of causality is always tied to an understanding of things which in a scientific view of the world could not be considered causality, for example, witchcraft (1987: 156–60). Under these circumstances, validity claims are assessed according to criteria which are universal within the society in question. However, in a modern society, massively differentiated into specialized spheres of action, this is not so, since each sphere of action has its own norms. For example, the operation of the economy is largely independent of the validity claims of morality, which are replaced by money values and legal norms such as contract and property. The capacity to make or meet validity claims which are localized within one or other of these spheres of action depends upon the acceptance of the rules of the game as locally established. Under these circumstances, it is always open to question how agreement about valid courses of action is possible when many different and potentially divergent value systems are involved (1987: 179–85): on what basis can validity claims be negotiated across the division between these spheres of action? how can social action in general be coordinated across these various spheres of activity and still meet with common approval? In other words, on what grounds can action claim legitimacy in a society differentiated by function?

Habermas' answer is that in all societies there are processes which in their simplest forms – in archaic societies – consist of prestige and influence. He speculates that these are originally attached to individuals and subsequently transferred to groups, who then claim objective legitimacy for their actions and enforce it in the form of coercive state power (1987: 179–80).[5] As societies become increasingly differentiated these legitimacy claims are based upon increasingly complex sets of criteria, but at their root always lie prestige and influence, and motives for accepting them. Put in the form of a universal matrix of possibilities, this gives us a schema in which prestige and influence are attributed to people or groups because of either their personal and/or moral attributes or because of the resources they have at their disposal. The motives for the attribution are either empirical (an assessment of the likely outcome of making the attribution) or rational (acceptance of the grounds upon which the prestigious and influential make their validity claims). A combination of these two sets of variables produces the schema shown in Table 8.1.

Habermas claims that in modernity legitimation is achieved through a mixture of all of these. In the economy, trust is largely empirically motivated, but, for example, in medicine trust depends upon a rational acceptance of the resource of valid knowledge. Rationally motivated trust is dependent upon a shared culture in so far as the grounds for exercising it are widely shared, even though the ability actually to assess its validity claims are very unevenly distributed across the population: consensus is achieved not through the actual acceptance

Table 8.1

	Attribution	
Motivation	*Attributes*	*Resources*
Empirical	Deterrence or inducement through expectation of success	Inducement through expectation of reward
Rational	Responsibility: trust in autonomy	Knowledge: trust in valid knowledge

Source: Habermas, 1987: 181–2.

of actual validity claims but through the acceptance of the grounds upon which specialized validity claims are made; dissensus occurs when this process breaks down, even in the absence of a shared capacity to accept or reject these validity claims.

In this situation, the mass media are central, since they are one of the forms in which validity claims, and the grounds on which they are made, are transmitted beyond their original location. Specifically, he says, it is the validity claims upon which rational trust is based that are transmitted by the mass media. The reason for this restriction is that empirically rooted trust is fundamentally grounded in instrumental action, whereas rationally motivated trust is grounded in communicative action and the normative regulation associated with the lifeworld; for him, the mass media are always essentially a mediation of communicative action (1987: 183).

At this point we may return to the earlier use to which Habermas has been put in debates about the mass media, where his theory of the 'public sphere' was the focal point of debate, despite criticisms of its adequacy for the task. For Habermas, the public sphere is a process – in fact the process of communicative action – taking place in a space, namely the public arena. This space is not an institution, although its existence and autonomy have to be institutionally guaranteed, ultimately by the state.[6] What makes it public is the range of topics and participants involved: the topics are of general and not just private interest, and anybody can join in; discussions are subject only to the criteria of reason – authority and interest play no determining role in settling what is acceptable in such discussions. This analysis has been criticized on various grounds, of which the main ones are: participation in the public sphere as Habermas describes it historically was in fact restricted, and therefore it was not truly 'public'; Habermas relies excessively on the self-image of those who originally composed it, and he therefore exaggerates its inner homogeneity and coherence; his comments on its role in the nineteenth and twentieth centuries are excessively pessimistic, and therefore he underestimates the importance of the mass media in modernity (Keane, 1991: 35-6, n. 31; Hermes, 1997: 69-74; Peters, 1993: 551-4; Calhoun, 1992: 32-7; Fraser, 1992: 112-16).

In large measure the theory of communicative action replaces the theory of the public sphere, in the sense that the processual aspect of the public sphere is relocated to this arena; the institutional element of the original theory is now replaced by the theory of systems differentiation, and the historical accounts of different spheres of action that this allows. In this new analysis of the role of mass-mediated communication, Habermas is not pessimistic in the manner characteristic of his original analysis of the public sphere. In the original argument, in 'post-liberal' or 'welfare-state' society the public sphere is 're-feudalised', in other words subjected entirely to the interests of economically and politically motivated groups. This process, he argues, is incompatible with the rational argumentation which was supposedly the core of the original historical version of the public sphere (1964: 54-5). However, in the version which derives from his analysis of the lifeworld and systems differentiation, he stresses the role of rational acceptance of specialized validity claims which are transmitted beyond their original location by the mass media, which 'permits public spheres to emerge' (1987: 389-90). The social impact which is the result of this process is ambivalent. On the one hand, it increases the level of social control because the mass media are characterized by a concentration of message senders and a diffusion of message receivers, which is a restriction on the intrinsically dialogic nature of communicative action. On the other hand, communicative activity is intrinsically dialogic and emancipatory. In particular:

- a plural social order means that interests are not homogeneous, and therefore the mass media transmit messages based upon potentially conflicting validity claims;
- it is clear that one cannot predicate the reception of messages upon their encoding at the point of emission;
- reception of the mass media involves the assessment of validity claims despite the restriction on dialogue noted above; and
- the professional ethics of journalism are an institutionalized site of reinforced assessment of validity claims (1987: 391).

At this point we have seen enough of Habermas' analyses to allow an overall assessment of the extent to which his framework will solve the dilemmas which led to reference to him. The dilemma, we may recall, is essentially this: through what process does event definition occur? What is the role of the news media in it? The earlier answers were defective in that one claimed that homogeneous 'maps of meaning' necessarily produced unified event definition, the other that meanings were fragmented according to group interests.

Habermas' own new defence of the mass media is based on the ambiguous presence of symmetrical, dialogue-based relations in the encoding and decoding of mass-mediated messages; I want to focus on a particular element of this claim, and that is the role of factual truth in it.[7]

In Habermas, factual truth appears in two linked processes: first, it is part of the process of control of the external environment, located in the feedback loop in which we check the efficacy of our instrumental actions in the world; second, as a result of this status it is one of the validity claims assessed in the dialogue which constitutes communicative action. In the first process it is not intrinsically dialogic; in the second it is. At this point it is important to recall that for Habermas differentiated action systems and institutions confront social agents as an externality, as reified practice whose ontological status is similar to that of the natural universe: it is that which we posit as external to us and wish to subject to instrumental, technical control. It is therefore subject to the same epistemological processes as the natural universe: cognitive adaptation to it is superior to lack of cognitive adaptation, and action in this context is subject to the feedback loop of testing – in short, scientific rationality is superior here to other forms of validity claim, as least where technical control is concerned. It is on these grounds that Habermas can say that the counter-intuitive truths of social science since the eighteenth century are an advance on previous knowledge of the social world in so far as they represent the application of scientific rigour to the social world (but at the same time 'technicize' the world, in other words produce a democratic deficit).[8]

The status of truth as established and legitimized in this way is especially important in modernity because of the results of system differentiation. First, this evolution produces a growing gap between the rational-purposive elements of the lifeworld and the consensus building elements of it – in other words between instrumental action and normatively regulated action; this is due to the ever-increasing space given over to sub-systems based on rational-purposive action, especially the autonomous economy (1987: 180). Rational-purposive action needs the feedback loop of empirical verification. In other words, wherever there is rational-purposive action, there is the need for factual information, a fortiori where there are entire sub-systems of social action geared to instrumental action. Second, as we have already seen, rational trust in validity claims is based in part on the acceptance of the validity of knowledge on the part of those whose actions are in conformity with the protocols of specialized spheres of action. The validity of such knowledge is surely not separable from demonstrations of cognitive adaptation. And we recall that the mass media play a central role in the dissemination of the activities and validity claims of specialized spheres of action.

Under these circumstances the role of fact in the mass media is central. 'Fact' should be understood here in Popper's sense: singular observation statements which are capable of being falsified. As is well known, Popper makes this the core of his argument about the superiority and universality of scientific reasoning; Habermas rejects this claim, but his thought still retains a clear margin of application for factuality. He rejects the universality of scientific reasoning on the grounds that it only applies in the arena of instrumental reason (1974: 264–8), and attacks Popper's theory of observation statements on the grounds that 'observations' are always preconstituted in the lifeworld, which introduces an element of tautology into observation-based testing. Observations derive from the lifeworld because observations are always made for a reason, and reasons derive from the lifeworld.[9] Despite this, he insists that observation of the real world and inductive reasoning have to be accepted as the basis of the success of science (1972: 124–34). Essentially his argument is that even if observation can never be entirely separated from the lifeworld, this does not alter the fact that empirical validity claims about the world are validated by reference to the real, and that it is through this that cognitive adaptation to the real progresses; indeed, in his account it is central to ego formation (1984: 67–74).

Now it must be made clear that Habermas himself does not defend the mass media in this way – for him the media are always essentially an arena in which discussion occurs. But the implication of his ideas seems to point in the direction I am taking, for the circulation of factual information in the form of validity claims is central to communicative action and also to rational trust in specialized validity claims. Additionally, his theory of 'second nature' in modernity enlarges the arena of instrumental action and thus the scope of empirical validity claims as an integral part of social action. We should consider this in relation to his reasons for rejecting his earlier pessimism about the mass media in contemporary society, which include both the variety of interests bearing upon the mass media and journalistic ethics: both of these occupy a place in modern society because of the existence of specialized spheres of action which confront outsiders as 'second nature', as the arena of instrumental action. In so far as trust in them is rational and not purely instrumental ('empirical', in his terminology), it is based in an assessment of their legitimacy, which includes the claim to valid knowledge.

I have stressed the role of factual knowledge not because Habermas himself makes it central to his new-found respect for contemporary mass media, but because it seems to me to be implied in his arguments about modernity, and because it has been clearly established that the credibility of information is central to news values and journalistic ethics. Although credibility and 'factual truth' are not identical, they are closely related. None of this is tantamount to saying that everything in the news is factually correct; but it does amount to saying that one of the ways in which the news media operate is by entering it into the public record that such-and-such was said or done. It is because of this that news sources put a good deal of effort into credible event-definition.

In Habermas' terms, event definition is always a form of validity claim: 'this statement really tells us what happened'. It is subject to counter-claims in the way that all validity claims are: claim and counter-claim are rooted in empirical evidence about events, and such claims are – for Habermas – always a form of instrumental action. In the lifeworld of archaic societies, this instrumentality would not often involve differentiated social functions and group interests, but in modernity, where differentiation confronts all agents as 'second nature', instrumentality and group interest are inseparable. Writing in the 1960s, this led Habermas to a pessimistic conclusion: the predominance of group interest made the operation of reason and the emergence of a 'general interest' impossible although he later revised this opinion. He conceded that the divergence of group interests and the possibility of assessing conflicting counter-claims made the operation of reason possible.

Thus far the turn to Habermas seems to support a claim about event definition which denies the Marxist version. However, validity claims are always rooted in the lifeworld: they are rooted normatively and in the maps of meaning that constitute the lifeworld. They are normative because validity claims which are purely instrumental in their intention none the less always open up the terrain of normative judgement – the claim that 'this happened' always potentially opens up the debate 'but should it have happened?' They derive from the 'maps of meaning' of the lifeworld in the sense that definitions of events must refer to categories of entities that are defined there: everything that we refer to in validity claims of any sort exists in some space in the lifeworld, defined in terms of the commonplace stock of knowledge which constitutes it. In the lifeworld, all definitions are bound up with experience, and all definitions are potentially normative as well as factual. Validity claims are always miniature narratives, in which various entities are brought into some relationship with each other; the attempts at event definition which we have looked at all have this basic structure: an attempt is made in a narrative of the event to show that it consisted of a certain set of entities, in a certain relationship to each other; of course, the narrative is motivated by a reason for preferring this version of the event.

A random example: divorce. In any individual case, the parties to it have their own reasons for wanting (or not wanting) it, and their own narrative of what has happened, with greater or lesser divergence between the versions. What is said is also inseparable from the public status of divorce, and this is especially true in the case of a divorce which attracts news media attention. Divorce is defined in the specialized sub-system of the law, but anyone wishing to define an event as a divorce outside the courts cannot avoid making reference to all the implicit meanings attached to it in the common-sense world. For example, is a divorce the recognition that a relationship has failed or is it a betrayal of trust? Two or three generations ago it was a betrayal. A generation ago either answer was possible. Today it is probably consensually defined as recognition of failure. Any individual narrative of a particular divorce inevitably has to be couched in terms deriving from this commonplace set of definitions, which change over time. The process is clear: causality is ascribed in the definition of the event, and the attribution of causality derives from the commonplace stock of knowledge that the lifeworld provides us with.

In the process of event definition, social agents attempt to bring factual claims about events into line with elements of the common-place maps of meaning that constitute the lifeworld. The role of the media in the transmission of specialized knowledge makes it clear that there is a tight link between group interest, event definition and the transmission of lifeworld meanings. Commonly, as we have seen, agents attempt event definition in order to pursue strategic interests in a society that is fundamentally split by functional differentiation. Journalism itself should be seen as one of those sub-systems, with its own specialized set of norms, including both journalistic ethics and news values. The role of factual reference and of agreed grounds for rational trust constitute a basis for assessing the validity claims implied in the narrative of any particular event. They also provide a basis for claims about media performance, against which media can be judged.

At this point we can review the comparison between the conceptions of source domination over information flows deriving from theories of 'primary definition' and its critics, with the conception of communication flows deriving from Habermas.

In the version of Marxism associated with the work of Hall and his associates, the source of power lies in the simultaneous domination over the economy and the polity by a single class, albeit a class whose existence as such includes the constant jockeying for a place between a number of factions in a never totally stabilized alliance. It is unlikely that the critics of the theory of primary definition quoted above would fundamentally disagree with this conception of class power, for the disagreement about 'primary definition' is over one modality of the exercise of such power. In Habermas, on the other hand, there is no single locus for the exercise of economic and political power. While the theory of 'system differentiation' certainly includes a theory of differential access to power – achieved through gaining acceptance for legitimacy claims – this is a very different conception of the basis of the social structure from the Marxist definition of a ruling class. Therefore it is not possible to claim that a Habermas-based model of mediated information flows can be used simply to supplement the Marxist-derived models analysed above: Habermas' insistence on the centrality of communicative action is explicitly based in part on a rejection of Marx' central claim of the dependence of all forms of social interaction upon forms of production. It is this that grounds his argument about competing legitimacy claims and the role of the mass media in the process. On the other hand, Habermas' conception of communication has the advantage that instrumental disagreements over event definition are inseparable both from lifeworld definitions and from every form of validity claim, including the factual. They are also thoroughly integrated into power relations. For Habermas, the role of the media in the circulation of legitimacy claims is ambiguous, as we have seen: in so far as they reproduce the claims made from within existing centres of power, they tend to increase social control. At the same time, the plurality of and competition between these power centres tends to destabilize this process. I have argued that the role of factual reference is central here.

Marxists commonly point to a severe restriction on the role of the circulation of factual information in the articulation of resistance to the power of the ruling class: they point out that many competing alternative voices, which attempt to gain a hearing for analyses of the world incompatible with 'official' ones, are marginalized or silenced (Parenti, 1993; Herman and Chomsky, 1988). The power of the state is used to prevent journalism from realizing the potential that it might otherwise have in this respect. The empirical evidence for this case is indeed strong, and the capacity to produce systematic silence or marginalization is certainly a form of power. By the same token, it is often said that the unwelcome revelations of scandalous behaviour are ineffective as attacks on the power of the state or the ruling class. No doubt scandals have limited disabling power due to their overwhelmingly individualistic focus: it is only if scandals come to be cumulatively seen as systemic that they acquire the real capacity to damage claims to legitimacy. Yet at the same time, denunciations of the 'irresponsibility' or 'unethical' behaviour of the press suggest that the cumulative power of scandal in destabilizing legitimacy claims should not be underestimated. The real restriction on the destabilizing power of scandal – at least from a Marxist point of view – is that it is impossible to derive any alternative from it: that is because scandal is a perfect example of purely negative, cynical reasoning about the world. At best, it articulates the burst of derisive laughter that is one of the voices of permanent distrust of all power centres (Sloterdijk, 1988: 102–32). The role of source control over information flows in this process is understood essentially as a way of achieving a restriction on information flows which is functionally similar if not identical to the restrictions achieved by the direct use of state power. Indeed, the point has been well made that the role of secrecy legislation, and the apparatus that accompanies it, is to securely ground the state's control over communication strategies by giving the essential initiative to the state: secrecy allows the state to set the boundaries to legitimate public communication and thus to communicate selectively (Downing, 1986).

These restrictions on the role of information flows as instruments of democracy are real, no doubt. However, the empirical evidence of their existence is as compatible with the Habermas model as it is with the Marxist. Indeed, we cannot choose between these two models on grounds given by this analysis of information flows. Both the state's restrictions on the democratic role of information, and the existence of 'spinning' – which is also evidence that the powerful can use information flows to their own advantage if their efforts are not subverted by other flows – are compatible with both models. If we restrict our basis for choice between a Marxist and a Habermasian model to these elements of information flows, we will have to make the choice on other grounds. It is more difficult to assign a place to the factually based validity claims central to Habermas' model, but my tentative conclusion is that this is determinant in the argument.

In the Marxist model, knowledge must fall into the category either of ideology, or of science and critique aligned with oppositional political forces. In this fundamentally split conception of knowledge, factual claims by themselves are arguably of less importance than their articulation into a strategic programme. Of course, in Habermas too, factual claims are always a form of legitimacy claim and only one form at that. Any factual claim is also simultaneously a normative and performative claim as well. None the less, the foregrounding of factuality in Habermas seems more compatible with the empirical evidence of the role of journalism in democracy than the role that would be assigned to it in a Marxist epistemology. To the extent that this argument is correct, the analysis of 'spinning into control' supports a model derived from Habermas rather than one derived from Marx, and avoids the situation where the choice between the two models would have to be made on grounds distant from such an analysis.

Annotated list of media sources

UK press titles

The Daily Telegraph: broadsheet daily, predominantly Conservative politically

The Guardian: broadsheet daily, predominantly left/liberal politically and culturally

The Independent: broadsheet daily, centrist/non-aligned politically

The Times: paper of record, broadsheet daily, predominantly Conservative politically

(All of these papers have affiliated Sunday papers: respectively, *Sunday Telegraph, The Observer, Independent on Sunday, Sunday Times*)

Daily Express/Sunday Express: mid-market tabloid, previously Conservative in orientation but currently moving to centrist position

Daily Mail/Mail on Sunday: mid-market tabloid, Conservative in orientation

The Daily/Sunday Mirror: Labour Party-supporting tabloid

Daily Record: Scottish affiliate of the *Daily Mirror*

Financial Times: business-oriented broadsheet daily

The Herald: Glasgow-based daily tabloid

News of the World: Sunday tabloid

The People: Sunday tabloid

The Scotsman: Scottish broadsheet

The Sun: tabloid that has traditionally been Conservative, but at the 1997 election supported the Labour Party

Other European press titles

Bild Zeitung/Bild am Sonntag: German national daily tabloid and Sunday edition

Focus: German weekly news magazine

Frankfurter Allgemeine Zeitung: national German daily with large business section

Hamburger Abendblatt: German regional evening daily

Handelsblatt: German national business daily

Der Spiegel: German weekly news magazine

Stern: German weekly news magazine

Die Welt: German national broadsheet daily

Die Zeit: weekly German broadsheet newspaper

Press agencies

DPA (Deutsche Press Agentur) German national news agency

North Scotland Press Agency: regional news agency

Press Association: nation-wide press agency

Television programmes

BBC1 *Panorama*: weekly news and current affairs magazine-format pro-gramme specializing in in-depth analysis, investigation and commentary

NDR *Panorama*: weekly news magazine programme produced by the North German broadcasting company, but networked nation-wide; specializing in in-depth analysis, investigation and commentary

Decisive Moments: two series of programmes on news photography – one annual series reviewing the past year, one series reviewing the history of news photography.

Notes

1. Similarly rare footage was obtained in New Zealand in September 1995, as a team of seismologists was monitoring a volcano which had been giving signs of returning to life. Other natural disasters, such as whirlwinds, which last for some time and occur in less remote places, are more regularly photographed.
2. Tagg (1982) shows how the history of photography is linked to its use in surveillance, record-keeping and investigation, and is thus a source of power; see also Goldberg, 1991: 59–62.
3. This theme is well established in commentaries on political communications. For the UK, see Cockerell (1984); for the US, see Sigal (1973). The Major and Blair Governments have both modified the degree of public accountability of government briefings since these standard texts were written. Details are to be found in the Mountfield Report (1997) and the Select Committee Report (1998).
4. In Revill's account the spin doctor is anonymous, but Nicholas Jones names him as Joe McCrea (1999: 76–7). See also Alison Pearson (*Evening Standard*, 14.10.98) on the BBC's use of leaked material apparently to lay the groundwork for the possible future redeployment of certain newscasters.
5. See for example Nicholas Jones' (1999) *Sultans of Spin*, which includes many examples.
6. Jones (1999: 209–10) clearly indicates that in his opinion Harman did talk to Toynbee. Parallel examples: Sigal (1973: 45–6, 53–6) gives a series of US examples; a detailed UK example is to be found in Cockerell *et al.* (1984: 130–3).
7. See, for example: Cockerell *et al.*, 1984: 130–8; Gans, 1980: 119–21; Hallin, 1986: 45–6, 163–7, 186–8; Harris, 1990: 13–14 (but contrast the account of the same events in Ingham, 1991: 333–7); Schlesinger and Tumber, 1994: 61.
8. This account follows the version in the *Observer* (14.12.97: 25) by Andy McSmith. Of course, this version is in its turn dependent upon confidential briefings, no doubt by those who had most interest in limiting the damage done by the original leak; this suggests that this version is prima facie no

more reliable than alternative ones. Only comparison of the two versions of the leaked document, together with firm attributions of dates to them, would settle the matter.

9. Macarthur (1992: 161-4); Taylor (1992: 10-17). *Decisive Moments 5* (BBC2) includes an extensive discussion of the taking of this photograph, of the editorial decision by the *Observer* to publish it, and US editorial decisions (*Life*, Associated Press) not to publish or distribute it.

10. In the UK, decorum in broadcasting and the press are also subject to regulatory guidance from the Press Complaints Commission and the Broadcasting Standards Commission, which have the power to adjudicate on matters of taste in reporting; the powers of the two organizations are not the same.

11. See also Thompson (1995) for a parallel argument. See Cannadine (1983) for a discussion of the history of English ceremonies, including an analysis of the role of the mass media (153-60). See Hay (1975) for an analysis of the role of ceremonial in the English criminal law in the eighteenth century intended to impress the public.

12. This distinction is similar to the well-known distinction between communication analysed as an empirical process (whose basic components are sender, message and receiver), and communication conceived as the result of generating meanings from codes, or from a semiotic system (see Chapter 7).

13. This is commonly the case with voluntary-sector organizations, whose main purpose in 'placing' material in the mass media is often only to maintain public credibility rather than to attempt to influence particular bodies of opinion; this does not imply that their press officers' motives are *always* such. See Palmer (2000).

14. Tom Wolfe's novel, *Bonfire of the Vanities* (1988), gives a good fictional example of these divergent strategies.

15. The following account of police and hospital press office activity comes from interviews with relevant press officers (January 1996).

16. The public information officer at Broomfield Hospital, Chelmsford, also commented in interview on the extent to which the police press office had been proactive because of the assumption of contamination.

17. The photograph was used as a poster in her home town in Northumbria (*Today*, *Daily Telegraph*, 15.11.95). But the event did not cause a widespread surge in media interest.

18. The details of this content analysis can be consulted on the London Guildhall University website: www.lgu.ac.uk

19. Because the mentions of her name are so protracted, the role of the 'girl next door' theme appears ambiguous in the content analysis. However, its centrality is stressed both by the public relations personnel I interviewed about this case, and tabloid journalists who covered her death extensively (Hilpern, 1995, quotes Gary Jones of the *News of the World* and Geoff Edwards of the *Daily Mirror* to this effect).

20. Police press officer, interview.

21. Interviews on 9 May 1996 with Mike Matheson of FFI and Andy Ray of

Knight Leach Delaney, the agencies responsible for the poster campaign. The cost of the campaign was donated by the poster site companies.

22. The details of this content analysis can be consulted on the London Guildhall University website: www.lgu.ac.uk. It is arguable that the duration of the use of a life-support system played a part in media interest. According to the hospital press officer who handled the case, one frequent question from reporters was about when the life-support machinery would be switched off. (The police press officer, on the other hand, argued that the duration of the coma was not significant.) Certainly, the nature of the media interest cannot be entirely separated from the duration of the coma, since this dictated one element of the scope of the story by setting its temporal frame and creating a period during which updates were indeed possible.

23. With one exception: over the Christmas period, many papers wrote about her story in their summaries of the year. Much of this material was very personalized, no doubt due to editorial decisions about suitability for publication at a time of year dominated by attention to the family.

24. We shall also see that this has implications for the use of content analysis in the examination of news values; see pp. 133–5.

CHAPTER 2

1. Interviews with national daily crime correspondent and news editor of a specialist news agency.

2. In this wider framework, the event entered a long-term debate about the nature of relationships in general; as the then *Guardian* columnist Suzanne Moore put it, famous stable heterosexual relationships have become a rare breed (G2, 29.6.95: 5); cf. vox pop interviews on BBC1, 9.00 p.m. News, 8.6.95.

3. According to the *Observer* on 2.7.95, by the time Grant's story broke, radio stations had started to receive phone calls from listeners complaining about the amount of coverage given to the Tory leadership campaign

4. I owe this point to Stig Hjarvard, Department of Film and Media, Copenhagen University.

5. For example, many rumours in the aftermath of Princess Diana's death – discussed on the Internet – were considered excessively implausible for news publication.

6. My source for this information, although confidential, is authoritative.

7. Would the revelation of sexual promiscuity on the part of another star whose 'image' was significantly different in this respect (say, Madonna or Mick Jagger) have had the same impact? It may be doubted; see Lull and Hinerman (1997: 17–18). On the other hand, promiscuity is not the same as prostitution. Comments about Jagger's promiscuity featured heavily in extensive press reporting of a rumour that his wife would seek a divorce (all UK national press, 16.10.96); the rumour was eventually proved true, but no doubt the reporting was part of the process of marital negotiation.

8. Charity press officers whom I interviewed in preparing an article (2000)

shortly after the Brent Spar affair said they were more wary about offering VNRs as a result of the controversy sparked by remarks by TV newsroom editors at the Edinburgh International Television Festival; see Chapter 6.

9. See Palmer (1998: 383–5). The discussion of 'breaking news' there is, in my view, inadequate; see p. 80. The second edition (2001) contains a fuller discussion.

10. Cockerell *et al.*, 1984; Negrine, 1989: 156–62; Sigal, 1973: 52–8, 111–15; Mountfield, 1997; Select Committee, 1999.

11. Some analyses distinguish three categories of national newspaper: tabloids, mid-markets and broadsheets; currently the national mid-markets, distinguished primarily by the demographics of their readerships, are the *Daily Mail* and *Daily Express*. In the interests of simplicity most of the following analysis will be based on format only.

12. The details of these analyses, which are all based on a series of chronologically random 'snapshot' comparisons, can be consulted on the London Guildhall University website: www.lgu.ac.uk/.... This point has created a rare example of methodology becoming a political topic: during the 'Back to Basics' scandals in 1994 the *Evening Standard* alleged that broadsheet newspapers were giving as much attention to sexual scandal as were the tabloids (in response to an accusation of tabloid sensationalism). However, the measure they used (total column inches) did not allow for differences in the size of the newshole and inevitably made the two treatments seem more similar in scope than a differentiated measure would have provided.

13. Details of the content analysis on which the following pages are based can be consulted on the London Guildhall University website: www.lgu.ac.uk/...

14. Sky TV, which had been carrying the trial live, claimed increased viewing figures from less than 0.5m at the beginning of the trial to over 3m shortly before the verdict (*Guardian*, 30.10.97: 19); in a press release on 24.10.97 Sky also claimed an increase of 500 per cent in its peak viewing figures during the same period, and subsequently claimed a vast increase in e-mail and dedicated website traffic in the immediate aftermath of the verdict (Sky News public affairs personnel, interviewed on 4.11.97). Andrew Marr, then editor of the *Independent*, wrote on 1 November that his staff had been regularly watching screens in the newsroom, speculating on the outcome.

15. Including four brief reports of similar events, which would probably not have been reported at all without the Woodward verdict as a 'peg' to hang them on.

16. See e.g. Peter Stothard, Editor of *The Times*, writing in the *Guardian*, 16.6.97; also Matthew Engel, *Guardian*, 3.10.96.

17. It could be said that these devices use space that could otherwise be given to 'information'; but the overall increase in newspaper sizes in the last twenty years makes it difficult to sustain this argument.

18. *Sunday Mirror, People, Sunday Express, Mail on Sunday, Observer*; the determining factor may have been the gender of the journalist in question, since in the majority of these cases the topics were raised in articles by women journalists; this is clearest in the case of the *Mail on Sunday*, in

which there was just over one page of coverage in the general news section, but five pages in the women's section. However, without being party to editorial discussions about who was going to cover what, it is impossible to be sure about the role of gender: it is possible that male editors decided that it would be women journalists who covered the issues in question; indeed, locating the reporting in the women's pages might imply a ghettoization of the topic.

CHAPTER 3

1. Ericson *et al.* (1989: 8) characterize this by distinguishing between the 'back space' and the 'front space' of organizations, combined with the capacity to either 'enclose' or 'disclose' information in either space. Crucially, control over the boundary between the two spaces lies with the organization in question. (although we shalll see examples where this control fails).
2. Our focus will be sources whose motives derive from their positions in large-scale organizations, since it is these circumstances that most clearly reveal the processes involved. This is not to deny that many sources act for purely personal reasons and often for financial gain, since news organizations pay well for useful information.
3. Macarthur's analysis points to a double bluff, in which the Saudi Embassy pretended to make life difficult for US media, in order to allow themselves to be persuaded by the State Department. Did something similar occur between the Navy and No. 10 over the Falklands? There is no public evidence.
4. This expression was introduced into academic literature on the subject by Gandy (1982). By this he means the decision to supply information to news media at below the cost which other means of obtaining it would create. The purpose of this subsidy is to exert influence by 'controlling access to and the use of information' (1982: 61). Another standardized term is 'below the line' communications budgeting.
5. See also Goldenberg (1975: 20) for a generalized discussion of such motives, followed by a wealth of examples.
6. See also Miller and Williams' discussion of the credibility-building strategy of the Health Education Authority during the early phase of the AIDS crisis (1993: 127-32).
7. See also ch. 1, p. 11. Further examples in Sigal, 1973: 136-8; Hallin, 1986: 15-19, 39-46, 70-5; Miller, 1993b: 84-5; Schlesinger and Tumber, 1995: 72; Cockerell *et al.*, 1984: 135-7.
8. An example of an unsuccessful attempt made by the City of Toronto police is given by Ericson *et al.* (1989: 117).
9. The number of government information officers has stayed roughly constant since 1970, according to a recent presentation by the Head of Profession. See also Select Committee (1999). But the recent increase in government special advisers, who are prime media sources, somewhat offsets this; see, e.g., Jones (1999).

10. Tulloch (1993) charts the growth of government information services in the UK from their beginnings in 1914 until the end of the first post-war Labour government in 1951. The growth of political television led to the creation of press secretaries for ministers and other senior political personnel (Seymour-Ure, 1989: 314-5). See Sigal (1973: 54) and Gold-enberg (1975: 79) for relevant examples of a parallel process in the USA. Mountfield (1997) and Select Committee (1999) give up-to-date information on the situation in the UK.
11. The catastrophic mishandling of the Lockerbie disaster by Pan Am's public relations department negatively illustrates the importance of this point; see Deppa *et al.*, 1993: 29-35, 223-36.
12. The UK TV current affairs programme *Dispatches* gave several instances of successful and unsuccessful placements of VNRs on 22.3.95. Gandy reports a claim by the PR agency Burston-Marsteller of a 50 per cent success rate in placing a particular VNR; VNRs may be released with pre-drafted scripts for news stations to use with their own reporters in additional cutaway shots (1982: 69). Their use fell somewhat into disrepute in the aftermath of the Brent Spar affair; see Chapter 6.
13. See for example: Gieber and Johnson, 1961: 295; Sigal, 1973: 47; Sigal, 1986: 21-2; Gandy, 1982: 104-7; Goldenberg, 1975: 79; Ericson *et al.*, 1989: 104-13; Morrison and Tumber, 1988: 95-130.
14. This consideration does not apply in the same way in the USA because of the First Amendment defence against contempt of court.
15. Sir Bernard Ingham states that this even-handedness must be the basis of the relationship between government press officers and the media (1991: 342-3).
16. See the case of Michelle and Lisa Taylor, who were convicted of the murder of Michelle's former lover's wife (*Guardian* 2, 28.8.95: 11).
17. To the extent that reports which are mainly verbal – for example, commentaries by political or economic journalists – are regularly filmed against a backdrop of a relevant location – the Houses of Parliament, the European Commission buildings or the United States Congress, the Bank of England or City dealing rooms, for example. See, e.g., Goddard *et al.*, 1998: 12.
18. Interviews with various charity press officers and other personnel; see Palmer, 2000.

CHAPTER 4

1. For example, various episodes analysed in Cockerell *et al.*, (1984) derive from such information sources; see e.g. pp. 77-9, 96-100, 130-34. See also Miller and Williams, 1993: 134; Hallin, 1986: 24; Sigal, 1973: 53-7. On two occasions in one of my case studies I was able to locate a significant silence; they are discussed on pp. 105-7.
2. It is clear from Engel (1996) that sensationalism was a normal feature of the popular press throughout its history, even if the degree of sensationalism and the language used varied (see esp. 207-215); see also

Lull and Hinerman, 1997: 7. To this extent, the famous examples such as the US tabloid treatment of the execution of Ruth Snyder in 1928 or the St Valentine's Day Massacre in 1929 are only the most visible, or exaggerated moments in a constant process. The New York *Daily News* managed to get a photographer into the execution chamber and published the picture the following day; sales increased by 1 million copies. The *Chicago Evening American* was tipped off by Al Capone himself to have a photographer in the neighbourhood of the massacre (*Decisive Moments*, BBC2, 4.10.97). Earlier denunciations of sensationalism are often misleading, as the charge commonly referred to the simple fact of reporting court cases without censoring out lurid details from the verbatim transcripts (Schudson, 1978: 23); denunciations of W. T. Stead's anti-vice campaigning in England in the late nineteenth century followed the same logic.

3. See for example the public arguments between Charles Moore (*Daily Telegraph*) and Sir David English and Paul Dacre (Associated Newspapers, *Daily Mail*) about their respective records in this respect, using their editorial columns in the days following the Princess' funeral; the spat is summarized, with one contribution to it by Paul Dacre in the *Guardian*, Media section, 15.9.97.

4. This case study was largely finished at the moment that Monica Lewinsky's name first appeared in US and UK news, and I have not been able to analyse the event. Passing reference is made at appropriate points.

5. See the London Guildhall University website for a content analysis of the distribution of the term 'scandal' across domains of social activity in recent press reporting: www.lgu.ac.uk/

6. See Leapman's analysis of the origin of the *Sunday Times* Insight pages (1992: 18–23).

7. On Tuesday, 21 March the *Guardian* editor Alan Rusbridger, interviewed on TV, said that Synon had approached the *Guardian* some weeks previously with her story, which they had refused on the grounds that it looked too much like a blackmail attempt; the following day the *Guardian* columnist Sarah Bosely wrote that they had rejected it because it didn't have enough public relevance. Subsequently, the then Deputy Editor of *The Spectator*, Anne Applebaum, revealed that Synon had approached her with the story but that she had refused it, not on the grounds that it was untrue, but on the grounds that the event was purely private and did not merit press attention (*Evening Standard*, 24.3.95). Rusbridger justified subsequent *Guardian* coverage on the grounds that while it was not the practice of broadsheet papers to break such stories, once they were broken it was necessary to follow them up if there was any element of public importance involved (ITN, 10.4.95).

8. In Parris (1995: 292–6).

9. News text available on FT Profile for this period indicates 102 reports between 20 and 28.7.92, 27 reports between 29.7 and 6.9.92 and 70 reports between 7.9.92 and 24.9.92, the date of Mellor's resignation. These figures are not a totally reliable indication of press interest since neither the *Sun* nor Mirror Group newspapers are available for these dates. However, the

contrast between the levels of coverage suffices to indicate the ebb and flow of the story; the fact that the 'silly season' intervened does not alter the significance of the information flows. The *Independent* (23.9.92) pointed out that during that summer Mellor had had more press coverage than most other public figures, including the royal family.

10. In Max Clifford's case, we should add that he himself subsequently stated, in a televised interview with Andrew Neil, that he was additionally motivated by political antagonism to the Tory government.

11. The *Sunday Times* (26.7.92) did an 'anatomy of the story' which attributed its prominence to the constant renewal, listing the following elements: Mellor's resignation offer, de Sancha's past, the privacy debate and charges of tabloid hypocrisy, the editor of the *Sun*'s accusation about Tory election conduct, Mellor's parents-in-law's accusations, more about de Sancha's past, the visit to Mellor's in-laws, yet more about de Sancha's past.

12. Senior broadcast political journalist, in interview with JP.

13. In the televised version of his autobiography, *The Major Years* (BBC1, November, 1999), Major protested that his personal history made it highly unlikely that he would seek to make life difficult for single mothers. This ignores the clear guidance at the press briefing that accompanied his speech.

14. Senior *Daily Mail* journalist, and other tabloid reporter, interviews.

15. Senior BBC journalist, interview.

16. Interviews with Tory broadsheet Westminster correspondent and broadcast political correspondent. The journalist who conducted the radio interview, Nick Jones, said in interview that he had offered Fowler the chance to re-record the segment of the interview in which he supported Yeo as he was not happy with the question being raised, despite the convention that once the tape recorder was known to be running, anything said was officially on the record; the re-recorded version was even more strongly supportive than the original version.

17. Sir Bernard Ingham describes this process as looking for 'destructively newsworthy' reactions to any political statement or action (1991: 303).

18. Interview with local newspaper reporter who covered the story. All the local activists I contacted were unwilling to be interviewed, either on or off the record. Every journalist with whom I discussed these events commented on the centrality of this omission, many of them spontaneously. Some journalists claimed that this was the main news value of the story. However, this does not accord with the common admission that the local dimension did not become clear to them for some days. In other words, my informants were probably confusing a retrospective understanding of the underlying cause of the events (or one of the causes) with the day-by-day flow of news judgements. My interviews were done late in the sequence of events in question.

19. Interview with local newspaper reporter who covered the story. Cf. Goldberg (1991: 117): 'It is possible to say "no comment" to an interviewer without losing all credibility, but covering one's face from an advancing photographer practically guarantees that the resulting photograph will be the perfect image of a crook.'

20. Senior BBC journalist in interview.
21. Michael Ricks of the *Independent*, unpublished paper at the conference on 'Reporting Financial Crime: Complex Cases in a Media Age', Institute of Advanced Legal Studies, London University, 21.10.97. According to Ricks, recent decisions in the European Court of Human Rights – which place the need for public interest revelation above commercial confidentiality – are unlikely to change the situation substantially as fear of the consequences of breaching confidentiality will still operate. Such considerations enter non-commercial spheres in so far as confidentiality is enforceable in them: for instance, scandalous mismanagement of cervical cancer tests at an English hospital remained undetected for a long time due to the confidentiality of the governing body's board meetings, according to Health Minister Baroness Jay, speaking on Channel 4 news, 20.10.97. Another investigative journalist with whom I discussed this matter, and who had extensive experience of investigating financial scandals, felt that confidentiality clauses were not a very effective barrier to sources 'blowing the whistle', since the crucial element was fear of being found out, and the antidote was personal trust in the journalist's ability to maintain secrecy.
22. Other journalists speaking at the same conference supported Ricks' contentions, but the inhibitory nature of the cost factor was challenged by another investigative journalist with whom I discussed this matter; it was a matter of the size of editorial budgets and of priorities, he said. According to journalists speaking at the Advanced Legal Studies conference, the total number of investigative journalists on national newspapers regularly covering financial matters is in single figures.
23. *Guardian*, 12.12.89; *All England Law Reports* (1996) 4 All ER: 769–71 (4.12.96) Smith New Court Securities Ltd. V Scrimgeour Vickers (Asset Management) Ltd.; *Washington Post*, 13.3.97; *New Law Journal* 137 (6330), 6.11.87: 1034. I owe these references to Helen Parry, Law Department, London Guildhall University. See also Stewart (1991: 125).
24. Schlesinger and Tumber, 1994; Golding and Middleton, 1982.
25. I owe these points about alternative information sources to Professor Michael Levi.
26. According to a '*Panorama* insider', her motive was to gain 'credibility among opinion formers and the public' (quoted in the *Observer*, 19.11.95).

CHAPTER 5

1. See a January 1994 survey reported in *The Times*, 17.1.94. See also the account of the Robin Cook separation scandal in Jones (1999: 185–98), in which he speculates that had the matter been handled differently, there would have been no scandal. The implication is that media attention is out of tune with public values, and it is only the handling of information flows which keeps such forms of scandal alive.
2. However, where norms of public propriety in politics and business are concerned, this shift is less evident.
3. Contrast the many examples of court reporting of sexual deviance

contained in Engel's (1996) history of the popular press, where the textual structure is such as to give closure to the event through unequivocal moral condemnation.

4. In a study of the difference between political scandals in Britain and the USA, Anthony King (1986) argued that the predominance of sexual scandal in the UK, as against the predominance of financial scandal in the USA, derived not from differences in the sexual morality of the two countries, but from the different roles that money played in the two political systems. The 'Parliamentary sleaze' scandals that were prominently reported in the UK press between the 1992 and 1997 elections, and in November 1997, must lead to a re-evaluation of that thesis, for what is striking about the 'crop' of scandals during that period is the mixture of sexual and other themes, and the clear role of money in many of them. The Clinton/ Lewinsky scandal may be relevant here too.

5. This photographic 'intimacy' was an invention of the inter-war years, when news photographers started actively seeking opportunities to bypass official photographs of political leaders and other public figures. For example, the abdication speech of King Edward VIII was accompanied by an official photograph, posed in Windsor Castle. A freelance photographer managed to snatch a candid, and less flattering, photograph of the now ex-king leaving the castle by car which was largely preferred by the British press the following morning (*Decisive Moments*, BBC2, 4.10.97). According to Victoria Goldberg, it was at this time that such photographs, portraying 'unguarded moments', came to be seen as the 'truth' about the person in question (interviewed *ibid.*).

6. Reviewing books about the death of the Princess, Adam Mars-Jones referred to her as 'everybody's imaginary friend' (*Observer*, 30.11.97, Review Section, p. 17); this is a reference to a theory of celebrities as the adult equivalent of the childhood 'imaginary friends'. See also Thompson (1995: 219–225) for further discussion of 'non-reciprocal intimacy'.

7. Except perhaps in totalitarian systems based on a cult of the personality, where the control over information flow can prevent disillusion. Even under these circumstances it may be difficult to ensure that the meanings attached to media output are identical to the meanings encoded in them at the point of transmission. Attempts to control meaning attribution can be more thorough in a totalitarian system, as can be seen from the history of radio in Nazi Germany: the cheap sets manufactured for the general populace were only capable of receiving German-originating broadcasts, and the Nazi Party tried (with what degree of success is unclear) to organize supervised collective listening to radio.

8. The Code is available on the Internet: www.pcc.org.uk

9. Indeed, when warnings about financial wrongdoing are not brought into the public domain, this is considered detrimental to the proper functioning of the market. This point was made apropos the BCCI scandal by the Professor of International Banking, Southampton University, speaking to the BBC's *Panorama* programme (18.11.91).

10. Moreover, the nature of the manner in which the events were revealed, via a

mixture of court cases, a judicial enquiry, parliamentary debate and media investigations ensured that the events never acquired a clear public profile in the way that (say) David Mellor's affair with de Sancha did; the media played a relatively restricted role in the definition of these events; the primary profiling was done in other institutional settings (Negrine, 1997).

11. Any account of the Aitken affair must distinguish between the original issue and the subsequent libel case. Granada TV's *World in Action* programme and the *Guardian* alleged that Aitken's hotel bill in Paris had been paid for by a business contact, and that this was in breach of guidelines for ministerial conduct. Aitken then sued for libel, claiming that the allegation was factually inaccurate. He subsequently withdrew his case, after the revelation in court that a central element in his evidence was invented. As a result he was subsequently convicted of perjury.

12. She colludes in the kidnap of a famous TV comedian with whom she is obsessed because she deludes herself into thinking that she will be able to seduce him. Many instances of apparently confused behaviour are to be found in the literature about fans and about soap opera. See, for instance, Hobson (1982: 99–104).

13. Although serial TV regularly promotes confusion about the border-line between the identities of performers and characters, a confusion in which 'showbiz' reporting regularly acts as a relay and incentive (see Engel, 1996: 280, for a clear example). Journalists who mock the naivete of viewers who make this confusion would do well to remember that some journalism is complicit in the process.

14. See Chapter 2.

15. These theorizations have their grounding in observations about funda-mental elements in the culture of modern societies, especially the role of bodily pleasures and intellectual and aesthetic refinement; see Bourdieu (1979), Bakhtin (1970), Stallybrass and White (1986). For the postmodern theorists quoted above, the tabloid excesses are a celebration of the grotesque, a reinstatement of 'low' pleasures at the heart of our culture. But see also Greenberg *et al.* (1997) who find that the prevalence of such content on US TV talk shows is massively exaggerated.

16. Note that obtaining scandalous information about the rich and famous is not a cheap option: the costs are high.

17. These examples tell us nothing about the motives of those who expose themselves on confessional TV. It would be very interesting to know how their behaviour reaches the attention of the researchers who find them, and how they are persuaded to appear on such shows; I have never seen any systematic analysis of this. The *Jerry Springer Show* is said to receive 3000 calls a week from volunteers (*Evening Standard*, 17.2.99). Reports of 'faked' confessional appearances on UK TV by actors, paid and recruited via agencies, suggest that the process is not simple or unequivocal (reported in all UK press in the week beginning Monday, 8 February 1999).

18. See, for example, H. Kurtz, 'The White House at War', *Vanity Fair*, no. 461, January 1999, which makes repeated references to this theme.

CHAPTER 6

1. Also to the later protests against the Nigerian Government's execution of Ken Saro-Wiwa and Shell's alleged inaction with regard to environmental damage and human rights' abuses linked to their operations in Nigeria. Herkstroter and Jennings are senior managers of the Shell Group and of Shell UK. The role of the confrontation with Greenpeace in this rethink is shown in *Sparring Partners* (BBC2, 31.1.98).
2. The capital structure of the Shell Group of companies gives the Dutch company a major role in the group as a whole. Scandinavian news coverage was no doubt also important in mobilizing the opposition of governments to Shell's plans. Because Scandanavian reports have not been translated into English I have not been able to draw on this material.
3. A fuller version appeared in an article in the *Journal of Communication Management* (Hampton, 1997: 280–4). The analysis here differs somewhat from the version given to the press, in that it includes an analysis of the role of 'factual' information; however, it would seem that the latter consists of the tone of the reporting of the key messages which were the basic data; see Hampton Tables 2 and 3. The conclusions derived from the data also include analysis of the background to the story and of Greenpeace's communications strategy.
4. Quotes taken from tapes of the discussion, available from EITF. In the seminar discussion, the availability of Greenpeace video footage, which was one of the main issues in the debate, was related to the widespread practice of VNRs (video news releases).
5. The content analysis is based on UK media. The results will be compared with a study done at the Vrije Universiteit, Amsterdam (de Haan and van Leur, 1996), comparing UK, Dutch and German media, but using a different set of analytic devices; also with a Deutsche Shell publication which contains summaries, extracts and statistical analyses of German media coverage, but no systematic thematic analysis (Mantow and Podeus, 1995). The technical details of the content analysis done for this chapter, as well as the full results, are available on the London Guildhall University website: www.lgu.ac.uk/...; here it is the outline of these results and their implications for the subject matter of this book which are the focus of our attention. I am grateful to Dirk Oegema of the Vrije Universiteit for making the Dutch study available to me, and to Deutsche Shell and to Wolfgang Mantow for the German study.
6. Although this chapter is concerned with information that had an impact upon events by its passage through the mass media, one small information flow that was not mass-mediated is significant. The public announcement of the Brent Spar disposal came on 16 February 1995. Clearly the plan was known within the oil industry before this date, and was known to Greenpeace. According to Simon Reddy of Greenpeace, his report for Greenpeace on sea disposal, which included discussion of Brent Spar, was written in the autumn of 1994 and sent to the DTI in December. Subsequently various people claimed credit for tipping Greenpeace off,

notably the lobbyist Andrew Gifford of the lobbying company GJW claimed credit for telling them (*Observer*, 12.7.98). According to Simon Reddy, they were tipped off in mid-1994 by an oil industry source, but did not come up with any plans to occupy it until after March 1995.

7. This information is derived from Shell UK Public Affairs records, which are the most complete national archive of broadcast mentions that I have found, plus the on-line index of BBC national radio news and current affairs output, and the ITN on-line index. I am grateful to the public affairs personnel of Shell UK, and to BBC and ITN archivists for their help.

8. Information based on personal telephone interview with Agency personnel.

9. Information obtained by checking the list of named reporters with BBC Newsgathering (London) and BBC Scotland Information Unit. It is difficult to establish where broadcast reports have come from since the identity of the original reporter is frequently omitted and the only name is that of the newsreader.

10. Here too this analysis runs counter to the Computerised Media Associates study, which sees little difference between the Scottish press treatment of the issue and the national press treatment.

11. Joe Quinn, who covered Brent Spar from the Press Association office in Glasgow, confirmed this for me in a telephone interview.

12. The relationship between these themes can be seen in the content analysis in the numbers of references to 'protest', 'environment' and 'political action' in the tables summarizing the themes of the reporting.

13. This finding is inconsistent with the results of the CMA study, where Shell and Greenpeace messages are identified in a way that allows analysis of the representation of exactly the issue addressed here. The difference between the two findings is probably due to the fact that the CMA study does not weight mentions of the messages according to the degree of emphasis given to them within each article where they appear, but only according to the degree of emphasis given to the article, considered as whole.

14. Shell, 36 per cent, to Greenpeace, 23.5 per cent; on a positive/negative scale from 1 to –1, where 0 means absolute neutrality, Shell average -0.42 and Greenpeace average +0.28.

15. More exactly, they were subsequently present at the eviction in an observer capacity to ensure that procedures were observed and no breach of the criminal law occurred.

16. Interviews with Greenpeace personnel, in which this speculative hypothesis was discussed, showed that they agreed that police action in the immediate aftermath of the occupation would have made the realization of their objectives far more difficult, and might have made a sustained campaign impossible. Of course, this is speculation.

17. Interview with Mike Sutherland, spokesperson of the Scottish Fishermen's Federation, 17.3.97.

18. E.g. *Die Welt*, 8.5.95: 'Shell: a company between claim and reality', which comments on the contrast between Deutsche Shell's 'claims' about social

responsibility and the 'reality' of the 'poison cocktail' of Brent Spar. This was one of the first national press reports of the Spar in Germany.

19. PA report of 30.4.95; DPA report as printed in *Hamburger Abendblatt*, 2.5.95, credited to DPA London and Hamburg. The DPA computer search provided a limited selection of reports from this period; I have been unable to identify which ones are missing. I am grateful to DPA staff in Hamburg for access to their archives and for their help in retrieval.

20. Radio and TV news on 30 April, satellite link from the Spar to a commercial TV station magazine programme on 3 May; ARD TV covered it on 4 May; little further mention of the occupation seems to have been made on German national TV until 11 May, when the London correspondent for ZDF TV originated a substantial report with location video footage. The first press reports I have found in a sample of German national newspapers (*Die Welt, Frankfurter Allgemeine Zeitung, Bild*) were on 8 and 27 May (*Die Welt*), 15 May (*FAZ*), and 17 and 23 May (*Bild*); the report on 8 May in *Die Welt* announces the occupation of the Brent Spar as a new event.

21. The German media system is more regionally based than the UK, and news values are correspondingly different from the UK. I had substantial help from the following German journalists, to whom I am grateful: Thomas Schreiber (NDR/WDR), Jochen Graibert (NDR/ARD) and Theo Koll (ZDF TV), who also gave me access to the ZDF online news index.

22. Information derived from a list of participating personnel obtained from Greenpeace Germany.

23. Interviews with Christian Bussau, Simon Reddy and Remi Parmentier of Greenpeace. Greenpeace have claimed that they did not call for a boycott. This is true, in the sense that they were not the first to mention it. However, (a) according to Jochen Graibert, Greenpeace activists discussed the possibility of a boycott as a viable tactic during the voyage back from the Brent Spar to Germany around 6 May; (b) Greenpeace commissioned an opinion poll on support for a boycott in Germany and published the results shortly after the Junge Union call. The question which was put to the public recapitulated the Greenpeace analysis of the situation in a way that reduced the risk of an unfavourable result (the question and poll results are in Mantow and Podeus, 1995: 255).

24. Both journalists spontaneously introduced this topic in interviews with the author.

25. Interview with JP.

26. Telephone interview with the author.

27. According to a Greenpeace circular to supporters dated after 20 June, Greenpeace spent some £350,000 (out of £1.36m total) on communications, excluding the marginal costs of transporting journalists, a cost beyond even the BBC's means (Richard Sambrook). The fact that the camera crew was paid for by Greenpeace was not a problem for Jochen Graibert since he had worked with Greenpeace with his own crew previously and knew that Greenpeace would not seriously impede access to material he wanted; in fact, access was entirely adequate.

28. Press releases obtained from Greenpeace officers. I am grateful for this cooperation.
29. All information about Greenpeace International's communications tactics comes from an interview with Cindy Baxter, 7.11.95.
30. Interview with Fran Morrison, Head of Shell UK media relations, 10.4.97. All subsequent information about Shell UK strategies derives from this interview unless otherwise stated. I am grateful to Ms Morrison for a generous allocation of time and effort to helping me.
31. Interview, 3.6.97. All other information about Deutsche Shell communications strategy comes from the same source.
32. According to one German reporter with whom I discussed this, Shell were not cooperative and refused access to their ships to himself and a colleague from another German newspaper.
33. According to Shell media records.
34. This episode is commented by Richard Sambrook in his EITF seminar contribution. According to Shell media personnel, they were 'naive' about the possible use of this video for PR purposes.
35. At the time of writing, (Spring 1999), they could still be seen on the Greenpeace website; the Shell Brent Spar website has an engineering diagram.
36. Subsequently Greenpeace won a libel case against the BBC which repeated this allegation (*Guardian*, 26.11.99).
37. They also point out that under the terms of the Esbjerg OSPAR agreement there was a moratorium on sea dumping pending the Lisbon conference (July 1998) regardless of whether the structures contain poisonous residues or not (para. 54 of the ministerial agreements, formalized as decision 95/1 of OSCOM). I am grateful to Remi Parmentier of Greenpeace for making the text of relevant documents available.
38. Interviews with Greenpeace activist Christian Bussau, TV journalist Jochen Graibert, spring, 1997.

PART II: CONCLUSION

1. Elsewhere Ingham makes it clear that Government 'credibility' is a question of three things: truthfulness, consistency between departments, and timely information release. On the matter of 'fairness' in general, cf. Leapman, 1992: 239–68, and esp. 254.
2. See also (a randomly chosen example): Miller and Williams, 1993: 132–3.
3. Mantow and Podeus, 1995. De Haan and van Leur come to a compatible conclusion on the basis of a content analysis which includes an 'authority' indicator.
4. See his role in two cases in November 1999: Gary Glitter's trial and Lord Archer's abrupt exit from the London mayoral election.
5. This claim is still central to their case; see Rose, 1998: 23–33.
6. The same point is made, more critically, by Willis (1991: 2–4) who distinguishes 'objectivity' from 'accuracy'. Cf. Weaver (1994), *passim*. To what extent readers make this distinction is unknown.

7. Ika Siswati (1998).
8. Monica Lewinsky's name was first publicly linked with the president's by the Drudge Report (a US-based news website) during the third weekend of January 1998. Ten days later, on 27 January, Hilary Clinton denounced a 'vast right-wing conspiracy' against the Clinton presidency on television.
9. A good example of a journalist analysing the process is Polly Toynbee's comments on a leak of the forthcoming Budget in the *Guardian*, 10.2.99.
10. See also Jones, 1999 for an extended denunciation of excessive use of government power in this respect.
11. Cf. other examples on pp. 332–3 and 348. He has been accused of the same tactic himself, smearing Tory politicians in order to justify their sacking or to belittle their motives for resignation. See Harris, 1990; Leapman, 1992: 243–5.
12. In his 'farewell' speech to the Tory Party conference in October 1997, John Major obliquely referred to the role of unattributable media briefings in destabilizing his Government (*Daily Mail*, 8.10.97); he returned to the subject in *The Major Years* (BBC1, October 1999).
13. See, e.g., *Die Welt*, 17.3.99; *Le Monde*, 17.3.99; *Daily Telegraph*, 17.3.99; *Guardian*, 17.3.99; *Observer*, 21.3.99. To be more precise, the exchange rate of the euro went down and back up during the day after the resignations.
14. Interview with Catherine Nestor, British Red Cross communications department.
15. For example, in a case involving someone who had allegedly had a homosexual relationship with a Tory MP, Max Clifford arranged for a radio interview, and arranged for a camera crew to film him going into the studio and commenting on what he would say; the story was also picked up by the morning papers. Other examples are to be found in Jones, 1999.
16. The Mountfield report comments on the relevance of this development for the Government Information Service.

CHAPTER 7

1. This argument is also central to Miller's study of news management in Northern Ireland (1993), which shows that we cannot necessarily 'read off from textual characteristics the interests which are served by particular television programmes or news items' (1993: 389–90).
2. As a contrast, we could think of the very great difficulties posed for the French by the recent trials of Paul Touvier and Maurice Papon for crimes against humanity in the Second World War. An approximately parallel instance would be the enormous difficulties that the demands of British and Commonwealth veterans' organizations for compensation for victims of Japanese war crimes create for the Japanese Government because of the fundamentally conflicting definitions of the Japanese role in the Second World War that still divide Japanese political opinion.
3. If only out of caution, we should say of Maastricht that it has not yet, at the time of writing (October 1999), provoked a major ideological crisis; at the

time of the promised EMU referendum we may wish to reconsider this remark.

CHAPTER 8

1. For the clearest and most complete outline of Habermas' conception of communicative action, see his *Theory of Communicative Action* (1984), vol. 1, Part 1.
2. Habermas incorporates Freud into his scheme by thinking of repression as the internalized disruption of communicative processes; see his 1972: 217–228.
3. See his *Theory of Communicative Action*, vol. 2 (1987), esp. ch. 6, part 2, pp. 153–97, for a detailed analysis of this concept.
4. The structure of communicative action is analysed in his *Theory of Communicative Action*, vol. 1, part 1. Its relationship to the lifeworld is analysed in vol. 2, pp. 20–52.
5. Habermas' argument here addresses the commonplace modern Marxist recognition that power cannot be maintained by repressive power alone, but must be based upon at least partial consent. Indeed, the Marxist debates about the role of ideology from Althusser onwards were expressly intended to deal with this matter.
6. Habermas' main text on the subject is his *Structural Transformation of the Public Sphere* (Habermas, 1989). For convenience I am here referring to the abbreviated version published under the title 'The public sphere: an encyclopaedia article' (Habermas, 1964).
7. I am using the commonsensical phrase 'factual truth' – despite its well-known problems – to summarize Habermas' own discussion of the concept in *Knowledge and Human Interests*, Part II.
8. See his *Theory and Practice* (Habermas, 1974: 41–81). See also the translator's introduction to his *Communication and the Evolution of Society* (Habermas, 1979). See also *Theory of Communicative Action*, vol. I, pp. 59–66. My formulation here ignores some elements of the negative side that Habermas attributes to the claims made in favour of scientific objectivity as a universal good.
9. In theory, the separation of science as a sub-system should modify these comments, since both identities and reasons may derive from the internal structure of this sub-system alone.

References

Adams, J. R. and Frantz, D. (1991) *A Full-Service Bank*. New York: Simon and Schuster.

Alberoni, F. (1976) 'Stars: the powerless "elite": theory and sociological research on the phenomenon of the stars', in D. McQuail (ed.), *Sociology of Mass Communications*. London: Penguin Books.

Bakhtin, M. (1970) *L'Oeuvre de François Rabelais*. Paris: Gallimard.

Bird, S. E. (1997) 'What a story! Understanding the audience for scandal', in J. Lull and S. Hinerman (eds), *Media Scandals*, Cambridge: Polity Press.

Boorstin, D. (1961) *The Image*. London: Penguin Books.

Bourdieu, P. (1979) *La Distinction*. Paris: Editions de Minuit.

Bruce, B. (1992) *Images of Power*. London: Kogan Page.

Calhoun, C. (1992) 'Habermas and the public sphere', in C. Calhoun (ed.), *Habermas and the Public Sphere*. Cambridge, MA: MIT Press, pp. 2-37.

Cannadine, D. (1983) 'The context, performance and meaning of ritual: the British monarchy and the "invention of tradition", *c.*1820-1977', in E. Hobsbawm and T. Ranger (eds), *The Invention of Tradition*. Cambridge: Cambridge University Press.

Chibnall, S. (1977) *Law and Order News*. London: Tavistock.

Cockerell, M., Hennessy, P. and Walker, D. (1984) *Sources Close to the Prime Minister*. London: Macmillan.

Collins, J. (1998), 'Food Scares and the Mass Media', unpublished PhD thesis, London Guildhall University.

Curran, J. (1990) 'The new revisionism in mass communications research', *European Journal of Communication*, **5**: 135-64.

Curran, J. (1991) 'Mass media and democracy: a re-appraisal', in J. Curran and M. Gurevich, *Mass Media and Society*. London: Arnold, pp. 82-117.

Curran, J. and Seaton, J. (1985) *Power without Responsibility*. London: Methuen.

De Haan, M. and van Leur, B. (1996) De Strijd om de Brent Spar in de Media: De Vrije Publiciteit en het Imago van Shell en Greenpeace. Unpublished dissertation, Vrije Universiteit, Amsterdam.

Dearing, J. and Rogers, E. (1996) *Agenda-Setting*. London: Sage.

Deppa, J. (1993) *The Media and Disasters: Pan Am 103*. London: Fulton.

Downing, J. (1986) 'Government secrecy and the media in the USA and Britain', in P. Golding, G. Murdock and P. Schlesinger (eds), *Communicating Politics: Mass Communications and the Political Process*. Leicester: Leicester University Press, pp. 153-70.

References

Engel, M. (1996) *Tickle the Public.* London: Gollancz.

Ericson, R. V. (1991) 'Mass media, crime, law and justice: an institutional approach', *British Journal of Criminology,* **31**: 219–49.

Ericson, R. V., Baranek, P. M. and Chan, J. (1989) *Negotiating Control: A Study of News Sources.* Milton Keynes: Open University Press.

Evans, H. (1978) *Pictures on a Page.* London: Heinemann.

Financial Times (1991) *Behind Closed Doors,* London: Financial Times.

Fisher, T. (1995) *Scandal: The Sexual Politics of Late Victorian Britain.* Stroud: Alan Sutton.

Fishman, M. (1980) *Manufacturing the News.* Austin: University of Texas Press.

Fiske, J. (1989) *Understanding Popular Culture.* London: Unwin Hyman.

Fraser, N. (1992) 'Rethinking the public sphere', in C. Calhoun (ed.), *Habermas and the Public Sphere.* Cambridge, MA: MIT Press, pp. 107–42.

Freud, S. (1979) *Notes upon a Case of Obsessional Neurosis (the 'Rat Man'),* in J. Strachey and A. Richards (eds), *Pelican Freud Library,* vol. 9.

Galtung, J. and Ruge, M. H. (1970) 'The structure of foreign news', in J. Tunstall (ed.), *Media Sociology.* London: Constable, pp. 259–98.

Gamson, W. (1984) *What's News?* New York: Free Press.

Gandy, O. (1982) *Beyond Agenda Setting.* Norwood, NJ: Ablex.

Gans, H. J. (1980) *Deciding What's News.* London: Constable.

Gaster, R. (1988) 'Sex, spies and scandal: the Profumo affair and British politics', in A. S. Markovits and M. Silverstein (eds), *The Politics of Scandal: Power and Process in Liberal Democracies.* New York: Holmes and Meier, pp. 62–88.

Gieber, W. and Johnson, W. (1961) 'The City Hall beat: a study of reporter and source roles', *Journalism Quarterly,* **38**: 289–97.

Gitlin, T. (1980) *The Whole World Is Watching: Mass Media in the Making and Unmaking of the New Left.* Berkeley: University of California Press.

Glasgow University Media Group (1976) *Bad News.* London: Routledge & Kegan Paul.

Glasgow University Media Group (1993) *Getting the Message: News, Truth and Power.* London: Routledge.

Glyn, K. (1990) 'Tabloid television's transgressive aesthetic', *Wide Angle* **12** (2): 22–44.

Goddard, P., Corner, J., Garvin, N. and Richardson, K. (1998) 'Economic news and the dynamics of understanding', in N. T. Garvin (ed.), *The Economy, the Media and Public Knowledge,* London: Cassell, pp. 9–37.

Goldberg, V. (1991) *The Power of Photography.* New York: Abbeville Press.

Goldenberg, E. (1975) *Making the Papers: The Access of Resource-Poor Groups to the Metropolitan Press.* Lexington, MA: D. C. Heath.

Golding, P. and Middleton, S. (1982) *Images of Welfare: Press and Public Attitudes to Poverty.* Oxford: Robertson.

Greenberg, B. S., Sherry, J. L., Busselle, R. W., Hnilo, L. R. and Smith, S. W. (1997) 'Television daytime talk shows: guests, content and interactions', *Journal of Broadcasting and Electronic Media,* **41**: 412–26.

Greenpeace (1997) *Brent Spar und die Folgen.* Gottingen & Lichtenau: Die Werkstatt and AOL-Verlag.

Habermas, J. (1964) 'The public sphere: an encyclopaedia article', trans. S. and F. Lennox, ed. P. Hohendahl, *New German Critique.*

References

Habermas, J. (1972) *Knowledge and Human Interests*, trans. J. Schapiro. London: Heinemann.

Habermas, J. (1974) *Theory and Practice*, trans. J. Viertel. London: Heinemann.

Habermas, J. (1979) *Communication and the Evolution of Society*, trans. and ed. T. McCarthy. London: Heinemann.

Habermas, J. (1984) *The Theory of Communicative Action*, vol. 1, trans. T. McCarthy. London: Heinemann.

Habermas, J. (1987) *The Theory of Communicative Action*, vol. 2, trans. T. McCarthy. Cambridge: Polity Press.

Habermas, J. (1989) *Structural Transformation of the Public Sphere*. Cambridge: Polity.

Hall, S. (1973) 'The determinations of news photographs', in S. Cohen and J. Young (eds), *The Manufacture of News*. London: Constable.

Hall, S., Critcher, C., Jefferson, T., Clarke, J. and Roberts, B. (1978) *Policing the Crisis*. London: Macmillan.

Hall, S. (1982) *Managing Conflict, Producing Consent*. Milton Keynes: Open University, Course Unit D102/21.

Hallin, D. (1986) *The Uncensored War: The Media and Vietnam*. Oxford: Oxford University Press.

Halloran, J., Murdock, G. and Elliott, P. (1970) *Demonstrations and Communications*. London: Penguin.

Hampton, F. (1997) 'Integrating PR monitoring into the overall corporate product marketing function', *Journal of Communications Management 1*, **3**: 280–88.

Harmsen, M. (1996) Conflict in beeld: Theorie en Onderzoek naar beelden van een conflict tussen actiegroep en onderneming. Unpublished dissertation, Vrije Universiteit, Amsterdam.

Harris, R. (1990) *Good and Faithful Servant: The Unauthorised Biography of Bernard Ingham*. London: Faber and Faber.

Hartley, J. (1982) *Reading Television*. London: Methuen.

Hay, D. (1975) 'Property, authority and the criminal law', in Hay *et al.*, *Albion's Fatal Tree*. London: Allen Lane.

Herkstroter, C. (1997) Speech at Erasmus University, Rotterdam, 16 March.

Herman, E. and Chomsky, N. (1988) *Manufacturing Consent*. New York: Pantheon.

Hermes, J. (1997) 'Gender and media studies: no woman, no cry', in J. Corner, P. Schlesinger and R. Silverstone (eds), *International Media Research*. London: Routledge, pp. 65–95.

Hilpern, K. (1995) Unpublished undergraduate dissertation, London Guildhall University.

Hobsbawm, E. (1975) *The Age of Capital*. London: Weidenfeld & Nicolson.

Hobson, D. (1982) *Crossroads: The Drama of a Soap Opera*. London: Methuen.

Horton, D. and Wohl, R. (1956) 'Mass communication and para-social interaction: observations on intimacy at a distance', *Psychiatry*, **19**: 215–29.

Ingham, B. (1991) *Kill the Messenger*. London: Fontana.

Jones, N. (1999) *Sultans of Spin*. London: Gollancz.

Keane, J. (1991) *The Media and Democracy*. Cambridge: Polity Press.

King, A. (1986) 'Sex, money and power', in J. Ceaser and R. Hodder-Williams (eds), *Politics in Britain and America*. Durham, NC: Duke University Press.

Kochan, N. and Pym, H. (1987) *The Guinness Affair*. Bromley: Croom Helm.

Kurtz, H. (1999) 'The White House of war,' *Vanity Fair*, 461.

Leapman, M. (1992) *Treacherous Estate*. London: Hodder and Stoughton.

Lichtenberg, J. (1991) 'In defence of objectivity', in J. Curran and M. Gurevich (eds), *Mass Media and Society*. London: Arnold, pp. 216–31.

Lowi, T. (1988) 'Foreword', in A. S. Markovits and M. Silverstein (eds), *The Politics of Scandal: Power and Process in Liberal Democracies*. New York: Holmes and Meier.

Lull, J. and Hinerman, S. (1997) 'In search of scandal', in J. Lull and S. Hinerman (eds), *Media Scandals*. Cambridge: Polity Press.

Macarthur, J. (1992) *Second Front: Censorship and Propaganda in the Gulf War*. New York: Hill and Wang.

McCombs, M. and Bell, T. (1996) 'The agenda-setting role of mass communications', in M. Salwen and D. Stacks (eds), *An Integrated Approach to Communication Theory and Research*, Hillsdale, NJ: Lawrence Erlbaum Associates, pp. 93–110.

McQuail, D. (1991) 'Mass media in the public interest: towards a framework of norms for media performance', in J. Curran and M. Gurevich (eds), *Mass Media and Society*. London: Arnold, pp. 68–81.

MacShane, D. (1979) *Using the Media*. London: Pluto Press.

Mahoney, P. J. (1986) *Freud and the Rat Man*. New Haven: Yale University Press.

Manoff, R. K. and Schudson, M. (eds) (1986) *Reading the News*. New York: Pantheon Books.

Mantow, W. and Podeus, J. (1995) *Die Ereignisse um Brent Spar in Deutschland*. Hamburg: Deutsche Shell Aktiengesellschaft.

Marchina, M. (1997) Unpublished essay, MA in Communications Management, London Guildhall University.

Markovits, A. S. and Silverstein, M. (1988) *The Politics of Scandal: Power and Process in Liberal Democracies*. New York: Holmes and Meier.

Mellencamp, P. (1992) *High Anxiety*. Bloomington: Indiana University Press.

Miller, D. (1993a) 'Official sources and "primary definition": the case of Northern Ireland', *Media Culture and Society*, **15**: 385–406.

Miller, D. (1993b) 'The Northern Ireland Information Service and the media: aims, strategy, tactics', in Glasgow University Media Group, *Getting the Message: News, Truth and Power*. London: Routledge.

Miller, D. (1997) 'Promotional strategies and media power', in A. Briggs and P. Cobley (eds), *The Media: An Introduction*. Harlow: Addison Wesley Longman.

Miller, D. and Williams, K. (1993) 'Negotiating HIV/AIDS information: agendas, media strategies and the news', in Glasgow University Media Group, *Getting the Message: News, Truth and Power*. London: Routledge.

Molotch, H. and Lester, M. (1981) 'News as purposive behavior: on the strategic use of routine events, accidents and scandals', in S. Cohen and J. Young, (eds), *The Manufacture of News*, 2nd edn. London: Constable, pp. 118–37.

Morrison, D. (1992) *Television and the Gulf War*. London: John Libbey.

Morrison, D. and Tumber, H. (1988) *Journalists at War*. London: Sage.

References

Mott, F. L. (1950) *American Journalism*. London: Macmillan.

Mountfield, Sir R. (1997) *Report of the Working Group on the Government Service*. London: Cabinet Office.

Murphy, D. (1976) *The Silent Watchdog: The Press in Local Politics*. London: Constable.

Murphy, D. (1991) *The Stalker Affair*. London: Constable.

Negrine, R. (1989) *Politics and the Mass Media in Britain*. London: Routledge.

Negrine, R. (1993) 'The organisations of British journalism and specialist correspondents: a study of newspaper reporting'. University of Leicester: Discussion Papers in Mass Communications MC93/1.

Negrine, R. (1997) 'The Scott Inquiry's media coverage', *Parliamentary Affairs*, **50** (1): 27–40 (special edition on the Scott Inquiry).

Newman, K. (1984) *Financial Marketing and Communications*. London: Holt, Rinehart and Winston and the Advertising Association.

Palling, B. (1996) *The Book of Modern Scandals*. London: Orion Books.

Palmer, J. N. J. (1978) *Thrillers: Genesis and Structure of a Popular Genre*. London: Edward Arnold.

Palmer, J. N. J. (2000) 'Les associations caritatives anglaises et les médias', in J. Walter (ed.), *Télévision et Exclusion*. Paris: Editions l'Harmattan.

Parenti, M. (1993) *Inventing Reality*, 2nd edn. New York: St. Martin's Press.

Parris, M. (1996) *Great Parliamentary Scandals*. London: Robson Books.

Pearce, F. (1973) 'How to be immoral and ill, pathetic and dangerous, all at the same time: mass media and the homosexual', in S. Cohen and J. Young (eds), *The Manufacture of News*. London: Constable.

Peters, J. D. (1993) 'Distrust of representation: Habermas on the public sphere', *Media, Culture and Society*, **15**: 541–71.

Pugh, P. (1987) *Is Guinness Good for You?* London: Blackstone Press.

Robertson, G. and Nicol, A. (1984) *Media Law*. London: Sage.

Romano, C. (1986) 'The grisly truth about bare facts', in R. Manoff and M. Schudson (eds), *Reading the News*. New York: Pantheon Books.

Rose, C. (1998) *The Turning of the Spar*. London: Greenpeace.

Rosnow, R. L. and Fine, G. A. (1976) *Rumor and Gossip*. The Hague: Elsevier.

Scheufele, D. (1999) 'Framing as a theory of media effects', *Journal of Communication*, **49**: 103–18.

Schlesinger, P. (1987) *Putting Reality Together*, 2nd edn. London: Methuen.

Schlesinger, P. (1989) 'From production to propaganda', *Media, Culture and Society*, **11**: 283–306.

Schlesinger, P. (1990) 'Rethinking the sociology of journalism: source strategies and the limits of media-centrism', in M. Ferguson (ed.), *Public Communications: The New Imperatives*. London: Sage.

Schlesinger, P. and Tumber, H. (1994) *Reporting Crime*. Oxford: Clarendon Press.

Schudson, M. (1978) *Discovering the News*. New York: Basic Books.

Schudson, M. (1986) 'Deadlines, datelines and history', in R. Manoff and M. Schudson (eds), *Reading the News*. New York: Pantheon Books.

Schudson, M. (1991) 'The sociology of news production revisited', in J. Curran and M. Gurevich (eds), *Mass Media and Society*. London: Arnold.

Select Committee (1999) *Proceedings of the Select Committee on Public Administration*. London: HMSO.

References

Seymour-Ure, C. (1989) 'Prime ministers' reactions to television', *Media, Culture and Society*, **11**: 307-25.

Shell (1995a) Press release, 20 June.

Shell (1995b) Press release, August (no date given).

Shibutani, T. (1966) *Improvised News*. New York: Bobbs-Merrill.

Siebert, F., Peterson, T. and Schramm, W. (1963) *Fourt Theories of the Press*. Urbana: University of Illinois Press.

Sigal, L. V. (1973) *Reporters and Officials*. Lexington, MA: D. C. Heath.

Sigal, L. V. (1986) 'Sources make the news', in R. Manoff and M. Schudson (eds), *Reading the News*. New York: Pantheon Books, pp. 9-37.

Siswati, H. I. (1998) Unpublished essay, MA in Communications Management, London Guildhall University.

Sloterdijk, P. (1988) *Critique of Cynical Reason*. London: Verso.

Stallybrass, P. and White, A. (1986) *The Politics and Poetics of Transgression*. London: Methuen.

Stewart, J. R. (1991) *Den of Thieves*. New York: Simon and Schuster.

Stone, L. (1977) *The Family, Sex and Marriage in England, 1500-1800*. London: Weidenfeld and Nicholson.

Stone, N. (1995) *The Management and Practice of Public Relations*. London: Macmillan.

Stone, J. and Yohn, T. (1992) *Prime Time and Misdemeanours*. New Brunswick, NJ: Rutgers University Press, pp. 13-25.

Tagg, J. (1982) 'Power and photography', in V. Burgin (ed.), *Thinking Photography*. London: Macmillan.

Taylor, P. M. (1992) *War and the Media: Propaganda and Persuasion in the Gulf War*. Manchester: Manchester University Press.

Thompson, J. O. (1995) *The Media and Modernity*. Cambridge: Polity Press.

Tillyard, S. (1994) *Aristocrats: Caroline, Emily, Louise, and Sarah Lennox, 1750-1832*. London: Chatto and Windus.

Truell, P. and Gurwin, L. (1992) *BCCI: The Inside Story of the World's Most Corrupt Financial Empire*. Boston: Houghton Mifflin.

Tuchman, G. (1978) *Making News*. New York: Free Press.

Tulloch, J. (1993) 'Policing the public sphere: the British machinery of news management', *Media, Culture and Society,* **15** (3) 363-83.

Tumber, H. (1993) '"Selling scandal": business and the media', *Media, Culture and Society*, **15**: 345-61.

Tunstall, J. (1971) *Journalists at Work*. London: Constable.

Vorfelder, J. (1995) *Brent Spar oder die Zukunft der Meere*. Munich: C. S. Beck.

Weaver, P. H. (1994) *News and the Culture of Lying*. New York: Free Press.

Weekes, J. (1981) *Sex, Politics and Society: The Regulation of Sex Since 1800*. London: Longman.

Wernick, A. (1991) *Promotional Culture: Advertising, Ideology and Symbolic Expression*. London: Sage.

Willis, J. (1991) *The Shadow World: Life between the News Media and Reality*. New York: Praeger.

Wolfe, T. (1988) *The Bonfire of the Vanities*. London: Picador.

Index

Note: 'News values' and 'sources' are only cited in the index when a relevant theory is discussed or there is discussion of substantial examples; media are only referenced where they are cited as an authority, or where there is some substantial discussion of them.